UNCOMMON
GROUND

UNCOMMON GROUND

White Women in Aboriginal History

Edited by Anna Cole, Victoria Haskins & Fiona Paisley

ABORIGINAL
STUDIES
PRESS

First published in 2005 by Aboriginal Studies
Press for the Australian Institute of Aboriginal
and Torres Strait Islander Studies
Reprinted 2021
GPO Box 523, Canberra, ACT 2601
sales@aiatsis.gov.au
www.aiatsis.gov.au

Reprinted in 2026

National Library of Australia cataloguing-in-
publication data:

Cole, Anna, 1969– .
Uncommon ground : white women in
aboriginal history.

New ed.
ISBN 0 85575 485 0.

1. Feminism — Australia — History. 2.
Aboriginal Australians — History. 3. Australia
— Race relations. I. Haskins, Victoria. II.
Paisley, Fiona. III. Title.

305.40994

This project has been assisted by
the Australian Government
through the Australia Council,
its arts funding and advisory
body.

Cover illustration: Jennie Smith working as
the matron, at Manunka, South Australia.
Photo Gretta Matthews © Sorrelle Smith,
North Rockhampton.

Contents

Aboriginal and Torres Stait Islander people are respectfully advised that this book contains names and images of deceased persons, and culturally sensitive material.

Illustrations

The contributors

Margaret Allen teaches Gender Studies and History at the University of Adelaide. She has published a number of articles in the fields of feminist history and literary history. She is currently completing a biographical study of the writer Catherine Martin. Her current project explores Australians within empire, looking particularly at links between India and Australia *c*. 1880–1925. Margaret's research interests include feminist and post-colonial histories.

Jim Anderson is a PhD student at Flinders University in Adelaide, engaged in doctoral research on the life and work of the late Dr Annie Heloise Abel, a pioneer in the history of US policy towards the indigenous nations of North America. He is also Editor of the *Flinders Journal of History and Politics*, a forum for graduate research.

Christine Brett Vickers is a postgraduate student in history at La Trobe University, Melbourne, where she is writing the biography of her great-grandparents. She is also a clinical social worker. Christine is interested in the nexus between history and anthropology and how psychoanalytic ideas might contribute to interpretation.

Anna Cole completed her doctorate on the gendered politics of assimilation at the University of Technology, Sydney in 2000. She has since worked as Project Historian for the 'Shared Aboriginal and

Non-Aboriginal Histories of Pastoralism' project with the New South Wales National Parks and Wildlife Service, Cultural Heritage Division, and is currently employed as Research Associate and Coordinator in the Department of Anthropology, University of London on an international research project on cross-cultural exchange in Oceania. She has published articles in the area of race, gender and colonialism, and is currently co-editing, with Bronwen Douglas and Nicholas Thomas, *Tatau/tattoo: bodies, art and exchange in the Pacific and Europe* (forthcoming from Reaktion Books).

Cynthia Coyne is a member of the Djukun-Yawuru clan, which is located in Broome in Western Australia. She works as an Indigenous academic support lecturer at the Charles Darwin University. Her work has been published in the catalogue *Buku Larrnggay Mulka Printmakers Exhibition*, which informs about printmaking produced by Yolngu people from North-East Arnhem Land. She has also published work on the contemporary sounds, movement and words of Indigenous people living in Broome, and is currently working on two papers that focus on Kimberley art and culture. Cynthia is a PhD candidate with the University of Melbourne, primarily investigating place, space and identity of Indigenous art in Broome, the Dampier Peninsula and Lagrange, the West Kimberley region of Western Australia.

Franchesca Cubillo is a Larrakia, Bardi, Wardaman and Yanuwa woman from the 'Top End' region of Australia. She currently holds the position of Artistic & Cultural Director at Tandanya, National Aboriginal Cultural Institute. Prior to this appointment she held the position of Director of the Aboriginal & Torres Strait Islander Program and Manager of the Repatriation Unit at the National Museum of Australia from 2001–2003. She was employed as Curator of Aboriginal Anthroplogy at the South Australian Museum for eight years and was the Indigenous Curator who assisted in the redevelopment of the Australian Aboriginal Cultures Gallery, 2000. Franchesca has a Bachelor of Arts Degree in Aboriginal Affairs and Honours in Anthropology. She has worked extensively in the area of Indigenous Cultural Heritage for the past 15 years and currently holds several positions on various boards and committees around Australia.

Stephanie Gilbert is a lecturer in Aboriginal Studies at the University of Newcastle. She has published in the area of Aboriginal and gender studies. She is currently working in the area of Aboriginal child removals and remains working in Aboriginal bridging programs.

Victoria Haskins is a lecturer in Australian History at Flinders University, Adelaide. She has published a number of articles on colonialism, gender and race relations history in Australia, and is currently working on a book about Joan Kingsley-Strack. Her research interests include relationships between Indigenous domestic workers and their employers, frontier histories and cultural memory, and intermarriage between Aboriginal men and white women.

Alison Holland is a lecturer in Aboriginal History and Australian Studies at Macquarie University, Sydney. She has published widely in the field of race and gender relations history. Her other research interests include humanitarianism, racial ideologies and memory. She is currently thinking about formulations of citizenship (citizen rights) and human rights in Australian 20th-century history.

Karen Hughes is a postgraduate research scholar in Australian Studies at Flinders University, Adelaide who teaches Australian Studies at the University of South Australia. She has published widely in academic journals and has produced and directed a number of documentary films, including the multi-award winning *Pitjiri — the snake that will not sink*. With the assistance of an AIATSIS research grant she is currently writing a biographical work on Ruth Heathcock and the Aboriginal women domestic workers at the Roper Bar Police Station. Karen's research interests include women's cross-cultural relations in new world settler societies; Indigenous epistemologies and anti-colonial strategies; narratives and their social lives; visual and screen culture; social justice issues; and the blurring of boundaries between documentary and fiction.

John Maynard is an Australian Research Council post-doctoral fellow with Umulliko Centre for Indigenous Higher Education Research at the University of Newcastle. His traditional roots lie with the Worimi people of Port Stephens. He was the recipient of the Aboriginal

History Stanner Fellowship for 1996 and the NSW Premier's Indigenous History Fellowship for 2003–04, and is the author of *Aboriginal stars of the turf* (Aboriginal Studies Press, 2002). John was a member of the Executive Committee of the Australian Historical Association, 2000–02, and has worked with and within many Aboriginal communities, urban, rural and remote.

Fiona Paisley is the Co-Director of the Centre for Public Culture and Ideas, and Senior Lecturer in Australian History at Griffith University, Brisbane. She has published widely on internationalism and settler colonial history in the first half of the 20th century, and on Indigenous history and gender, including *Loving Protection? Australian feminism and Aboriginal women's rights, 1919–1939* (Melbourne University Press, 2000). She is currently completing a study of women internationalists and debates about culture and 'race' in the Pacific region, 1920s to 1950s.

Preface

Why not develop a certain degree of rage against
the history that has written such an abject
script for you that you are silenced?
—Gayatri Spivak, 1986

This collection grew out of several years of discussions during conference lunch breaks as we met and reported on the progress of our various projects with their shared focus on settler colonialism, white women and Aboriginal history. One day, we said, we must work on a book together. We had all contributed in one way or another to the debate concerning the ethics of historical research, and were challenged by the question of privilege and perspective, the importance of memory and reading against the grain of the official archives, and the moral issues surrounding the kinds of history we chose to write. We were conscious of an Indigenous argument that white historians' incorporation of Aboriginal subjects in historical work was yet another form of neo-colonialism. In putting together a collection primarily on 'white' women involved in the Aboriginal domain we have sought to respond positively to such criticism.

Firstly we point to the ways in which the category 'white' has entered into the historiography of Aboriginal history in the past several decades, drawing on the comments of anthropologist WEH Stanner in the late 1960s and leading into 1990s debates over the possibility or otherwise for white women to work ethically in the academy, especially in the area of Aboriginal history. Secondly, we acknowledge the influence of critical imperial histories from beyond Australia in situating the Australian white woman and her accounts of Indigenous women within transnational and international contexts. And thirdly we argue for the value of the biographical approach in providing for a nuanced reading of the entanglement of white and Indigenous subjects in history.

Throughout the book, we adopt the term 'white' for Anglo-Australian or settler women. This reflects the focus of the Indigenous and non-Indigenous contributors to this collection, who were concerned with Anglo-Australian women and their various interactions with Aboriginal women, mostly in the first decades of the 20th century which saw the consolidation of government intervention in Aboriginal lives. White women were involved in this process, whether directly as government employees or indirectly as members of the white community. These Anglo-Australian women were 'white' in the context of contemporary race relations, where white and black were the assumed dichotomy upon which racial policy and White Australia was founded. In this collection, reference to that dichotomy has been maintained but in changed form. 'Black' has been replaced for the most part by 'Indigenous', while the whiteness of Anglo-Australian women has been given new emphasis — whiteness, rather than the otherness of 'race' is given central stage.

As white women interested in the historical interactions between Indigenous and settler Australia, we were also painfully aware of the implicated status of white women in the settler colonialism of the past, and our own implication in the present. Not least, we were aware of the irony that our careers were to be established on grounds reminiscent of some of the protagonists in our research — white women concerned with the rights and status of Aboriginal people, particularly Aboriginal women. This doubling effect is something we neither seek to gloss over nor reify; unapologetically, but not unreflectively, three white women have edited this collection. From the outset, then, we each have our own account to give of the influences that have shaped our research and writing.

Anna Cole

Born in England and moving with my family to live in the West Indies as an infant, back to Britain and then migrating to Australia as a young child, questions of place and identity fuelled my earliest academic studies. For a while I thought I'd found a home in feminism, and in particular women's history, so in 1990, a few years before I began postgraduate studies, Jane Haggis's survey 'Gendering colonialism or colonising gender? Recent women's studies approaches to white women and the history of British colonialism' articulated some important concerns about a new and burgeoning area of research. Haggis argued that certain studies with a 'woman-centred' approach to colonial history had, by 'centring' white women, acted to 'un-gender the colonised people and contribute to silencing colonised women'.[1] Further, she said, the woman-centred approach failed to locate class divisions between both colonial and colonised women.

Influenced by such debates, and the argument that writing Aboriginal history as a white person was another form of neo-colonialism, the easiest option for me as a non-Aboriginal woman graduate student would have been to avoid working in the area of 'Aboriginal history'. It seemed to me, however, that the argument that it was just too difficult could easily become a rationale for writing segregationist history by default. As Carole Ferrier has argued, '[t]he problems of speaking about people who have been constructed in the dominant discourse as "other" cannot...be a pretext for not doing so.'[2] Rather than abandoning the field altogether in an intellectual and political climate that contested whites' roles in writing Aboriginal history, I felt a new way of understanding and writing this history had to be found.

This new way for me meant looking at the other side — not of the frontier, but of the administrative fences that had for so long enacted a form of unofficial political, social and emotional apartheid in Australia (and whose ghost I detected in the hostility I felt from some towards my interest in Aboriginal history). In pragmatic terms this meant considering those non-Aboriginal people who had worked closely with the administration and policy that constituted the conflicting but draconian context for Aboriginal history. But in order not to cast Aboriginal people as passive victims of white authority, this new history needed to recognise the agency of both sides and become a history of interrelationships. My aim was not to attempt to write 'Aboriginal' history but rather, from the position of my white subjectivity, to write a history of interaction, of relationship — a history that sought to desegregate the arena of Aboriginal history.

Further, rather than writing women's history, I wanted to extend Haggis's approach by writing a gendered analysis of both coloniser and colonised in the context of Indigenous policy in Australia.[3] I understood gender as a social relationship distinguishable from, but shaped by, other relationships in society, such as those of class and race, and by the meanings attributed to sexual difference.[4] I sought to analyse the ways in which public representations of gender interacted with the administration and discourse of race in post-war Australia. While this approach led to an original analysis of colonial administration and its wider discourse, it did not confront in a direct way the sticky problem of understanding the individuals who enacted and oversaw policy and administration.

Victoria Haskins

I learned early, growing up in the East Kimberley of Western Australia, that I was a '*kartiya*', or white: literally, 'one who cannot hear'. Out of politeness, attention was not drawn to my outsider status by my friends and, being a child, I was only dimly aware of the inexplicable privileges of race that so mortified my mother (such as being served first in the local shop). Paradoxically, it was not until my family moved to Sydney's comfortable North Shore that I really felt the peculiarity of being a white person in Australia. Part of a large, pallid majority, Aboriginal people nowhere to be seen, I became more and more curious to learn about the history of relationships between Aboriginal and white Australians.

When I started at university in the mid-1980s, as the 1988 bicentenary of white Australia approached, Aboriginal culture was experiencing an unprecedented renaissance in the urban mainstream. Accompanying the wave of Aboriginal music, Aboriginal art and Land Rights flags was the clarion call of the 1980s: 'White Australia has a Black history'. The demand that white Australians recognise that the history of invasion and racist oppression was indeed relevant to themselves, and needed to be addressed — and, hopefully, redressed — had a powerful resonance for me. But it was not until well into my postgraduate history studies on the vexed relationships between white and Aboriginal women that I discovered, by chance, that my paternal great-grandmother had been active in the Aboriginal rights movements of the 1930s.[5] As I began to tell a history that for the first time seemed to be a history that was truly mine to tell, I felt my understanding of the relationship between the past and the present shift. That nobody in my family had even remembered this story of a white woman in Aboriginal history, let alone seen fit to tell me about it, was, I realise now, part of the historical experience of 'whiteness' in this country.

Fiona Paisley

In her 1992 book *White, male and middle class*, Catherine Hall, the historian of Englishness, wrote: 'History, for me, is not just another fiction.'[6] Hall's assertion that imperial and colonial history is very much a matter for the present encapsulated the spirit of critical analyses of gender and empire in the 1990s. Her words also expressed my own concern, as I began my postgraduate research in 1991, to engage with Australian history from a settler colonial perspective, a concern that reflected as much my being a first-generation settler born in Scotland as it did my academic interest in white women and Aboriginal rights in the inter-war years. Deeply impressed by what I learned about a vibrant history of Aboriginal rights campaigns in the first decades of last century, and in the context of the new studies of gender and empire, I wondered how white women living at the time had contributed, if anything, to their struggle.

As I went on to describe in my thesis and later my book, behind the long-assumed silence on interracial relations there existed a genealogy of white women's political engagement with Aboriginal Australia.[7] Not coincidentally, this genealogy emerged during a decade of extraordinary interest, beyond as well as within the world of academic research, in the historical formations of whiteness and settler colonialism. As the history of Aboriginal child removal and its ongoing impact on Aboriginal communities entered public discourse through the moving testimonies of Indigenous people from around Australia, and as the centenary of Federation loomed, the future relationship between Indigenous Australia and 21st-century settler nationhood became a crucial issue for all Australians. For me, it brought with it a greater realisation that the question of which histories we choose to tell remains one of the most pertinent in the new century.

One of the things I learned from my research was that although the desire to enter into a more honourable relationship with Indigenous Australians in the 1980s and 1990s seemed to represent a new phase in white Australia's history, it was not the first time that the morality of policies like removal, or even colonisation itself, had been widely debated. Officials supporting the genesis of assimilation in the 1920s and 1930s, for example, were not merely the unfortunate advocates of an evil doctrine widely accepted in their day. As the new critical histories of humanitarianism in Australia have made clear, they persisted despite significant public criticism of government policies. Encouraging though the genealogy of white women's active engagement with Aboriginal status and conditions remains, opposition cannot in itself be assumed to signal progress. The hard lesson is that while racialist policy has never lacked critics, its advocates have justified nonetheless the suffering of a 'few' (the Aboriginal mothers of children taken, for example) in the name of a greater good, as they saw it, whether settler or Indigenous.

That white women have engaged in various ways in the rights struggle, both settler and Indigenous, individually or in organisations, also undercuts any sense we may have that previous generations were less aware, less strategic, or less motivated than those of today. In her 1992 work on British imperialism and feminism, Vron Ware set out to investigate how categories of racial, ethnic and cultural difference were constructed in the past and how they continue to be reproduced, albeit in changed form, in the present. Applying Walter Benjamin's notion of 'moments of danger', she asserted that only in the 'act of seizing hold of a memory' could the past be put to active use in the present.[8] Such a realisation that the past is not disconnected from the present leads to the recognition that neither are its actors: not to be condemned or praised, they need to be understood within the contradictory and complex parameters of historical possibility. It has provided me with a useful way forward over the years as I have moved from ignorance, through shame and guilt, into what I hope is a more nuanced and active engagement with history. And it is this recognition that illuminates the white women in Aboriginal histories in this collection, distinguishing our approach and that of our contributors from the extremes of either whitewash or black armband history.

***

It is against such questions and debates that this collection grew. We have deliberately chosen to produce a book about 'white women' as a partial response to the debates about the appropriation of Aboriginal history by white historians. But our response is not simply that. In this collection Indigenous women and men write about non-Indigenous women, offering fresh perspectives and viewpoints on neglected stories of our shared history. As well, Stephanie Gilbert, an Indigenous author, has chosen to write about Aboriginal activist Pearl Gibbs, seeing an essential place for her in a book about the history of white women. In so doing she acknowledges the longstanding collaborations and historical entanglement of women's lives 'across the racial divide'.

We have also deliberately chosen to focus on white women, as opposed to men, to address an imbalance in the historical record. Those familiar with both academic and popular representations of Aboriginal history (such as in the recent film *Rabbit-proof fence*) may well be familiar with the name of AO Neville, the notorious 'Native Commissioner' from Western Australia; AP Elkin, the anthropologist and senior administrator from New South Wales; or Cecil Cook, Chief Administrator of the Northern Territory.[9] Less well known are the women who appear in this collection, such as Ella Hiscocks, Matron of the Cootamundra Home for Aboriginal Girls in New South Wales, or Ruth Heathcock, the South Australian nurse working with Aboriginal people suffering from leprosy in the Roper River and Gulf Country of the Northern Territory. In answer to the critique that a woman-centred approach fails to locate class, the women represented in this volume are not classless, nor all from the middle classes. Indeed, as some of the chapters in this collection show, the 'racial' frontier in settler colonial societies was sometimes a place where class allegiances and constraints were worn thin or worn down altogether; for example, Jennie Parsons Smith, featured in this collection, was a former domestic servant and lady's maid from the working-class East End of London, transformed in colonial Australia into the matron of a home for Aboriginal children.

Our focus on the personal and private, as well as the public, interactions of white women with Aboriginal people, and their engagement with Aboriginal issues, has been more than simply a convenient way of negotiating our own positions as white women in Aboriginal history. Understanding the complexities, the multiple ways in which identities are forged, shaped and shifted, and the ways in which an individual's words and actions may have a wider or different effect than expected, enriches our understanding of the entanglement of ourselves and of others generally within history. Coming through the academy in the late 20th century we have been schooled in the understanding that we cannot address race relations history without taking our privilege and power as white women on board. To tentatively reach beyond this, to go beyond simple dichotomies of 'black' and 'white', is to reconstruct the complex enmeshment of experience that makes up the history of oppression, resistance and coexistence under colonialism.

Aboriginal historiography

In his 1968 Boyer lecture, anthropologist WEH Stanner talked about the ways in which Aboriginal people had been marginalised in Australian history, left out of most history books altogether, relegated to 'a melancholy footnote' in the pages of a few:

> ...inattention on such a scale cannot possibly be explained by absent-mindedness. It is a structural matter, a view from a window which has been carefully placed to exclude a whole quadrant of the landscape.[10]

It was a call to integrate the experience of dispossession and colonisation into the course of Australian history, to redress an exclusion dating back to the emergence of the modern Australian nation in the early 20th century, and the time was ripe for such a historical reassessment. At first, Aboriginal people appeared in histories in somewhat familiar guise: sad and bewildered victims of unstoppable Anglo-Saxon power in the past, outcasts of Australia in the present. It was the victors whose visage changed: from conquering hero to conquering villain, from civiliser to destroyer. But from the mid-1980s Aboriginal people underwent another reconstruction, appearing as patriots, warriors, guerrilla fighters for their country and culture. The whites remained the villains, and in the face of such concerted and undying resistance their power seemed even more inscrutable and unstoppable. Noting the paradox, from the late 1980s historians became more concerned with the nuances of colonisation, the shifting balances of frontier relations, the historical web of negotiations over language and spatial arrangements, the patterns of accommodation as well as resistance, the agency of Aboriginal people in this history, and the diversity of roles played by white actors.

An emphasis on place and on genealogical connections and responsibilities marked the entry of Aboriginal historians in the world of history-on-paper, reflecting an important transformation of the Western historical tradition. Enthusiastically, many white historians in the 1980s and 1990s took up projects to present an Aboriginal perspective by working collaboratively with Aboriginal people (in theory at least) to 'translate' Aboriginal histories to a non-Aboriginal audience. But the entry of Aboriginal historians also carried within it an inherent challenge to the presumed authority (and objectivity) of white historians. This challenge would run head on into the desire to write Aboriginal history back into the white Australian historical narrative.

In the lead-up to the bicentenary, a collective of Indigenous historians undertook to answer the question 'Why can't white historians write Aboriginal history?' Stating that Aboriginal people regarded the 'white version of history since colonisation as colonialist propaganda, as a denial of our set of truths', they asserted that Aboriginal and white approaches to history were fundamentally different. Importantly, they declared Aboriginal historians were 'ultimately responsible to "our own mob", and not to the discipline of history nor to the white concept of knowledge':

> This responsibility to family, kin and community is keenly felt. Our relations will edit and correct our versions of history and participate in the version of our histories which will be passed on to our children as our set of truths. Aboriginal people largely mistrust white historians because they know they cannot pass on all information in trust, and that they cannot participate in arriving at the final form...
>
> It must be clear that Aboriginal contributions to Australian history have fundamental cultural and political purposes. We are reclaiming our right to identify and define ourselves.[11]

The writers concluded with a call to Aboriginal people to write their own history, rather than a demand that non-Aboriginal people did not. But the very question that had been posed sent a clear message to non-Aboriginal historians.

In 1995, the writer Mudrooroo declared: 'It is our past and only we can write it, for in a sense we need history and it is not "ours" until we do the writing ourselves, giving importance to the stories which matter to us.'[12] In time to come his own position and authority as an Indigenous person would be challenged, but the point he made remains valid: history written by another cannot be claimed as one's 'own' history.

The following year, leading Aboriginal historian Jackie Huggins explained that 'reflection on the past for Aboriginal people' was 'quite different to non-Aboriginal people':

> White constructions of history have been charged with this ethnocentrism which keeps us by and large excluded and marginalised, on the peripheries of existence. What we are saying is, rather than be at the margins, we should be at the centre.[13]

The explosion of the so-called Bell–Huggins debate further cautioned those of us working in the field of 'women's history'.[14] The assertion that white women should not, and indeed could not, speak on Aboriginal women's issues touched a deep nerve among white feminists accustomed to being criticised for marginalising Aboriginal women and Aboriginal women's experiences. But in the heat of the argument the deeper issue — that white women needed to acknowledge and understand their relationship to Aboriginal women in the historical and ongoing colonial order of things — was obscured.

In fact, for some time a number of white female historians had been revisiting the position of white women in colonisation. The pioneer mythologising of white women as nurturing carers of Aboriginal people began to be reassessed in the 1970s, as did the idea, more favoured by white men, of white women as passive, helpless, unwitting ciphers and bystanders of colonisation. Others, conversely, took issue with the argument that the white woman was the catalyst for increasing racial divides, a belief that had emerged strongly in the post-war decline of the British Empire. In the 1990s, attention was drawn to the complex role played by women's groups, feminists and humanitarian women in moves to reform official policies on Aboriginal people, and towards Aboriginal women specifically. This provided an important foreground and corollary to recent studies of the white humanitarian movement generally. Such studies of white women's roles constitute the soil from which much of this collection grew.

The essays here, however, move beyond the earlier obsession with allocating blame, complicity and responsibility. Though a necessary exercise in revisionism, the unintended result of this earlier approach has been a reductionist debate on whether white women were 'good' or 'bad'. Ironically, such work not only tended to 'un-gender' Aboriginal people but, by focusing on the white actors, may have marginalised the Indigenous actors in their own past (as Jane Haggis has also pointed out). What has become obvious is the need to explore 'whiteness' as positionality — to squarely address the location of white women within their relationships with Aboriginal people, and within Aboriginal history generally. For regardless of how we judge them today, it is clear that all white women, as Ann Curthoys stated succinctly in 1993, 'were always already in situations of power in relation to Aboriginal people... [and they] inherit "agency" and "empowerment" as part of the triumphant colonial process of historic dispossession'.[15] As these essays show, such power relations were embedded in a structural as well as a personal complex of racial, gender and class inequalities.

In Australia, whiteness is 'itself a fantasy position of cultural dominance born out of the history of European expansion'.[16] Or, to put it another away, as did James Baldwin with regard to North America:

> ...the people who, as they claim, 'settled' the country became white — because of the necessity of denying the Black presence, and justifying the Black subjugation... White men — from Norway, for example, where they were Norwegians — became white: by slaughtering the cattle, poisoning the wells, torching the houses, massacring Native Americans, raping Black women... Because they think they are white, they dare not confront the ravage and the lie of their history... Because they think they are white, however vociferous they may be and however multitudinous, they are as speechless as Lot's wife — looking backward, changed into a pillar of salt![17]

The 'Great Australian Silence' noted by Stanner back in 1968 has been inextricable from the experience of imagining Australia and Australian history as being 'white'. The challenge for us now is to find the voice of the white woman to confront the 'ravage and lie' of a history that has, to paraphrase Spivak, written such an abject script for her.[18]

When we say that 'white women have a black history' — and that white women have a voice in this history — we do not intend to claim Aboriginal history as 'our own'. Nor do we intend to talk over or silence the voices of Aboriginal people. Indigenous scholar Aileen Moreton-Robinson interrupted any simplistic dichotomy between appropriation histories and 'autohistories' in her analysis of the whiteness of Australian feminism, tellingly titled *Talkin' up to the white woman*.[19] By choosing to write on and to white women from her subjectivity as an Indigenous woman, Moreton-Robinson reversed a standard and much criticised practice whereby white historians are the presumed authority on Aboriginal experiences, and Aboriginal historians' role limited to providing useful, if subjective, 'perspectives' on Aboriginal history. For the authors in this collection, white or Aboriginal, male or female, the relationship of themselves as speakers, as well as that of their individual subject, to Aboriginal history and people has been a crucial part of the writing process. Our challenge as editors has been to draw out the difficult question of how to represent such complex entanglements without appropriating Aboriginal history and without denying structural racial inequality.

Gender and imperial history

Historians of whiteness in empire, such as Catherine Hall, Vron Ware, Antoinette Burton and Ann Stoler, have pointed out the very material effects of discourses of race and gender employed in colonisation, both in the colonial past and continuing into the 'post-colonial' present. Moreover, their attention to formations of actual bodies, white and black, as well as to social bodies such as the colonial nation, has shown that frontier and metropolitan space are dynamically intertwined. Their vision of empire/colonial worlds as fluid, contingent and unstable domains crisscrossed by transnational imperial and colonial connections provides an important context for our reappraisal of white women in settler colonies without resort to the fixed binaries of centre/periphery, coloniser/colonised or imperial/national.[20] In her most recent book, *Civilising subjects*, Hall reminds us of the importance of asserting colonialism's place at the heart of national histories, both metropolitan and settler colonial. The nation is brought into being through 'particular discursive work', she writes, in which only certain individuals, identities and subjects are constituted within its imagined collectivity. Moreover, it is those marginalised subjects that consolidate metropolitan or national centres.

In Australia, as elsewhere, 'the white woman' was an important figure in the civilising mission of empire. Thus Antoinette Burton has shown that at the turn of the 20th century, British women were able to deploy their imperial maternalist duty to speak for their less fortunate colonised sisters in order to promote their own suffrage campaigns.[21] Following suffrage in Australia, as Joan Strack, Elizabeth McKenzie Hatton and others in this collection illustrate, some settler colonial women used their relatively empowered position to support Aboriginal people against authorities.[22] But a concern for Aboriginal people, a readiness to participate in their administration or a desire to contribute to their 'uplift' were welcomed by governments only as long as the women who felt this way did not advocate a change in policy, criticise Australian governments overseas, or support Aboriginal people against authorities.

White womanhood, particularly middle-class, although powerfully positioned was still constrained by dominant expectations of proper, white femininity, particularly in the settler colonies where these women were to found a new society.[23] Those who contravened expectations soon confronted disapproval. While white men had conquered the 'frontier', they would need 'properly' domestic white women in order to remake themselves as 'settlers'. Such women were seen as crucial in the modernisation of both white and black populations as the post-frontier settler nation took shape during the first half of the last century.

In this transnational gender configuration, white women were expected to play a humanising role in uplift. In this larger sense, feminist or not, white women were variously situated along a civilising continuum that straddled settler and crown colonies, colonial periphery and imperial metropole. But while white women might mobilise their subject position to disrupt dominant representations of settler colonialism, theirs was a highly contingent and fragile identity.

As well as looking at the location of white women, then and now, in the colonisation process, our collection brings into overdue focus the enormous influence of Indigenous women and men in articulating whiteness. Although formally ended, British imperial history, as with other imperial histories, continues into the present. As Catherine Hall explains, it is the recognition of the 'same but different' repetition between colonial and post-colonial power that has made possible a 'return to the past and [a] rewriting of connection histories', which are characteristic of recent critical imperial and colonial histories such as her own.[24] For Anne Stoler and Frederick Cooper, writing of Dutch colonialism, the fluid relationship between the categories 'colonial' and 'colonised' highlighted the impossible task faced by colonial regimes in aiming to fix racial distinctions that were 'neither inherent nor stable'. They argue that these categories — problematic, contested and changing — were imbued therefore with 'possibilities for empowerment among the colonised'.[25] Moreover, structured in gendered terms, they were supposedly secured through forms of sexual control. Hence, domestic arrangements in colonial communities have been significant to our understanding of colonialism, and play a significant part in each contribution to our collection.[26]

By refusing to accept colonial power as monolithic or all-encompassing, we are able to see those living under colonisation as engaged in diverse negotiations, including through complex sets of relationships with settler women. As Cooper and Stoler put it, 'the idea of indigenous "response" or "resistance" to an imperialist initiative no longer captures the dynamic of either side of the encounter'.[27] This rendering of intercultural and interracial exchange as an encounter — a moment in time and space occupied by both 'sides' of the colonial divide — is certainly evident in the biographical studies offered here.

Extending this reappraisal of agency to include the figure of the white woman, it is clear that notions of complicity with or resistance to colonisation as a universal expression of the 'good' or 'bad' woman are no longer applicable. At most, we can investigate how white women understood themselves in relation to a 'slippery and constantly negotiated series of exchanges embracing both rejections of and collusions with colonialism and with different forms of nationalism'.[28] The white women of our title are both subject to and the subject of complex sets of gender and racial ideologies — ideologies imbuing settler colonialism with a remarkable polyvalency. A diverse group, white women must be recognised as differently positioned in relation to class, and hence to racial hierarchies variously and particularly activated in individual lives. Intrigued by the interaction between (auto)biography and the shifting local impacts of imperialism and colonialism, one of our key themes in this collection is the way in which the global is intimately inflected through the local, daily, lived experiences of white women, not least in their exchanges with Indigenous people — both of their imagination and those they've actually met.

Biographical approach

Our biographical approach to the material means confronting the full range of subjectivities that women have occupied in colonial, and particularly settler colonial, contexts. Marg Allen, in her chapter on Catherine Martin, notes: 'While it might be easy to represent her as some sort of heroine…such a view would obscure the complexities and contradictions within her writing and of her own position as a settler woman.' The various chapters share an approach that highlights the ambiguities of these women's lives and work. As these stories show, there is no life lived without contradiction, and how each woman deals with the sometimes painfully conflicting demands and influences in her life and work is an important aspect of each.

A related question is how to understand the gap between the way people interpret their own histories and the biographer's analysis of that experience. To put it another way, we recognise that biography as a genre is by no means separate from the autobiography of those who produce it. The two chapters in this collection on Daisy Bates, written by different authors and highlighting different aspects of her relatively well-known life, illustrate this point. Cynthia Coyne's essay explores a little-known collaboration between Bates and Aboriginal senior man Billingee, revealing new information about both the woman and the language, the social and cultural rules, the history and material culture of the Jukun-Yawuru clan from north-western Australia.

The question of the relationship between researcher and subject is perhaps most keenly felt by those working on family history. In these cases the author's personal investment in the stories of the past presents a particularly stark challenge for the biographer: 'We may look with distaste at the tragic events preceding us; hiding, from unease, those parents or grandparents to whom we are the heirs', writes Christine Brett Vickers in her chapter on her great-grandmother Jennie Parsons Smith, 'mother' of the Singleton Aboriginal Children's Home. But, as she acknowledges, 'Jennie's involvement and struggle with a particularly difficult dimension of Australian settler experience, the removal of Aboriginal children from their parents and their relegation to the realms of uneducated servitude, is part of my family story'.

Memory and family reminiscences form the source material for a number of chapters in this collection. Family memories, oral history from both Aboriginal and non-Aboriginal individuals, and missionary archives are used to construct the life of Parsons Smith, for example. Victoria Haskins reconstructs the life of her great-grandmother, Joan Kingsley-Strack, using both family memories — and, crucially, family 'unrememberings' — to understand a complicated and disturbing story buried deep in her family history. In the past two decades, as Antoinette Burton has recently noted, scholarly attention to memory has given women's historical experience 'a foothold in history'.[29] In each of these chapters, memories are not used as a verbatim report on the past, nor are they seen as an 'unreliable' source; rather, the cultural and personal selection inherent in memory is seen as essential to the interpretation of each woman's life in the present. What is forgotten, the confusions and the silences, is as important to the interpretations in this collection as what is remembered.

Our critical use of memory, family recollections and oral history highlights the ways historical consciousness and individual identity dwell in varying forms of narrative.[30] For example, the analysis of Matron Ella Hiscocks of the Cootamundra Aboriginal Girls' Home is partially recalled through her own memories, recorded in an extended interview in 1980. Her account of her work and life, retold in a changed, and charged, political environment, is treated not just as evidence for the reconstruction of her life history but as part of her ambiguous self-narrative, intended to shape and reshape a persona in response to questions from a new era. This is not to claim that Hiscocks was 'making it up' in her interview with oral historian Peter Read, but rather that people adopt a variety of historically contingent narrative strategies in the telling and retelling of their lives.

Such an approach to self-narrative challenges notions of biography and autobiography as the 'coherent shaping of the past from the perspective of the unified self in the present'.[31] Instead, we become aware of the continuous reassessment of the past in the light of the present. As Peter Read notes, reflecting on writing the biography of Charles Perkins, our present interpretation of the past is influenced by multi-variant factors that include 'our sense of happiness and failure in the present, of achievement or missed-opportunity'.[32] These biographical explorations of women's lives do not assume a purely rational and coherent fixed identity in which being a Woman, White, Aboriginal, Working Class or Middle Class, is always the central element of identity. As John Maynard's chapter shows, Elizabeth McKenzie Hatton's identity as a white, middle-class missionary with a 'strong, condescending Christian ethic' did not finally obscure her view of the Aboriginal men and women she worked closely with. Her personal experiences led her, regardless of her class and 'race', to be at times 'a cutting-edge and astute political activist'.

Biography may seem to underpin models of analysis that honour the individual over the collective, giving sustenance to a common neo-conservative celebration of individualism. However, our approach is to consider the wider implications of an individual's life for the broader interpretation of Aboriginal history. Importantly, these biographies emerge as stories of interrelatedness, from the private domain of domestic service to the public work of women such as Constance Ternent Cooke and Mary Bennett. As a number of the chapters document, personal connection or contact with an Aboriginal individual or community at a crucial or formative time had a powerful influence on a number of the women in this collection, and more longstanding contacts and friendship could radicalise. Karen Hughes, for example, considers leprosy nurse Ruth Heathcock's early childhood contacts and abiding friendships with women from the Ngarrindjeri community around Wellington, South Australia, as influential in her radically anti-establishment approach to Aboriginal health. Alison Holland notes the impact of Aboriginal activist

Anthony Martin Fernando on the humanitarian Mary Bennett, arguing his accusation that Bennett's own interest was driven by 'cant and hypocrisy…to some extent stirred her to practical action…' For Constance Cooke, as Fiona Paisley writes, 'although her heartland was in the women's movement, her political agenda was grounded in the exchanges she had with Aboriginal people, whether indirectly through a train window in the outback or directly as a visitor to their communities'. It is clear that white women's lives in this collection were connected in significant and sometimes seminal ways to Aboriginal women's and men's lives. Each chapter, then, moves towards desegregating the area of Aboriginal history, showing the often intimate levels of engagement, both personal and political, between Aboriginal and non-Aboriginal women and men. As Victoria Haskins argues, the history of white women employers of Aboriginal domestic servants is revealing of the 'enmeshed relationships between white and Aboriginal women that generations of repression and denial have obscured…just as personal and colonialist histories are interwoven, so too black and white lives are inseparably enmeshed in our past.'

In the political climate fostered by the Howard government, where both Aboriginal and non-Aboriginal history is being stereotyped and polarised, an approach that seeks to get personal, to break down categorical statements and explore the nuances of lived experience and relationships, is crucial. Understanding the 'peculiar intimacy', as Sara Suleri calls it, between colonisers and colonised, without giving away the historical and persisting inequalities in those relationships, is an essential part of post-colonial research, and a prime motivation for this biographical collection.[33]

Finally, in the first few years of the new millennium in Australia some highly publicised debates, ignoring decades of historiography, have returned to questions of 'frontier wars' and their repercussions. Body counts of how many were 'really' killed in massacres and battles have taken centre stage in the Australian 'history wars' in the same miserable way that arguments about how many Iraqi civilians were 'really' killed in British, American and Australian bombings have taken centre stage recently in the world media. We take a stance outside such 'body count' debates, which return the focus to an apparently masculine domain of open warfare. This collection provides a space where the generational repercussions of colonialism can be recognised; where the nuances of policy devised in the 'best interests' of Aboriginal people can be fleshed out; where the subtleties, the depths and shallows of relationships between Aboriginal and non-Aboriginal in the past and present can be explored. Over a decade ago Nancy Hartsock argued for a more diverse feminism, and it applies well to Australian race relations history today:

> ...we need to dissolve the false 'we'...into its real multiplicity and variety...to develop an account of the world which treats our perspectives not as subjugated or disruptive knowledges, but as primary and constitutive of a different world.[34]

It is to aspects of this different world that this collection turns.

Notes

1. Haggis 1990.
2. Carole Ferrier, 'Resisting authority', in Ian Donaldson, Peter Read & James Walker (eds), *Shaping lives: reflections on biography*, Humanities Research Centre, Australian National University, 1992, p. 104.
3. Cole 2001.
4. Joan Wallach Scott, *Gender and the politics of history*, Columbia University Press, New York, 1988.
5. Haskins 1998b and Victoria Haskins, 'Skeletons in our closet: family histories, personal narratives and race relations history in Australia', *Olive Pink Society Bulletin*, vol. 10, no. 2, 1998, pp. 15–22.
6. Catherine Hall, 'Feminism and feminist history', in Hall 1992, p. 1.
7. Paisley 2000.
8. Ware 1992b, p. 116.
9. *Rabbit-proof fence*, directed by Phillip Noyce, was based on the novel by Doris Pilkington, *Follow the rabbit-proof fence*, University of Queensland Press, 1996.
10. Stanner 1991 (1968), p. 24.
11. Aboriginal historians for the bicentennial history 1788–1988 working party (Wayne Atkinson, Marcia Langton, Doreen Wanganeen & Michael Williams), 'Aboriginal history and the bicentennial volumes', A W Martin (ed.), *Australia 1939–1988: A Bicentennial History Bulletin*, no. 3, Australian National University, Canberra, May 1981, pp. 21–25.
12. Mudrooroo, p.178.
13. Jackie Huggins, 'Experience and identity', *Limina*, 1996, reprinted in Jackie Huggins, *Sister Girl*, University of Queensland Press, Brisbane, 1998, p. 122.
14. See Moreton-Robinson, pp. 111–25.
15. Curthoys, p. 174.
16. Hage, p. 20.

17. Baldwin, pp. 177–80.
18. Spivak & Gunew, p. 137.
19. Moreton-Robinson.
20. See Hall 1992; Ware 1992a; Antoinette Burton, *At the heart of empire: Indians and the colonial encounter in late-Victorian Britain*, University of California Press, London & Berkeley, 1998; and Ann Laura Stoler, *Carnal knowledge and imperial power:race and the intimate in colonial rule*, University of California Press, 2002.
21. Burton, 1994.
22. Koven & Michel; Newman 1999; Daley & Nolan; and Jayawardena.
23. Adele Perry, *On the edge of empire: gender, race, and the making of British Columbia, 1849–1871*, University of Toronto Press, 2001.
24. Hall 2002, p. 11.
25. Cooper & Stoler, p. 1.
26. Stoler 1989, pp. 634–36.
27. Cooper & Stoler 1989, 'Introduction', p. 1.
28. Ian Christopher Fletcher, Laura E Nym Mayhall & Philippa Levine, 'Introduction', in Fletcher, Mayhall & Levine (eds), *Women's suffrage in the British Empire: citizenship, nation, and race*, Routledge, London, 2000 , p. xiv.
29. Burton 2003, p. 21.
30. Amin.
31. Paula Hamilton, 'Inventing the self: oral history as autobiography', in Ian Donaldson, Peter Read & James Walker (eds), *Shaping lives: reflections on biography*, Humanities Research Centre, Australian National University, 1992, p. 112.
32. Peter Read, 'A phantom at my shoulder: the final draft of *Charles Perkins: a biography*', in Donaldson, Read & Walker, 1992, p. 168.
33. Sara Suleri, *The rhetoric of English India*, University of Chicago Press, 1992, p. 69.
34. Nancy Hartsock, 'Foucault on Power: A theory for women?' in Linda J Nicholson (ed.), Feminism/Postmodernism, Routledge, New York, 1990, p.171.

Part 1
On the home front

1. 'Light in the darkness'
Elizabeth McKenzie Hatton

John Maynard

From the earliest point of white settlement in Australia, many people came forward with ideas about what the non-Indigenous authorities could best do to 'help' Aboriginal people — most of them put forward without input from Aboriginal people themselves. The main thrust was in terms of Christianising, civilising, caring for or saving a projected 'doomed race'. At the time, the British Empire was regarded as one 'on which the sun never sets' and the British themselves were believed to have attained 'the highest point of human progress and development'.[1] Wealthy socialites, working-class heroes, righteous intellectuals cr those imbued with nationalistic fervour stepped forth, especially in the early decades of the 20th century. Many were white women campaigning for the feminist platform, or simply in need of an interest.

Although many of these people had good intentions, deeply ingrained assumptions and perceptions of European superiority undermined much of their work. One woman who initially carried such baggage of the period was Elizabeth McKenzie Hatton. But unlike others, McKenzie Hatton, through her contact with Aboriginal people, would undergo a major shift in thinking that was decades ahead of its time.

In the early 20th century the Aboriginal population of Australia was largely controlled by church missionaries or state-operated Aboriginal protection boards, with their enforced, restrictive and destructive policies. In New South Wales two major initiatives of the Aborigines

Protection Board were to revoke former Aboriginal reserves that had been independently and successfully farmed, and to callously strip away Aboriginal children from their parents.[2] The children were subsequently placed in the so-called 'apprenticeship scheme', far removed from their families. Many never returned. These events were the catalyst for an eruption of Aboriginal political protest and the formation of the Australian Aboriginal Progressive Association (AAPA).

It was into this cauldron of agitation and fierce opposition to government policies that Elizabeth McKenzie Hatton found herself drawn. At the height of the AAPA's political agitation over the issue, she cried, 'Day after day letters come from the people, pleading for their children, asking me to find the girls, long lost to them — in service somewhere in this State — taken away in some cases over seven years ago and no word or line from them.'[3] Her deep empathy with the grievances of Aboriginal people and her political alliance with the Australian Aboriginal Progressive Association would put her in opposition to church, state and her own Christian beliefs.

It was not, however, as a political ally but as a white missionary and social worker that Elizabeth McKenzie Hatton began her connection with Aboriginal people. Mrs Hatton's earlier activities are described in the pages of *Our Aim*, the Aborigines Inland Mission (AIM) newsletter, and in letters to its founding members. A missionary at the Walla Street Evangelical Mission in Bundaberg, northern Queensland, 'Mrs McKenzie' had been through her own experience of personal loss when she married her second husband, a Mr Hatton of the same mission, in July 1908. Her first husband had died in a drowning accident at Bundaberg around the turn of the century.[4] Then, just six days before her marriage to Hatton, her 11-year-old daughter died: 'Thus joy and sorrow had been interwoven once more in this honoured servant's experience.'[5]

Before marrying Hatton, Elizabeth McKenzie had spent some 16 years working as a missionary in northern Queensland with the Kanaka communities, part of that time with the people of Pialba–Hervey Bay.[6] An Aboriginal missionary, Mrs Charles, worked closely with McKenzie Hatton during those years, and was described by her as a woman carrying a 'high standard of Christian character — a clever, refined, and educated woman, she has been used to help in the translation of the scriptures in the language of the Solomon Islands...'[7]

During this period McKenzie Hatton was also in touch with Aboriginal people living in the region. According to *Our Aim*, about 40 people at Tweed Heads 'had heard the gospel mainly through intermarriage with the Kanakas and Mrs McKenzie Hatton's work amongst the latter'.[8] She had originally hoped to go to the Torres Strait, but had declined the offer of a post there in order to care for her invalid father.[9]

During the First World War, McKenzie Hatton took up pen and paper to assist the war effort — a practice she would repeat a decade later with her prolific correspondence and petitioning on behalf of the AAPA and the Aboriginal political fight. Her efforts during the war were recognised by Rev. W Cleugh Black, who 'spoke in eulogistic terms of Mrs Hatton's splendid work with her pen…when by such means she brought comfort to thousands of stricken hearts'.[10] In stark contrast, her alignment with Aboriginal political campaigners would meet with ridicule, opposition and open hostility. Her relationship with the Aborigines Inland Mission, and in particular with its founder, Retta Dixon Long, was also destined to disintegrate. McKenzie Hatton's

Elizabeth McKenzie Hatton takes up the pen of political protest. Courtesy Mitchell Library, State Library of New South Wales.

make-up and fierce resolve would lead to a falling out not only with the AIM but with the whole process of Christian civilising.

McKenzie Hatton moved to Melbourne after the war. Her old friend and missionary colleague Mrs Charles had returned to Queensland after 14 years service in the Solomon Islands and was 'shocked to find, in this Christian land of ours, so little being done for her own people and the half caste girls'. Mrs Charles was so distressed by the conditions, she travelled to Melbourne to beseech McKenzie Hatton to 'go back and help her to rescue these young and helpless girls'.

A letter McKenzie Hatton wrote to Prime Minister Billy Hughes in 1921 as a result of Mrs Charles's grim story can be read as a prelude to what would eventuate some three years later. She asked for Commonwealth Government assistance to enable her 'from a moral standpoint' to look after Aboriginal girls. Her communication revealed her sympathy for the horrific impact of child separation on Aboriginal families: 'One of the saddest sights ever witnessed was the sorrow of an old man wailing for the loss of his little daughter, who, with no gentle hand, was being dragged off before his eyes by the officer of the law.'

She questioned the actions of the police in removing such children: 'Where do you take these girls, and what do you do with them when you remove them from the station?' The answer, McKenzie Hatton proffered indignantly, was 'we take them to the city and *lose* them.' Her letter was full of the need to *protect* and *Christianise* Aboriginal girls and to have 'inculcated [in them] those high ideals, which form the basis of our civilization'. She continued: 'No wonder some of us cry out with longing and ask to be allowed to *save* them'. However, McKenzie Hatton also praised state governments, particularly New South Wales, for their efforts regarding the 'educational scheme and the generous provision' made to Aboriginal people.[11] At this point the tone, direction and knowledge base of McKenzie Hatton's argument and comments were largely similar to those of most evangelical humanitarians of the time.

McKenzie Hatton's driving desire was to establish an Aboriginal 'girls' home'. Despite the Commonwealth Government's negative response to her proposal, it was not to be subdued. The Australian Aborigines Mission (AAM) newsletter, the *Australian Aborigines Advocate*, reported in April 1921: 'A strong Mission Council has been formed in Melbourne — Mr. Thos. Graham being President, and Mrs. McKenzie-Hatton Secretary. They have begun work in real earnest, and already successful results have been achieved by our Victorian Council.'

But only months later McKenzie Hatton would cut ties with the AAM, soon after visiting Sydney to initiate links with the AIM. The abruptness of the split suggests it was not amicable, particularly as the AAM had its headquarters in Sydney and it would have been easy for McKenzie Hatton to continue the relationship there. In siding with the AIM in preference to the AAM, she undoubtedly raised the ire of the National President of that association, TE Colebrook, the results of which would surface later. Colebrook still carried deep-seated resentment over the split of the New South Wales branch of the AAM, which had resulted in the formation of the AIM some 13 years earlier. According to the mission's newsletter:

> For years the work of God amongst this people went on undisturbed by internal friction; but there came a day when the Evil One succeeded in creating discord, which led to the retirement of Miss Dixon, and the establishment of work now controlled by that lady and her husband (Mr. and Mrs. Long) under the name AIM or Australian [sic] Inland Mission. Since then the work has been carried on by two forces instead of one, whether with better or worse results time alone will reveal.[12]

Obviously Colebrook would take any defection to the AIM very badly.

The AIM had been founded by missionary Retta Dixon Long. After her marriage in 1906 to another missionary, LW Long, Retta and her husband became the driving force behind the AIM's organisation and direction. From its inception in 1905, the AIM newsletter *Our Aim* carried the rather grandiose banner, 'to give Light to them that sit in Darkness'.[13]

During her visit to Sydney in 1921, McKenzie Hatton became aware that the AIM had a similar vision to her own of instigating an Aboriginal girls' home. She at once offered to take up the challenge. But her proposal was delayed when, after returning to Victoria the same year, she was struck down by illness. It was only at the end of 1923 that 'she was set free' and well enough to return to her work.[14] During the course of the next three or four months, the AIM, through Retta Dixon Long, attempted to secure on behalf of McKenzie Hatton a suitable house in Sydney for the proposed home. McKenzie Hatton returned to Sydney in late November. During her stay she found a house at Burlington Road, Homebush, but had not yet gained permission from the NSW Aborigines

Protection Board (APB) to use it 'as a home for Aboriginals'.[15] The board duly noted correspondence received and, in a sign of bitter confrontations to come, its members dismissed McKenzie Hatton's overture for assistance: 'A Mrs E McKenzie Hatton offering to care for incorrigible Aboriginal girls & asking whether the Board would pay a small allowance. Board unable to assist in direction mentioned.'[16]

Not yet accustomed to opposition, and unaware of the board's negativity, McKenzie Hatton remained quietly optimistic of gaining its support. She advised the AIM that she 'intended to take the place hoping that permission would be given'.[17] In January 1924, however, she was already facing difficulties. She had taken a lease on the house in Homebush, outlaying a substantial sum to furnish it, but soon had to seek a means of breaking the lease. Although the place was already operating as a boarding house, it had proven 'impossible to get permission to carry the place on as an Aboriginal Girls' Home and Mrs Hatton was now trying to dispose of her interest in the place'.[18]

Unfazed, McKenzie Hatton found another suitable home in the same street, a 12-room house named 'Comarques', on large grounds. It was obvious that she fully intended to push ahead, with or without backing of the AIM or consent from the APB. She proposed taking in two Christian workers as helpers, and sought to establish 'a small council to control the lease or purchase of the property'. The AIM fully endorsed her proposal and advised her to take the property on a year's lease at the weekly rental of £4, 'subject to the formation of a council to work in affiliation with the AIM'.[19]

Two weeks later McKenzie Hatton entered into a 12-month lease on the property, with the AIM contributing £22 to assist with the first month's rent and the purchase of some furniture.[20] She took possession on Monday, 14 January, and the first girl, Emily Melrose, was admitted on Wednesday, 23 January.[21] Two fellow missionary women had taken rooms at the property and 'both ladies would assist Mrs Hatton in various ways'. At an official opening ceremony held on 1 March the home was renamed 'Rehoboth'.[22] The biblical significance of the new name and the benevolent purpose of the property were highlighted in *Our Aim*: 'And he removed from thence and digged another well; for this they strove not; and he called the name of it Rehoboth; and he said, For now the Lord hath made room for us and we shall be a fruitful land.'[23]

Initially neither AIM nor McKenzie Hatton intended the home to run in opposition to other missionary or government institutions, believing it should instead provide a haven for girls the board deemed 'incorrigible'. Once labelled by the board, these girls were destined for institutionalisation in mental asylums. The AIM asserted that: 'It is our intention to take in girls — not children — who have proved unsuitable for domestic service and have otherwise given trouble and failed.' A report in its paper declared:

> The A.A.M are endeavouring to meet the need of the children in their Bomaderry Home and the Government Home at Cootamundra caters for girls requiring training before going to situations, but so far no provision has been made for the class of girl we hope to help. For lack of just such a home the Aborigines Board have had to place these girls in any institutions who would take them — for instance, two were in Rydalmere mental hospital, and at times Newington Asylum and other Institutions have sheltered them.[24]

The opening of the home, held on the front lawn, was given extensive and excited coverage in *Our Aim*:

> After a few introductory remarks by Mr. Long, Director of AIM, who presided, the A.I.M. treasurer, Mr. A.L. Perry, mounted a ladder and with a few strokes of the hammer nailed the gold and black letters in place. Mr. G.J. Tomkins, Vice-President offered a dedicatory prayer, presenting the house to God and calling upon Him to make it a veritable "Rehoboth" for Aboriginal girls in N.S.W.

The occasion highlighted a significant early link with the future Australian Aboriginal Progressive Association (AAPA). 'Mr Long then called upon Miss Cora Robertson, one of our early Singleton Home Girls, to sing and with pathos and power she exhorted us in song to "Cast thy bread upon the waters".' Cora Robertson was the cousin of future AAPA President Frederick Maynard and she would later marry Sid Ridgeway, who in 1927 would hold the position of AAPA secretary.

Two guest speakers, Rev. W Cleugh Black and Rev. E Davies, praised and encouraged McKenzie Hatton in the new enterprise. They appealed to the audience and the 'people of Homebush to support Mrs Hatton in her work'. Rev. Cleugh Black 'delighted the audience with incidents of his early association with Mrs Long and Aboriginal work'. The two final speakers were McKenzie Hatton herself and Retta Dixon Long:

Rehoboth Aboriginal Girls' Home, Sydney. **Our Aim**, *20 March 1924. Courtesy AIATSIS.*

> Mrs Hatton told how God had in her girlhood days revealed to her that He would come in and sup with her, and that while still in her teens she had heard His call to service and arose and followed. And now at the age of 54 He had again called and had shown that 'the lame shall take the prey'. She had answered…

The address by Mrs Long officially closed the opening. She described the lead-up to the establishment of the home, closing with the words: 'The glory of this latter house shall be greater than of the former, saith the Lord of Hosts: And in this place will I give peace, saith the Lord of Hosts.'[25]

The strong religious tones of the occasion reverberate through the archival sources. Hatton was at this point still clearly at one with the call and duty of the church. Yet only weeks later, the AIM council began to show signs of doubt about the activities of the home. This may well have been an early indication of disquiet over McKenzie Hatton's close contact with Aboriginal leaders and 'agitators'. Minutes recorded that: 'It was understood by the council that should any alteration be made in the management of the Home at any time the A.I.M would be entitled to the furniture purchased with the money voted from the Home fund for that purpose.'[26]

Meanwhile, McKenzie Hatton was unaware of any misgivings on the part of the AIM. Buoyed by her success to that point, she wrote in excited tones of the progress being made: 'It scarcely seems credible that only a few weeks ago Mr and Mrs Long and I sat on the front steps of this beautiful home and accepted it as God's provision for us to use as a Home for Aboriginal girls.' She reflected that from the outset there had been 'two outstanding facts: the NEED of the Girls' Home and God's unfailing CARE'.[27]

Shortly after, a second 'inmate' was welcomed to the home: 'We have prayed very definitely about those who shall be admitted to the Home and there are some points in this girl's story which make it seem as if the Good Shepherd has been seeking her out, for many days, and her coming here is a part of His plan for her salvation.'[28] McKenzie Hatton's delight in the house and in the prospects for the future were clearly evident: 'Now as I sit writing in the beautiful prayer room, so sweetly decorated and furnished, I wonder if it was all a dream, for Lo! The whole house is fully furnished and equipped from top to bottom in a most wonderful way.'[29] And the joy and attachment she felt for the Home were reflected in its increasing occupancy. In April 1924 she reported to AIM that another girl and baby had been admitted.[30] Knowledge of the house and its operations was also being transmitted around the country. Retta Dixon Long wrote to Janet Matthews in Adelaide: 'On Saturday last we opened a home for Aboriginal girls in Homebush near Sydney and we are trusting it will be a haven of rest and peace for them.'[31]

In May, a women's committee was established to act as an advisory council for Rehoboth. This body was to be an auxiliary of the AIM, the funding being 'altogether separate from the General Fund of the AIM. Ear-marked donations to Mr. A. L. Perry, AIM treasurer, will be passed on to Mrs Hatton.'[32] Mrs Long was elected president, Mrs Murray vice president, with McKenzie Hatton on the committee. At its first meeting, the Rehoboth Women's Committee 'resolved to convey to Mrs Hatton appreciation of her work'.[33]

A quality that set McKenzie Hatton apart at this time was her awareness of the need to take Aboriginal issues to the wider public forum, and a willingness to do so. In this respect she was very much a forerunner of feminist activists like Mary Bennett, Joan Kingsley Strack and Jessica Street, who began their rise to prominence during the 1930s.[34] At the invitation of the president of the Women's League of Church Aid, McKenzie Hatton pleaded for their interest in her cause:

[The] needs of the Aboriginal Girls of N.S.Wales and Queensland were placed before the kindly women and as it became clear to them that it is a work in which women must take a hand — their interest grew accordingly — before the meeting closed. The President handed the whole of the afternoon offering (£1/2/6), over to me for use at 'Rehoboth'.

The women of the league also decided unanimously to visit Rehoboth with the express desire of stocking the home's pantry. 'I met them at the door, to welcome such good friends in most heartily. My pantry had a very comfortable look the next morning, when all the parcels were opened and the goods, placed upon the shelves.' A similar generous response was triggered from the Granville Women's Guild: '…such a list of good things they brought the table was loaded and had all the appearance of a harvest festival in a very prosperous year.'[35]

This interest in developing and fostering awareness of Aboriginal issues through the wider community aligned McKenzie Hatton more with Aboriginal politics of the time than with the AIM. The contemporary Aboriginal leadership sought to educate and pursue the conscience of the largely ignorant wider public, initiating a campaign to 'enlist the sympathy and support of the public in urging the Government to repeal the *Aborigines Act* as it existed on the Statute Book'.[36] But the stance, objectives and argument of the Aboriginal political agitators radically contravened the notions of care promoted by both the church and government at this time.

McKenzie Hatton's wider public agenda situates her solidly with this Aboriginal political argument. The Aboriginal leaders would argue vehemently that they were well able to look after their own affairs and families, and they were sickened by policies and actions that continued wrongly to portray them as 'helpless children'.[37] McKenzie Hatton would, with Aboriginal backing and direction, eventually take the message of Aboriginal disadvantage to the wider populace herself, and come to know the Aboriginal communities with an intimacy that very few white people had developed. The independent Adelaide-based journal *Daylight* commented: 'Mrs Hatton has stayed in their homes, and states that they are very clean; sweet and wholesome food is prepared by painstaking wives and mothers. Further, she is proud to be associated with a people who have overcome the difficulties of racial feelings.'[38]

Yet it was this very awakening, through coming to know Aboriginal people and their families in their world, that would soon cause her estrangement from the AIM and everything she herself had taken as gospel.

Despite the glowing praise that both the home and McKenzie Hatton had received from local women's groups in such a short space of time, the mobilisation of opposition was already underway. In the following months, her behaviour was placed under serious scrutiny. Moreover, AIM Director LW Long showed that his (and therefore the AIM's) allegiance was not with McKenzie Hatton, and certainly not with the emerging Aboriginal political movement. In September the Secretary of the Aborigines Protection Board contacted Mr Long and relayed the news that the board was 'dissatisfied' with McKenzie Hatton's work:

> Amongst other things she [Hatton] was said to have told them that in her opinion there was no need for such a home as "Rehoboth". She had also told them she did not endorse our methods & operations. The Board were insisting on the return of one of the girls to Newington Asylum. It was left to Mrs Long to see Mrs Hatton.[39]

The board's motive was to destabilise and undermine McKenzie Hatton's activities. Despite the evidence that Rehoboth was providing a caring and genuine alternative environment for Aboriginal girls, the board demanded that one of the girls be returned to its care and placed back into Newington Asylum. The ambiguous relationship between the AIM and the board was clearly revealed in AIM documents from November that year: 'Mrs Long reported that she had a very favorable interview with the Chief Protector. He appeared to be very sympathetic with the work of the Mission.'[40] He was less sympathetic, it appears, with the AIM's involvement with Rehoboth. Only weeks later, Mr Long reported that 'he and Mrs Long had an interview with Mrs Hatton with reference to the future of the girls' home. The interview had been unsatisfactory — Mrs Long undertook to see Mrs Hatton again before next meeting.'[41]

It soon became obvious that McKenzie Hatton's close contact with the Aboriginal community in Sydney and beyond, and her willingness to visit the people and listen to their objections, was raising the eyebrows of some within the corridors of power. AIM documents from December record that Retta Dixon Long told McKenzie Hatton she'd 'received letters from Mr Colebrook & Miss Barker [another AAM missionary] complaining that she [McKenzie Hatton] had gone to La Perouse'. It was also noted: 'She had promised not to go again but had done so.'

Hatton's earlier defection from the AAM, controlled by TE Colebrook, had created another adversary. Despite the tensions between the AIM and the AAM, the Longs chose to admonish McKenzie Hatton and side with Colebrook and the board. These combined forces constituted a developing united front against her operations and association with Aboriginal political activists. For McKenzie Hatton, the painful realisation that the church and mission groups stood opposed to Aboriginal recovery was like a stinging slap to the face. The AIM was prepared to sacrifice the genuine needs of Aboriginal people for concessions and favour, bowing down and aligning itself with the Aborigines Protection Board and its policies.

McKenzie Hatton went on the offensive, undoubtedly with the backing and support of the Aboriginal political leadership. In a defiant declaration to the AIM, McKenzie Hatton responded that 'the Homebush Home was now the centre of the "Australian Aboriginal Progressive Association"'. The AIM minutes reveal its membership's distaste that the objects of this association 'appeared to be purely political and social'.[42] McKenzie Hatton's defiance prompted a further visit by Mrs Long to the home and a disciplinary interview after which the AIM severed its ties with Rehoboth:

> The auxiliary had been disbanded and Mrs Long had notified Mrs Lowe [Miss Alice Lowe, NSW Aborigines Protection Board 'homefinder'] that the mission disassociated itself entirely from Mrs Hatton's present activities. Resolved that Mrs Hatton be informed that the objects of the Home as presently conducted, being altogether different from those of the Mission and that for which it was instigated. We withdraw all support and sever all connection with the Home.[43]

By informing the board, and notifying the intimidating Miss Lowe, the AIM let loose a pack of hounds baying for blood. The board quickly instigated an investigation into McKenzie Hatton's back-ground, and implemented directives to make life as difficult as possible for her and the Aboriginal political activists with whom she was aligned. The board Secretary, AC Pettitt, requested information from Victorian counterparts regarding Hatton's activities 'amongst natives in Victoria'.[44] They called for police surveillance and a report on the activities of the girls home, a clear attempt at intimidation.[45]

For Aboriginal people during this period, rules, regulations and restrictions represented a strictly enforced police state of control. In a clear act of continued rebellion, McKenzie Hatton contacted the board seeking approval to visit its Aboriginal reserves. She received a polite, patronising response: 'Mrs Hatton to be advised that her application to visit reserves cannot be approved, but that the Board is always ready to consider any grievances she might think the [A]borigines may have.'[46]

The director of the AIM inserted a thinly disguised rebuke of McKenzie Hatton and her activities in the next issue of *Our Aim*, which officially announced the severance of relations:

> Our readers will no doubt remember that early last year an Aboriginal Girls Home was opened and named "Rehoboth" at Burlington Road, Homebush. Mrs Hatton had come over from Victoria and offered with our help to establish such a Home for girls, which we had considered a felt need for a long time.
>
> The A.I.M. promised to stand by Mrs Hatton for the first year, although she was to be entirely responsible for the control and upkeep of the Home.
>
> Mrs Hatton some months ago felt led to introduce other work into the Home which quickly changed its character, and has finally resolved itself into an Aboriginal Institute, and is the present headquarters of an 'Aboriginal Progressive Association' for both men and women, having for its object the social betterment of the people.
>
> As the 12 months lease has expired and it is necessary to re-lease, Mrs Hatton placed the change of project before the A.I.M. Council, who considering that the Home no longer came under the specific object of the A.I.M., viz., the evangelization of the [A]boriginal races of Australia, passed a resolution severing our connection.[47]

Although McKenzie Hatton had cut ties with the AIM, the termination of their relationship was not without a petty and laughable aftermath. Fuelled by a sense of perceived injustice, the AIM launched a crusade to strip her home of its furniture. McKenzie Hatton was asked 'if she had any suggestion to make regarding the furniture purchased with Mission funds for the benefits of the inmates'.[48] She replied that 'she anticipated no difficulty in adjusting the matter when the furniture was required'.[49]

The furniture issue continued to rankle the inner sanctum of the AIM for the next three months:

> Mrs Hatton wrote to Mrs Long (June 11th) offering to let us have the organ and table back (our property) as she had no further use for them, but asked to be allowed to keep the beds. It was reported that she was going to Kempsey and it was resolved to ask her if this was so, to return all the furniture belonging to the Mission.[50]

Too late, the AIM was alerted that McKenzie Hatton had advertised a furniture sale at Rehoboth. They demanded to know what she had done with their property.[51] She replied that she had sold the furniture at Rehoboth to pay her debts. The AIM inquired if the furniture had in fact been sold to a man now resident at Rehoboth. If this were the case, it said, 'the council may have to consider the question of taking possession of that portion belonging to the Mission'.[52] McKenzie Hatton for her part treated the AIM with the contempt that their idiotic behaviour deserved. AIM correspondence noted: 'If she could learn anything of the furniture belonging to the Mission what was reported to have been sold when the furniture of the Girls' Home was disposed of, she would let us know.'[53]

This signified the end of any cordial or civil diplomacy.

***

The period where the Aboriginal political leaders had been hidden from public view was now over. As a white woman, McKenzie Hatton had previously been able to pursue their agenda with a degree of secrecy. It could be argued, perhaps, that to this moment she had been used as a public front by the imaginative and committed campaigners of the AAPA. Quite clearly there were things a white person, especially a white woman, could achieve on the quiet that were an impossibility for Aboriginal people.

In April 1925 the AAPA burst from veiled obscurity in a blaze of publicity. The launch of its first annual conference was front-page news in the Sydney press. This was held in Sydney at St David's Hall, Surry Hills and over 250 Aboriginal people attended, many travelling great distances from across the state to be there. The President, Fred Maynard, opened proceedings with the call: 'Brothers and sisters, we have much business to transact so let's get right down to it.'[54] His inaugural address rang with the influence of civil rights advocate Marcus Garvey: 'We aim at the spiritual, political, industrial and social. We want to work out our own destiny. Our people have not had the courage to stand together in the past, but now we are united, and are determined to work for the preservation for all those things which are near and dear to us.'[55]

Significantly, this Sydney conference was 'entirely run by the [A]boriginals themselves — chairman, secretary and treasurer included — and even the business paper was the work of these people'.[56]

It has been wrongly interpreted that the AAPA had white membership and office bearers or was influenced by white Christian, humanitarian or nationalistic groups.[57] Nothing is further from the truth, and McKenzie Hatton herself revealed the error of those assumptions. In correspondence with *Voice of the North* Editor JJ Moloney, she wrote that the AAPA would not allow anyone 'to hold any position but Aboriginals'.[58] Similarly, writing to J Chas Genders, Editor of *Daylight*, she stated that the AAPA organisation was one where all 'the officers are [A]boriginals. The President a man of very great ability as an orator. The Secretary, Treasurer, and all the secretaries of country branches, and Presidents of country branches and all officers have carried out their duties in a manner which provides them to be capable of conducting their own business affairs.'[59]

McKenzie Hatton was herself a Christian humanitarian, albeit one undergoing a major shift of understanding. Her correspondence with Genders, a noted humanitarian campaigner of the period, is illuminating. She had written to the secretary of the Aborigines Protection League of South Australia in regard to that organisation's push to establish a model Aboriginal state in the Northern Territory (see Chapter 8).[60] She also requested information from Genders on the proposed petition, indicating her willingness to distribute it on her travels and revealing that it would be a topic of discussion at the forthcoming AAPA conference in Grafton.[61] This indicates that she had not discussed the issue with the Aboriginal leadership in any great detail, as they would later vehemently oppose the proposal at the Grafton conference and in the press.[62]

It is noteworthy that when the petition was finally submitted to the federal House of Representatives in October 1927, McKenzie Hatton's signature was not among the 7113 that supported the proposal.[63] It seems she was more influenced in her political mindset by the Aboriginal leaders than by fellow white Christian humanitarians.

For her efforts and insider's understanding, Aboriginal communities and political leaders held McKenzie Hatton in high accord. At the AAPA's half-yearly meeting, held in July 1925, President Fred Maynard expressed the gratitude of his people:

> I must congratulate Mrs McKenzie Hatton on having organised so successfully the branches in these country towns. The difficulties of access and also opposition and intolerance on the part of the provincial towns were quite enough to have disheartened any worker but Mrs McKenzie Hatton had gone ahead ignoring all difficulties and had succeeded in firmly establishing the AAPA.[64]

At the second annual AAPA conference, held in Kempsey, Maynard again offered praise on a report delivered by Hatton, which detailed her membership drive. The Aboriginal leader reflected that 'behind that report lay months of self-sacrificing toil'.[65]

Although not an official member of the Aboriginal organisation, Hatton was a committed supporter, campaigner and organiser. At her own expense, she made an exhaustive trip across the state, travelling 'over 5,000 miles on a membership campaign in the country places'. The inspirational news of the AAPA and its work 'preceded her at every point of the tour'.[66] As the Kempsey-based *Macleay Chronicle* reported in August 1925:

> Everywhere she went she was met by deputations of coloured people asking that branches should be formed. From the remotest part of the state calls were still coming in asking for a visit from the organising Secretary. One man wrote from a far back settlement, asking that some one should come and tell them about the 'freedom Club'.[67]

Within six months, the AAPA had established 11 branches and a membership of over 500 Aboriginal people. When one considers that the entire Aboriginal population of New South Wales at the time (on APB figures) was 6270, and that many were under tight control with access denied them, this was a remarkable achievement.[68]

The board, however, viewed the AAPA's growing support with a jaundiced eye. They were infuriated with McKenzie Hatton and Maynard when 'with the aid of the Nambucca Aboriginal community they removed an Aboriginal girl Eileen Buchanan from the Protection Board's control'. Such successes in openly defying the board were having an inspiring impact on Aboriginal communities, but the board regarded them as rebellious and confrontational. They responded to the Eileen Buchanan incident by placing the matter 'in the hands of [the] Inspector General of Police'. They also sought advice from a Crown Solicitor 're Bd — power to deal with activities of Mrs Hatton of Homebush'.[69] Their paranoia concerning AAPA actions was increasingly visible. In response to the AAPA's application for registration as a company, the board informed the registrar general that it was:

> ...very strongly opposed to the granting of the application on account of the unfitness of the promoters who, with the exception of Mrs Hatton, are all [A]borigines, certain available particulars re the character of whom are to be furnished; and

also because many of the objects set forth in the articles of the Association of the proposed company are already included among the duties imposed upon the Board of the Aborigines Protection Act.[70]

In an act that showed she had not altogether given up on the missionaries, McKenzie Hatton offered the AIM the opportunity to stand with the Aboriginal population against such clear acts of oppression by the board. She invited the AIM to unite with the Australian Natives Association and the AAPA in a deputation to the prime minister. They declined, however, saying they 'could see no utility in the proposed deputation & that the A.P Board were quite conversant with the needs of the Aborigines & had the power to deal with the specific matter mentioned in her letter'.[71]

Initially McKenzie Hatton had believed that the New South Wales Government and its Aborigines Protection Board had honourable intentions in their actions and directives towards the Aboriginal population. But in recent months her thinking had changed:

> I came over here with the idea of joining one of the existing missions at work amongst them, but after serving some months in the capacity of missionary amongst the [A]borigines I came into possession of facts regarding the legislation of New South Wales in the affairs of the [A]borigines which seemed to need readjustment and in response to a direct appeal from the more enlightened of these people, we formed the Australian Aboriginal Progressive Association.[72]

Her clash with the AIM had left her disenchanted with the mission, and convinced of the malevolence and sinister motives of the board itself. In a clear call to arms, McKenzie Hatton recounted her revelation: 'I came over here from another state expecting to preach to heathen people. But I found an eager keen people who demanded a voice in their own destiny. You have come through the fires of persecution, insult and opposition. You refused to be pushed out of your own country...'[73] She was forthright in her opinion that the current Aboriginal dilemma was a consequence not only of church ignorance and government bungling but of a deliberate campaign to oppose their rights and opportunities:

> The greatest hindrance to the welfare of these people was the system so long in vogue of handing out rations to the people and nursing them. These people were well able to work and support their own families and the AAPA was out to teach the

people self respect, and that could only be brought about when they took on the responsibility of their own support and development.[74]

In a long letter published in *Daylight*, McKenzie Hatton was scathing in her appraisal of the invaders: 'The fact that certain [A]borigines are camped under petrol tins and without certain knowledge of where their next meal is to come from is a reflection on our boastful civilization.' Some of our contemporary analysts do not possess the same insight and compassion for the horror of the Australian historical experience. She could well be answering the erroneous contemporary argument of right-wing intelligentsia (and the current prime minister) that the actions of the past hold no relevance to present-day injustice:

> We may claim that we are not responsible for the actions of the original British invaders who violated their homes, shot, poisoned, burned and mutilated the natives; but we cannot claim immunity from the conditions existing at the present time, and what should not be tolerated for one moment longer than it will take to rectify matters.

In her view, Aboriginal people's right to recognition and equality in every aspect of Australian life deserved the overwhelming attention of Australian governments. She attacked the 'blame the victim' mentality that continues to pervade much of Australian thinking. In trying to rectify this mentality, she targeted the more privileged sections of the wider community, who were able to ignore the fact that their prosperous existence and lifestyle was a direct result of Aboriginal dispossession. She wanted them to know that Aboriginal people were subjected to the continued abuse of even their most basic rights: 'The citizens comfortably situated on the shores of Port Jackson are, in the main, absolutely ignorant of the conditions under which the natives are existing. Publicity will cause a revolution in this regard...' She believed that —as had occurred in her case — once the majority of people became aware of injustice towards Aboriginal people they would take action:

> The moment this sore is opened up, there will be a rush of apologists from the ranks of parliamentarians, parsons, priests, pedagogues, pedants, and peripatetic philosophers, but such belated excuses will be promptly brushed aside, for the fiat has gone forth — JUSTICE TO THE NATIVES — and the people of Australia will not be satisfied until that full measure

of compensation has been accorded to a much injured and sadly wronged people.

What is striking in McKenzie Hatton's letter is the wrath and condemnation that she directs at church, government and the wider community. Her understanding of the situation is truly amazing, so modern is it in its conceptualisation. She realised over seven decades ago the importance of giving control of Aboriginal issues to Aboriginal people and taking heed of their perspectives. This was an extra-ordinary piece of insight for its time, and the failure to understand this fundamental concept has had a detrimental impact on Aboriginal people ever since. Sadly, so many years later we still confront those who dispute the horror history of the past 200 years, and we still await the healing process of acknowledging and under-standing these issues. The ghosts of the past still cannot be laid to rest.

As a consequence of her association with Aboriginal people and communities, Elizabeth McKenzie Hatton eventually came to share their political mindset, including a deep distrust in the motives of the church. She declared that the 'position of the remnant of the original owners of this land and at present resident in New South Wales is a blot on State and Church alike'.[75] Her change of heart had been inspired by the Aboriginal leaders of the AAPA, who were educated, gifted and inspirational political campaigners. President Fred Maynard was described in the press as 'an orator of outstanding ability' who 'in the not far distant future will loom large in the politics of this country for the reason that the [A]boriginal question is becoming a very important one'.[76] Similarly, the AAPA Treasurer, Tom Lacey, was described in the Newcastle *Voice of the North* as 'not only a fluent speaker but a veritable Lincoln of phraseology. He is possibly the best-informed man in the State regarding the movement for the emancipation of the slaves in America and Cuba...'[77]

The impact of these men and the other members of the AAPA on McKenzie Hatton was startling. She had relinquished her strong, condescending Christian ethic and become a cutting-edge and astute political activist. Through their agitation, Elizabeth McKenzie Hatton and the Aboriginal leaders of the 1920s would remain defined outsiders to government authorities, denied the opportunity to express their views to official government bodies in an organised public arena.[78]

In 1928 there was a move for a national and united focus on Aboriginal issues, one the *Voice of the North* hoped would involve the likes of 'Mr J C Genders (Adelaide), Dr A P Elkin (Broome, W.A.) and

Mrs E McKenzie Hatton in Queensland'.[79] Genders and Elkin were welcomed by Commonwealth and state bodies and inquiries, but not Hatton, and certainly not the Aboriginal leaders like Maynard or Lacey. A decade later, in 1937, with a proposed government inquiry into Aboriginal affairs on the horizon, JJ Moloney again nominated the AAPA old guard to present evidence to the inquiry, stating that Mrs Elizabeth McKenzie Hatton (now resident in Queensland) would be a very important witness: 'She can give evidence such as is not procurable from any other person on account of her work amongst the Aborigines of the North Coast and N.S.W. generally.'[80] Moloney advocated the importance of including 'another witness and very reliable man...Mr Maynard, an Aboriginal who resides at Lakemba'.[81] But the government agencies were well aware of the price they would pay if either Maynard or Hatton gained the opportunity to present the horrific realities of government policies.

For her allegiance to Aboriginal people, Hatton paid a price in the wider community, and was still doing so many years later. As a woman in her 70s she appeared in court and successfully assisted in the defence of an Aboriginal man. Even decades after her experiences with the home and the AAPA, she was confronted with the same racism. Describing the way the defendant and his supporters were treated, she remarked: 'I will not go into details of the sneering we received at the hands of the four or five solicitors present before the opening of court.'[82]

Hatton spent her later life in Queensland working with the South Sea Islander communities at Hervey Bay and Tweed Heads, and evidence of her contribution can be found in the records of the local historical society:

> Mrs Hatton lived in Coolangatta, circa 1935. Phyllis [Corowa] recalls that Elizabeth was in her eyes another 'Mother Teresa' working mainly with the South Sea Islanders. She became a 'Guardian' for many and assisted them when they were threatened with deportation, or had money troubles. She used to attend the Methodist Church in Tweed Heads and a Minister used to visit from Vanuatu and he would take back needy supplies and clothes made by the Islanders, to help the poor.[83]

Jack Horner, a founding member of FCAATSI, recalls visiting the north coast in the 1960s and meeting with Aboriginal leaders. One man he met was Pastor Alf Bekue, who introduced him to the South Sea Islander community at a public meeting near Tweed Heads:

...their hall — freshly whitewashed weatherboard it was (as I recall it) — was *theirs*, owned by their Australian South Sea Islander Association, donated and paid for years before by Mrs EJ McKenzie Hatton. I read this information myself, inscribed on a small brass plate, screwed to the front wall.[84]

At the local level, Hatton continued to campaign for Aboriginal justice and rights until the end of her life, although she was never allowed to regain her place of prominence in the Aboriginal political fight. Despite all the heartache and opposition she had endured, reminiscences reveal that to the very end of her life she was a woman of great and unflinching faith. Carl Redman recalls an active Mrs Hatton visiting his mother at their home at Cudgen: 'On one of her visits Mum was concerned how Mrs Hatton would get home. Mrs Hatton replying "My father will provide for me", she walked out the door and stood at the curb and within minutes a car pulled over and she was offered a lift.'[85]

Elizabeth McKenzie Hatton died at Tweed Heads on the 13 June 1944. The local South Sea Islander community erected a large tombstone in her memory, with the inscription: 'Erected by the New Hebridians of the Tweed River in memory of their beloved missionary Elizabeth McKenzie Hatton'. She had remained a committed champion of Aboriginal and South Sea Islander people and one prepared to stand up in the face of hostility to speak out against the oppression, racism and prejudice manifest in the wider community. From the perspective of an Indigenous man, I applaud the courage of this woman and take pride and strength from her stance. All sections of the community can learn from her journey. Her willingness to listen was fundamental in the process that revealed the truth.

Notes

1. *Daylight*, 15 May 1920, p. 139. *Daylight* was an independent, Adelaide-based 'journal for the man on the Land and Everybody'.
2. Maynard 2002, 'The 1920s Aboriginal and political defence of the sacred "ancient code"', in Deborah Bird Rose & Ian Macintosh (eds), *Cultural Survival Quarterly*, vol. 26.2, Cambridge, MA.
3. *Wingham Chronicle and Manning River Observer*, 10 June 1925; *Voice of the North*, 12 June 1925.
4. Personal conversation with Carl Redman, 22 July 2003. Carl Redman was born in 1930 and is a member of the South Sea Islander community in the Tweed Heads region. Carl Redman's father, Archie, and Uncle Otto were the driving force behind the erection of a memorial to Elizabeth

McKenzie Hatton, donating £100 towards its construction. At the time of our conversation, the memorial had fallen into disrepair and Carl was responsible for having it restored.

5. *Our Aim*, August 1908, p. 3. There appears to be little material available on Mr Hatton, other than that he was very supportive of his wife's activities, especially later with the AAPA. He died in 1927, according to a report in the *Voice of the North*, 10 February 1927, which stated: 'You will learn with regret of the sad bereavement sustained by Mrs E. McKenzie Hatton, whose honoured husband died very suddenly at his home in Queensland during the current week.'

6. National Archives of Australia: McKenzie Hatton, 1921, series AI/15, item 21/6686; J Christiansen, *They came...and stayed: a history of Hervey Bay*, R & J McTaggart & Co., Hervey Bay, 1991. The book contains photos (pp. 115–16) of McKenzie Hatton with members of the Kanaka community. She is mistakenly referred to as 'Mrs Hutton'.

7. NAA: AI/15, 21/6686.

8. *Our Aim*, February 1909, p. 6.

9. McKenzie Hatton to Retta Dixon Long, Aborigines Inland Mission correspondence, donated by Christine Brett, uncatalogued, in possession of the Mitchell Library, Sydney.

10. *Our Aim*, 20 March 1924, p. 12.

11. Documents relating to Mrs Charles's request and the letter to Prime Minister Hughes contained in NAA: AI/15, 21/6686.

12. *Australian Aborigines Advocate*, 28 February 1918.

13. Retta Dixon Long was one of the early missionaries connected with the Christian Endeavour Union which began a full-time mission at La Perouse in 1894. In 1899 it was renamed the New South Wales Aborigines Mission (NSWAM) and broadened its base of operations around the state. In 1905 Retta Dixon Long was one of the NSWAM missionaries at Singleton who broke away to form the Australian Aborigines Mission (AIM). See Harris 1990, pp. 554–55.

14. *Our Aim*, 20 March 1924, p. 12.

15. *Our Aim*, 14 September 1923, 11 October 1923 & 29 November 1923.

16. Aborigines Protection Board Minutes, 14 December 1923, ref. nos 4/7108–7127, Archives Office of NSW (AONSW), Sydney.

17. AIM correspondence and reports, 19 November 1923, Minute Books, MSS 7167, Box 1, Mitchell Library, Sydney.

18. AIM correspondence and reports, 10 January 1924.

19. *Our Aim*, 20 February 1924, p. 14; AIM correspondence and reports, 10 January 1924.

20. AIM correspondence and reports, 31 January 1924.

21. *Our Aim*, 20 February 1924, p. 14 & 20 March 1924, p. 13.

22. AIM correspondence and reports, 31 January 1924.

23. *Our Aim*, 20 March 1924, p. 12.

24. *Our Aim*, 20 February 1924, p. 14.
25. Quotes relating to the opening ceremony of 'Rehoboth' are from *Our Aim*, 20 March 1924, pp. 12, 13.
26. AIM correspondence and reports, 27 March 1924.
27. *Our Aim*, 20 April 1924, p. 12.
28. *Our Aim*, 20 June 1924, p. 13.
29. *Our Aim*, 20 April 1924, p. 12.
30. AIM correspondence and reports, 24 April 1924.
31. Daniel and Janet Matthews established Maloga mission. Confrontation with the Aborigines Protection Association (APA) in 1888 resulted in the Aboriginal population being moved to Cumeroogunga and the Matthews resigning from their reduced responsibilities as 'religious teachers'. The Matthews suffered much criticism, losing credibility and much of their financial support. They relocated to South Australia, founding a mission at Mannum and naming it Manunka. Daniel Matthews died in 1902. Janet carried on the Manunka mission until 1911, when she retired. She died in Adelaide in 1939 (Harris 1990, pp. 220–28); Retta Dixon Long correspondence to Janet Matthews, Mortlock Library, South Australia (now missing).
32. *Our Aim*, 20 March 1924, p. 13.
33. AIM correspondence and reports, 29 May 1924
34. Holland 2001, 'Wives and mothers'; Paisley 2000; Sekuless 1978; Haskins 1998a; Lake 1996.
35. *Our Aim*, 20 June 1924, p. 12
36. *Grafton Daily Examiner*, 29 December 1926.
37. Maynard 2003.
38. *Daylight*, 31 August 1926.
39. AIM correspondence and reports, 4 September 1924.
40. AIM correspondence and reports, 13 November 1924.
41. AIM correspondence and reports, 27 November 1924.
42. AIM correspondence and reports, 11 December 1924
43. AIM correspondence and reports, 24 January 1925.
44. Victorian Board for Protection of Aborigines correspondence, 8 January 1925, Register of Inward Correspondences, ref. 10768 16, Public Record Office Victoria.
45. APB Minutes, 23 January 1925, ref. nos 4/7108–7127, AONSW, Sydney.
46. APB Minutes, 6 March 1925, ref. nos 4/7108–7127, AONSW, Sydney.
47. *Our Aim*, 20 March 1925.
48. AIM correspondence and reports, 24 January 1925.
49. AIM correspondence and reports, 26 February 1925.
50. AIM correspondence and reports, 4 August 1925.
51. AIM correspondence and reports, 1 September 1925.
52. AIM correspondence and reports, 1 September 1925.
53. AIM correspondence and reports, 10 November 1925.

54. *Daily Guardian*, 7 May 1925.
55. *Daily Guardian*, 7 May 1925. Marcus Garvey and the doctrine of his Universal Negro Improvement Association were the biggest influence over the awakening of Aboriginal political activism with the rise of the Australian Aboriginal Progressive Association in 1924. See Maynard 2003.
56. *Macleay Argus*, 7 April 1925.
57. McGregor 1997, p. 115; Attwood & Markus 1999, p. 59; Goodall 1996, p. 152.
58. McKenzie Hatton, correspondence to JJ Moloney, in possession of the Newcastle Regional Library (Society of Patriots Archives), 1926.
59. *Daylight*, 30 September 1926.
60. I am currently undertaking a major study of this topic, entitled 'The Aboriginal political response to the model Aboriginal state', through an AIATSIS grant in 2002.
61. *Daylight*, 30 September 1926
62. *Sydney Morning Herald*, 15 November 1927; *Northern Star*, 19 November 1927.
63. Australia, House of Representatives 1926–28, *Votes and Proceedings*, vol. 1, pp. 691–94. My thanks to Mark Hargans of the staff at the Bills and Papers Office, Parliament House, Canberra.
64. *Voice of the North*, 10 August 1925.
65. *Macleay Chronicle*, 7 October 1925.
66. *Voice of the North*, 10 August 1925.
67. *Macleay Chronicle*, 19 August 1925.
68. *Sydney Morning Herald*, 11 February 1925. The following year, board figures published in the *Newcastle Morning Herald* (10 February 1926) showed the New South Wales Aboriginal population had risen to 7072. This contradicts the theory so popular at the time of the rapidly 'dying race'.
69. APB Minutes, 24 April 1925, ref. nos 4/7108–7127, AONSW, Sydney.
70. APB Minutes, 23 October 1925, ref. nos 4/7108–7127, AONSW, Sydney.
71. APB Minutes, 23 October 1925, ref. nos 4/7108–7127, AONSW, Sydney.
72. *Daylight*, 30 September 1926.
73. *Daily Guardian*, 24 April 1925.
74. *Macleay Argus*, 7 April 1925.
75. *Daylight*, 30 October 1926.
76. *Voice of the North*, 11 January 1926.
77. *Voice of the North*, 10 October 1927. The newspaper's editors, JJ Moloney and his wife, Dorothy, were staunch AAPA supporters.
78. *Voice of the North*, 10 August 1927.
79. *Voice of the North*, 12 March 1928.
80. Premier's Department correspondence files, ref. 12/8749A, State Records NSW, Sydney.

81. Premier's Department correspondence files, ref. 12/8749A, State Records NSW, Sydney.
82. *Uplift*, February 1941, National Library of Australia.
83. Personal correspondence with Gwen Hart, research officer at the Lower Tweed Historical, 27 September 1999.
84. Personal correspondence with Jack Horner, 2000.
85. Conversation with Carl Redman, 22 July 2003.

2. 'The mother of the home'
Jennie Parsons Smith

Christine Brett Vickers

> Perhaps the most interesting figure of all is the mother of
> the Home. How Mrs Smith accomplishes all she does,
> seeing to washing, ironing, cooking, sewing, cleaning,
> and dozens of other things, and yet has the leisure,
> when you call in, to help and serve you is a marvel...[1]
> —Retta Dixon Long

On the evening of 3 August 1919 my great-grandmother, Sarah Jane (Jennie) Parsons Smith, Matron of the Singleton Aboriginal Children's Home, sat down to write to her eldest son, Percy. 'I feel I must write to you tonight. I feel condemned receiving so many letters and not one answered.'

Percy was recuperating in London from war injuries, where he was visited by family friends and relations, 'the dear ones at Home', left behind when Jennie had followed her fiancé, George Colton Smith, to Australia 25 years before.[2]

'We have had a lead turn of Influenza here in Singleton,' Jennie wrote. 'There has been between 5 and 6 hundred cases...everyone down together. There were 7 deaths all men.' As a result of the epidemic, the 'home children' had been unable to attend school for five weeks. Jennie was tired. An admission escaped her pen. 'Don't you pity us with 34 of them?' Two children had just arrived, she noted, and four more were expected the following week, 'which means forty'.[3]

With her husband, George, Jennie had been superintending the Singleton home for the Aborigines Inland Mission since April 1910. In the pages of the mission's monthly paper, *Our Aim*, there unfolds a narrative of family life through George Smith's monthly accounts of the home's doings. Unusually for the women of the AIM, Jennie did not write about herself nor contribute to the paper, allowing herself to be represented by her husband and other contributors. She is said to have seen herself first and foremost as a wife and mother.[4]

As a 'missionary wife' her role was to complement her husband, and the direction of their missionary endeavour was supposed to be — always — his responsibility.[5] Yet such is the vitality of her presence behind the scenes, it appears that the home was the project of this most private person.

'Poor old Mum, alone again,' her second daughter Lou would say. George was often away on mission business, and her children wondered why Jennie tolerated as much as she did. To her children, Jennie's life was one of sheer drudgery and toil: long hours working behind the scenes at the home looking after up to 50 children at a time — although with the assistance of one or two young women missionaries and the older girls living at the home.[6] My grandmother, Tilda, described Jennie as 'a saint'. It seemed she was always left behind, busy at the home while her husband and children went about their lives outside. In Lou's and Tilda's opinions, Jennie carried the burden of her husband's missionary dream.[7] But Jennie was said to have 'liked her life', to have been more than a helpmeet following her husband's path. And there appears to have been a collaborative relationship between husband and wife as both pitched in to care for the children. Although her children don't remember it, Jennie also represented the home at public meetings while George remained behind to mind the children.[8] She was part of a couple living though all the complexities, ambivalences and practicalities of marriage. She chose to emigrate. She could have remained safely tucked up in England.

As Jennie's great-granddaughter, I have drawn upon family memories and discussions among Jennie's children and grandchildren to reconstruct her story.[9] Reminiscence occurs in the space between past and present. Neither one nor the other, it is about attempting to understand oneself in terms of one's particular sense of the past.[10] Family memory has its own subjectivity, expressed by the myths and beliefs family members create together. Each brings their particular perception, challenging then adding to each other's search for truth. In its negative form, family memory might try to deny, if not rewrite, a past nevertheless revealed through public accounts. On the other hand, personal, family memory can assist and challenge historians' interrogation and interaction with the archive: the two can enrich each other. Like family reminiscence, history exists in a 'space between'. Both are underscored by a drive to find the truth. But truth is elusive and ultimately unknowable, glimpsed maybe through myriad lenses, stories, and perspectives.

We of the present social mind may look uneasily at our kin — mothers, fathers, grandparents, the ancestors of others in our community of settler descent — and wonder about their actions. We wonder, too, about those threads — conscious and unconscious — that link and reflect us through the generations.[11] Missionaries were part of settler society's delegation to redress the wrongs of whites' arrival. Now these arguments and debates have an uneasy familiarity as contemporary culture seeks to articulate what has been spoken of before. The genuine desire of those living decades before us to do something, to stand against what they saw to be wrong, is lost in the tumult of overwhelming human suffering that suggests the chosen solution was worse than the illness. Now we may look with distaste at the tragic events preceding us, hiding from unease about those parents or grandparents to whom we are heirs. They lived in their time. They are part of our formation.

My knowledge of the Aborigines Inland Mission, and the life story of my great-grandparents, led me to the mission itself, and to the opening of records kept since its inception in 1905.[12] Within this missionary archive there unfolds a humane view of Aboriginal people, an alternative to that developed within the Aborigines Protection Board, whose underlying paradigm turned from philanthropy to control between 1910 and 1920. Jennie and George, caught in this change, were confronted with the puzzle of reconciling the board's notions of Aboriginal people with their own experience and perceptions. Their views of Aboriginal people differed from those of the board and ultimately put them on a collision course with it. After the board took over the home, George is said to have written to his son: '…with government money comes government control, and they didn't know the blackfellow as the missionaries did.'[13]

We shall never be able to get inside the minds of those personages and subjectivities from the past. We too have our subjectivity, which colours interpretation. Or is it that meaning is always changing? In this essay, personal memories gathered from Jennie's descendants, and remaining letters and photographs will blend with archival material to form an intimate portrait of the 'mother of the home'. Oral history provided by Wonnarua woman Pansy Hickey, a descendant of the Waters family from the Singleton area, adds to the mix. Jennie's involvement and struggle with a particularly difficult dimension of Australian settler experience — the removal of Aboriginal children from their parents, and their relegation to the realms of uneducated servitude — is part of my family's story. It is also, as Pansy Hickey points out, part of her people's story.[14]

The Singleton home

Opened by the missionary Retta Dixon in August 1905, the Singleton Aboriginal Children's Home initially catered to 'orphaned and neglected Aboriginal girls up to the age of eighteen or nineteen years'. The intention was 'preserving them morally, and preparing them for their future lives as wives and mothers' before returning them to their communities.[15] 'It was the fearful need of rescuing these [Aboriginal] children,' she wrote in 1909, 'especially the young, half caste girls from their evil surroundings, which led us to establish our Home in Singleton.'[16]

Dixon and several single women missionaries ran the home in its early years. Some of the latter were assigned to it; others worked there during their probation before leaving to live among Aboriginal people on government reserves. But by 1908, married to Leonard Long and in her childbearing years, Retta Dixon Long wanted to relocate mission headquarters to Sydney.[17] Envisaging the home as a self-supporting industrial school, taking in sewing and dressmaking, she began advertising for a matron who was both sympathetic to the AIM's cause and capable of teaching the home girls sewing.[18] In early 1910 George Smith wrote offering the services of 'Mrs. Smith' and himself, and between 1910 and 1919 the Singleton home was largely in the Smiths' hands.

Government legislation affected the workings of the home from the beginning of the Smiths' tenure. From 1910, children were placed in the home under the auspices of the *Aborigines Protection Act 1909* (NSW).[19] The home was obliged to take in boys as well as girls, with the intention of preparing them for employment. It also took in infants and very young children removed from their families by the board upon application to a magistrate.[20] Arrangements were more permanently, and differently, enforced from 1915. It was the lighter

Jennie Parsons Smith and George Colton Smith with two family groupings (unidentified) of the 'home' children, c. 1918–1920. The Smith Family Collection, courtesy Betty Dupleix.

children who went away, Pansy Hickey told me. Her mother remarried a 'full blood' (Pansy's words) in 1916 and those children were left alone.[21]

For Jennie and George, Aboriginal children were not specimens of an inferior race, but young people, part of an extended family, worthy of the same guidance as their own children. They brought to their task their lower middle class background and values of family closeness, practicality, self-development and improvement, and belief in hard work. Jennie's role as 'the mother of the home', as written about by Retta Dixon Long, George and others, underscored the couple's parental relationship with the home children. This had scant regard for Aboriginal culture, and indeed, much of the work done at the home appeared structured around the maintenance of an 'English family home'. But as Pansy Hickey observed, life was very tough for her people at that time.[22] 'Going with the missionaries', for some, meant survival. The missionaries, in turn, offered what they knew.

***

There are the facts: Jennie's birth in Battersea in 1861, her mother's death during childbirth in 1863, and her father's remarriage two years later to an aunt of young Jennie's future husband, George Smith.[23] There is a photograph of Jennie at the age of three or four, taken around 1865. She is a sad-faced little girl standing alone on a chair gazing at the camera. I will see those eyes in all of her photos and wonder about her response to her own motherhood and to the children at the home.

Jennie's father was an artisan, a wheelwright with his own business. George's family were shopkeepers, his grandfather a pipemaker who became a tavernkeeper.[24] Jennie's stepmother was an invalid, disliked by her stepchildren, but Jennie found love and acceptance from other members of George's family. Her stepmother nevertheless taught her to read and write, and Jennie remained a keen letter writer, and reader, for the rest of her life.[25] Upon her stepmother's death, Jennie, then 12, like so many girls of that time, assumed domestic responsibilities, which later proved useful. By the age of 14 she was working in service.[26]

Jennie was a striking woman: in her youth she had curly hair with red lights in it, and her hair held its colour until the end. Her skin was dark olive, complementing her dark brown eyes. She spoke with a strong Cockney accent, calling her granddaughters 'brazen hussies' and telling them stories of 'pea souper' London fogs for their entertainment.[27] Maybe Australia provided more than those pea souper fogs that froze and stifled her breathing. She eschewed 'straightjacketing', following her own mind and choices. She and George wanted their children to have an education, and sacrificed their daughters' help at the home to enable this.[28] Both girls matriculated from Maitland Girls High (south of Singleton) where they had scholarships. Lou would graduate from university. And an argument with the Aborigines Protection Board about the right to a good education for Aboriginal children would see the couple out of the home.

In 1892, Jennie followed George to Australia. Inspired by the missionary Daniel Matthews during the latter's lecture tour seeking support for his work, George, missionary secretary with the Ealing YMCA and a member of the Church of England Temperance Union, left England with him in July 1890.[29] Jennie waited behind in London, working to save her fare. She had a good wage, having risen through the ranks of service to become a ladies' maid. She loved sewing and fashion, and could run a household. She attended classes in home nursing and anything else that would be useful to her as a missionary's wife.[30]

In Australia, after a brief spell and miserable Christmas at Maloga Mission, George defected to the Aborigines Protection Association, moving to Cumeroogunga Aboriginal Mission in January 1891.[31]

In September that year he was appointed the APA's overseer at Warangesda Mission on the Murrumbidgee River.

Jennie set out from London on 9 September 1892. Anticipating marriage to George on her arrival, her plan was to work alongside him as a matron at the APA's Brewarrina Mission while he was employed as an overseer and teacher.[32] It did not work out that way. Jennie arrived in Australia to find that George needed to qualify for this position, the undersecretary in the Department of Public Instruction having insisted that he undertake training and pass the prescribed examinations before being considered for an appointment.[33] As an unmarried man, however, George could not work at an APA mission (despite his earlier position at Warangesda) and there was no other vacancy.[34] In their practical way, Jennie and George decided to adjust and wait until they were more financially stable before marrying. So, ironically, Jennie went to Brewarrina, alone and unmarried, to work as a matron.[35]

In 1895 she was appointed dormitory matron at Warangesda Mission by the APA. Jennie's task was to:

> ...have special charge of all unmarried women, girls and young children, [to] daily visit the dwellings of the married women and give instruction in cooking, sewing and other domestic duties and shall be held, subject to the superintendent, responsible for the order and cleanliness of the women and children.[36]

Jennie took her duties seriously. The Aborigines Protection Board noted the tidiness of the dormitories, 'the dormitory girls and also of the women and children outside', under the joint supervision of Jennie and the manager's wife, Mrs Pridham.[37] Close study of the Warangesda Manager's Diary shows Jennie ensured that the activities of the dormitories were fully reported; with her absence, on the other hand, dormitory life did not come within the ambit of the manager's thinking. Jennie, who was to run a 'tight ship' organisationally at the Singleton home in the future, struggled with issues of discipline and order.[38]

In 1896 George was living in Queensland and involved in the Church of England in Brisbane.[39] He had found his way to Queensland's Myora Mission on North Stradbroke Island, after meeting with Daniel Matthews again.[40] Matthews was looking to establish a mission — a children's home — in Queensland. Jennie and George decided to marry at this point. Jennie left Warangesda on a month's leave in August and travelled to Brisbane for the wedding. Precisely a month later she returned to Warangesda, alone.[41]

Interestingly, from this point Jennie began to report instances of 'illicit' sexual activity to the manager. These might have been taking place for a long time, but Jennie, now a married woman, was perhaps a little more aware of them — or, more practically, in a better position to intervene. A day after Jennie's return, Louisa Barlow 'was interviewed for receiving letters from Harry Wedge and answering them'.[42] A month later, Harriet Paroo was alleged to have 'stayed overnight with the white men' and could not be permitted to leave the station.[43] Jennie, a white woman working for an organisation that was particularly concerned with the moral rectitude of its charges, believed her job was to control the young women.[44]

Daniel Matthews had purchased a property, 'Coonowrin', in the Glass House Mountains, and late in 1897 installed Jennie and George as the future managers of the Aboriginal children's home he proposed to establish there.[45] They remained until 1905 while Jennie bore four of the couple's five children. During these years George was often away for up to four days at a time on pastoral business, visiting isolated settlers.[46] As plans for a children's home did not eventuate, George sought a place as a missionary, travelling as far as Mapoon and the Roper River region. Jennie was not going anywhere. In December 1898 Jennie, pregnant with their first child, was alone when, terrifyingly, she went into labour two months prematurely. George returned to find Jennie had delivered a baby boy, Percy, so small he could fit into a jug.[47] She made sure she was in Brisbane when she gave birth to three other children: Tilda, born in September 1900; Louisa (Lou) in June 1902; and Syd in 1904.[48] Always Jennie was busy and anxious for her children to grow up. Percy, it was noted in a card sent to relatives, liked going out riding on horseback, and, at eight months old, liked doing things himself.[49]

In 1902 Daniel Matthews died. In his letter of condolence, George offered the couple's services to Mrs Matthews, who had just begun the mission at Manunka on the Murray River in South Australia.[50] The call came late in 1905. The Matthews' son John, the overseer at Manunka, had fallen in love with an Aboriginal woman. He went to Canada and the Smiths were sent for.[51] The journey by steamer from Queensland to Adelaide seemed so long. Jennie was a terrible sailor, the children were all under seven and Percy was ill during the voyage. In a family photo taken on a break in Melbourne, Jennie looks thin, exhausted and ill. Possibly she was pregnant again.

The Smith family on the way to Manunka, c. 1906: (left to right) George, Sydney, Louisa, Percy, Tilda and Jennie. The Smith Family Collection, courtesy Betty Dupleix.

Manunka, on Walkers Flat near Mannum in South Australia, surrounded by high granite cliffs, is Ngarrindjeri country. The Matthews' large stone house was at the top of a cliff overlooking the campsite where Aboriginal families lived in tents. On the hill above, German families had built stone huts. Lower down, a creek marked the boundary between these houses and the mission site. The Smith family also lived on the river flat, in a slab hut with an earthen floor adjacent to the Aboriginal people's camp.[52] A storehouse and schoolhouse were part of the site and for about 18 months the government supplied a teacher.[53]

Jennie's main tasks were to take care of the older people as well as seeing to the children. Janet Matthews, then close to retirement, noted Jennie's particular empathy for neglected children. 'The children under her care have been well looked after,' she wrote. 'Sick and suffering little ones, neglected beyond description, have been brought in, and they have been fed and clothed and watched over until they look fine healthy children.'[54]

Tilda and Percy both recalled this time from 1906 to 1910 as the happiest of their childhood. But their reminiscences also reflected the family's reliance on the Aboriginal people for their safety. Percy recalled being saved from drowning after he fell into the river.[55]

Tilda remembered drifting downriver in the mission's rowboat into the path of a paddlesteamer and her rescue by one of the mission's boys.

But it was about 'Black Jennie' and her friendship with 'White Jennie' that they spoke of most. 'Black Jennie', as the children called her, believed the white people's education would benefit her children. Jennie Christmas, widow of the late 'king' of the region, 'Jerry Mason', had contacted Janet Matthews early in 1900 when Matthews established her first camp at Metco. When it was moved to Manunka, Jennie Christmas brought her family to live there.[56] The children of 'White Jennie' always remembered Jennie Christmas's warmth. She looked out for them, ensuring their safety when their mother was distracted by work and babies.

About three days before Christmas 1906, Jennie went into labour with her fifth and last child. An emergency unfolded as Jennie, then 45, began to have complications. The local white midwife was cut off from the site by floods covering the bridge between the Matthews' house and the camp. 'Black Jennie' took over and ensured that the baby was safely delivered. The mission people called baby Arthur 'the little white king of Manook', after the area. A queen had delivered him, after all. He was called 'King' for several years after the family went to Singleton.[57]

For the couple, this experience was seminal, a story told and retold for decades afterwards. Even Retta Dixon Long's 1917 tribute to the couple referred to it.[58] Jennie Christmas's presence and intervention, and her sheer integrity, awakened George and Jennie to a new view of the objects of their missionary zeal — one different from those recorded in the Warangesda diary.[59]

For Jennie and George, the Manunka years were transformative. Like their contemporaries, they believed in the Christian principle that all are equal under God, but they also absorbed, unconsciously, those cultural discourses rendering Aboriginal people lower on the scale of humanity than white, British people.[60] Now, beyond words, was a deeper apprehension of the universality of human experience. Perhaps Jennie, more practical than her husband, tempered George's zeal. Maybe there was a tacit acceptance among the missionaries that the Ngarrindjeri people responded to Christianity on their own terms.

The regard appears to have been mutual. 'I could not advise her to go [to the Manunka area],' Janet Matthews said in 1912 of a potential successor to the couple. 'I knew the natives would prefer the former overseer [and his wife] whom I had.'[61]

But Manunka did not thrive. Drought wrecked vegetable gardens and newly planted fruit trees. Tilda remembered her parents were often left to manage alone, doing all the work, she said, while the Matthews family took the credit. As the years passed following Daniel's death, ambivalence about his cause, which his family scarcely dared speak of during his lifetime, began to surface. The money for the mission ran out, and the Smiths were asked to leave.[62] The Smiths needed a place to go, so George wrote to Retta Dixon Long offering their services for the Singleton home — anywhere really, as long as he could continue mission work, even if this meant sacrificing their own children. They would leave the older children in 'Christian homes', if necessary. Percy, their eldest, had been boarding away from home since he was nine, working for his keep and going to school.[63] 'Mrs Smith will only have the two with her in her work for a time,' George assured Long. 'We would not mind taking charge of [the] home that is if you would like it.'[64]

One imagines the discussions behind the scenes. One scenario: Jennie refuses to leave her children. She had boarded out Percy. An attempt to board out Tilda failed when she developed whooping cough and returned to her family.[65] A second scenario: Retta Dixon Long does not endorse the notion of leaving the children and offers them the home appointment. The house, Glasgow Place in the centre of Singleton, was a convict-built mansion of 14 rooms. There was space for everyone and the Smiths were able to take four of their five children with them (Percy continued to board away from home).

From the beginning, the home was Jennie's project: she had got them the job through her experiences as matron at Warangesda and Manunka. Jennie valued, and boasted of, her Cockney birth, 'within earshot of Bow Bells'.[66] Her outlook was practical: doing what needed doing, getting on with it. In her own upbringing, everyone pitched in and helped, older ones looking after the younger children to free their parents for the work they had to do. When the home's numbers became too large for her to handle, she delegated responsibility for groups of younger children to the older home girls. Humorous and accepting, her capacity made her the home's focus as she worked to develop it as a space where the children could be themselves.

Jennie's background had schooled her in the requirements of service in a good English household. Pansy Hickey told me that her mother, who was at the home until 1912, was taught 'very English ways'. There was always a jug of milk and a loaf of bread in the centre of the table. The sugar and salt were put out in special bowls, as was the butter. All the girls learned to sew, knit and crochet, as well as manage a household.[67]

Jennie claimed for the Aboriginal children in her care the sense of self-pride and respectability that she thought would enable them to manage anywhere.[68] Respectability was valued. Jennie's idea would have been to ensure the children had a good sense of themselves. Begging, for example, was demeaning and diminishing. Allowing oneself to be ill-treated in such a way was to abrogate one's self-pride.[69] Outwardly she eschewed pretension and posturing but, proudly, promoted her father, a wheelwright, to the status of engineer on her marriage certificate. She and George put a high premium on education — for girls and boys. In their minds all children had the potential to be participating members of the community, whatever their individual abilities made appropriate.

Young missionaries who came to the home during their probation were educated by Jennie and George's attitude. Some were single women, immigrants in Australia on their own. Missionary life provided asylum and a respectable identity. Others sought independence and, like Retta Dixon Long, the possibility of a useful career. Time at the home was an opportunity to reflect upon their work, and upon their encounter with Aboriginal people.[70] They wrote about this, adding to a discourse that challenged prevailing negative views about Aboriginal people. On her resignation in June 1913, Emily Jackson wrote of having learned many things during her six years with the mission, 'one of the most important being the knowledge gained of the natives themselves'. Not only were they 'worth saving' and 'uplifting', she wrote, but 'I have found many of them to be possessed of splendid qualities, which the majority of people do not ascribe to'.[71]

George's monthly report contributed to the fabric of *Our Aim*, where readers learned not just about the Christian mission but about the relationships that developed between the missionaries and Aboriginal people.[72] Readers could see the children at work and play, the ordinary intimate moments in family life: the splinters in the fingers and bumps on the head, shopping for presents, and birthday teas.

There are sad times: George helps a dying child to 'let go to be with the angels' and Jennie sits with a dying babe.[73] Tilda sleeps with a sick child to keep it warm. At times readers are taken into the Smiths' bedroom — a couple's most private space — where a child is being cared for. They celebrate birthdays and Christmas, where the table is laden with goodies, where Santa Claus arrives to romp with the children and turns out to be Jennie.[74] George wrote happily in 1913: 'These little tots take a good deal of watching. They eat well and sleep well, and I was going to say, cry well — the world would be a miserable place without the cry of a babe. In our case the smile and merry prattle makes up for all.'[75]

Everyone had a place, a role within the home, even the smallest child. In 1914, Tilda, then 13, described a typical day:

> The getting-up bell has just been rung, and every child is now out of bed and dressing themselves — some only tiny tots of four years. There are still five little babies in bed, but they have not reached the dignity of "dwessing themselves" as little Rita says. When the ten little girls have got their clothes on they go to the landing, which serves as a kind of dressing room for them; there they get washed and their hair combed... The little girls go downstairs and some mind the babies, while others pick up pieces of paper and rubbish lying about in the yard. Mr Smith has, in the meanwhile seen that the boys are up and dressed, so that they will each get their piece of work done before breakfast. They see to the chopping of firewood, drawing of water cleaning of sheds, etc Laura and Florrie, the two elder girls, have their work cut out in getting the breakfast ready.[76]

Tilda implied that the day-to-day running of the home was her mother's responsibility. Her father helped, but his role also appears to have been outside the home, doing some work as a lay preacher when called upon, as well as representing the home and mission to the public. The two are complementary.

There is little direct information on the response of Aboriginal people to the home, or to the parental role the Smiths took on. *Our Aim* records the home as being a centre of mission activity in Singleton, providing services for Aboriginal people living in the town. Herbert Waters and his wife were frequent visitors, deciding to apply to the mission to become 'native helpers'.[77] In the Smiths' early years at Singleton some 'Home children', according to the columns of *Our Aim*, came from local families for their education, others because their parents were dead or otherwise unable to care for them. Several children stayed at the home temporarily, their parents utilising it while they went away to work. Faced with the board's new requirement that children should be sent from the reserves to work and earn their living, it may be that some local Aboriginal parents used the home as a way of complying and remaining close to their children.[78] Cards and notes written after the children left the home suggest that at least some of them valued their time there. 'Mary' and 'Lil' sent Tilda a photograph of themselves posing proudly in their uniform, taken by their employers. They were looking after five little boys in a big house in the city. Mary, though, was not having a good time. She wrote secretly to Tilda: 'Lindfield is not a very nice place, I think so... I am lonely down hear [sic] when I think of you and Louie. I miss you and Louie.'[79]

'The youngest boy in the Home, whose name is Albert Morgan, is her especial care,' Tilda wrote of her mother in 1914. 'Albert, although he is only a very tiny personage, makes a great deal of work at present as he has whooping cough and is teething.'[80]

Left with the Smiths shortly after his birth in 1913 by his 15-year-old mother, Dinah, from the Murray River region, Albert became the couple's 'baby'.[81] (There had been another 'home' baby, a little girl who died early in 1913.)[82] In June 1916, Albert died. Jennie and George were devastated by his death. Albert, George wrote, was 'so knitted to Mrs. Smith and myself. He was a weak child, we had him in our room and when we retired for the night, he slept in our bed with "Mumma" as he called Mrs Smith.' He continued: 'The last time I saw him alive was late on Saturday evening. He knew me and looked up in my face as soon as I reached the bedside, and said in a low voice: "me dadda's boy". It was the hardest matter to keep the tears back.'[83]

They buried Albert at Whittingham Cemetery near Singleton, in the white section. The couple found their own paths through mourning. Jennie went away for 10 days 'for a rest and a change' the following month.[84] She had never left the family or the home before. Symbolically, perhaps, George wrote of extremely cold weather — the home was without window glass — and the onerous task of keeping the fires going, as if to stave off death's chill.

Jennie and George were preoccupied with the home children. Jennie is always described as busy, attending to others but not herself. Her own children seem to have had to wait their turn. Percy, left behind, never regained his place in the family. He ran away, wandering up to Queensland where he enlisted for the war. In her adulthood Lou rarely spoke of these years. She seems to have been determined to go to university and leave it all behind. Tilda, whose dream had been to be a missionary, and who went teaching at Cumeroogunga to fill in time before commencing her training as a nurse, left altogether.

The Singleton Home, 1917. The Smith Family Collection, courtesy Betty Dupleix.

Witness to one of the first raids by the board, which 'carried off three girls to the Cootamundra Home' in 1918, after which she suffered a near-fatal attack of enteric fever, she moved on into marriage and a family of her own. The younger boys' schooling was interrupted by the closure of the home.

Perhaps Jennie, too, somewhere in the depths of her mind, remembered being orphaned. She lost her mother when she was three and was taken in by George's family. It may be that Jennie, whose organisational talents were realised in the management of the home, felt freer to connect with the home children without those personal and unconscious complexities biological motherhood can arouse. She may have been frightened after giving birth alone to her eldest child, never resolving whatever ambivalent feelings this entailed. As a new mother, too, she may have been too ready for her children to grow up, preferring their independence and assistance to their infancy.[85] There may have been too much to do, with five children and a husband to keep track of without the support of the extended family back home. It hindered her ability to express her maternal passions.[86] Her own children may have felt they had to grow up too quickly, given their parents' distraction with their mission. We don't understand, either, why Percy was left behind. A possible explanation is that Jennie and George were part of a contemporary culture in which the boarding out of children for their keep and to make ends meet in the family was accepted practice. Perhaps, too, Jennie Smith gained something from Jennie Christmas, whose generosity and maternal presence at Manunka had saved the family from disaster.

***

Removing children as 'young as possible from their families' could be seen today as an attack on identity and being by those in government and power. Robert Donaldson of the Aborigines Protection Board was aware that to argue for the removal of children from their mothers was to transgress a most fundamental relationship: that between parent and child.[87] The home Jennie and George developed was caught between the contingencies of state intervention which proved to be extremely destructive of Aboriginal being and their perception that the home children were in need of the parental care they could provide.

'Our Missionaries would seek to work in harmony with officials of the department and aid them in the work they have undertaken,' Retta Dixon Long wrote in 1909.[88] But divisions between missionary practice and government policy emerged very early in the home's history. George collided with the board in 1914, when he protested against a decision to place a boy in service at the age of 12 years. 'Sorry in a way to see him go,' George wrote of George Perry. 'It is simple child labour.'[89] The board then wrote to Mrs Long requesting that George be pulled into line, and a copy of the rules was sent for their perusal. George was not to make contact with the board other than through the Longs, nor to make independent decisions.[90] From 1915 the board began to implement a policy of child removal based on racial criteria, the children to be 'educated and fitted for domestic service, apprenticed out to approved homes, and become gradually merged in the general population of the State'.[91] In 1916 the Department of Education released its *Course of Instruction for Aborigines Schools*, 'with the object of assisting the boys to become capable farm or station labourers, and the girls useful domestic servants'.[92]

The AIM did not agree that opportunities should be restricted.[93] George pointedly praised the children's success at school in light of the board's determination that the children were incapable of mainstream schooling.[94]

In September 1918, the NSW Aborigines Protection Board purchased the Singleton home. Though it initially signalled nothing would change, the board soon after ousted the AIM, claiming it was responsible for the children and thus the home, too.[95] To implement the *Aborigines Protection Acts* of 1915 and 1918, legalising the removal of Aboriginal children from their families, it needed the premises for a boys institution. The Smiths, hoping to stave off this eventuality — they did not want the home, run for years on 'family' lines, to be turned into an institution for boys — decided to remain as board employees.[96] For Robert Donaldson, who had masterminded the 1918 purchase for the board, they were innocents, stubbornly running 'a home for waifs' with a frame of mind irrelevant to the efficiencies required of an increasingly totalitarian board.[97]

Retta and Leonard Long were devastated by the loss of the home. They accused the Smiths of disloyalty after the couple allegedly retained funds and items that had been donated. They argued that, because accepting salaries was against the principles and practices of the AIM constitution, the Smiths should resign.[98] 'Mrs Smith and Self are still Missionaries,' George Smith insisted. 'There ought not to be any hitch with us in any way,' he continued. He did not understand 'why we should be cut off altogether'.[99]

In September 1919 George asked the board for a salary increase on the 100 pounds a year they were receiving. 'Everything is so dear,' he said, and they had three adolescent children of their own to support.[100] A photo taken about this time shows them to be gauntly hollow cheeked. 'We are having a bad time just now for the want of rain,' Jennie wrote to Percy in November. 'Every place is suffering more or less. We are full up with children just now.'[101]

Jennie and George had apparently trusted Donaldson when he first began visiting the home in early 1916. 'His visits can and will be helpful,' George wrote. And there is evidence — at least through the columns of *Our Aim* — that the Smiths welcomed the board's intervention, hoping it would ease some of the financial pressures caused by so many children to care for.[102] But slowly the archives reveal a different story, where trust was betrayed as Donaldson schemed to gain control over Aboriginal matters in New South Wales.

The sale of the home coincided with a campaign to remove the home children from the local public school. It was a bitter debate which ultimately reached the minister for education. When the board assumed control of the home in September 1918, the teacher-manager of the Mount Olive (formerly St Clair) reserve, TH Austin, aligned himself with the Parents & Citizens Association of Singleton Public School to campaign — successfully as it turned out — for the exclusion of the home children from the town school. An Aboriginal school was established on the home's grounds.[103] The board planned that Thomas Schadrach James from Cumeroogunga would take up the teaching post.[104]

At the home, conditions worsened: the premises were run down and rat-infested, food was short, and support from the board limited. The children kept on coming, sent by an organisation that neither knew nor cared about the conditions in which its wards would be living.[105]

James declined the transfer and George had a nervous break-down.[106] He was dismissed for 'improper conduct alleged by some of the inmates' of the home. There is no record of an investigation, merely a note of the decision. The board's plan in 1920 was to break up the home. It recorded '...the smaller boys in the home should be transferred to Bomaderry Mission Home and the girls to Cootamundra Home, so that Singleton may be placed on a proper footing as an institution for boys.' Austin was appointed to George's position.[107]

After his dismissal, George sought an AIM position at Karuah, near Newcastle. The AIM referred it to the board, which refused to sanction the appointment. Broken and emotionally exhausted, George Smith severed contact with the AIM and left, alone, for Queensland, where he found work as a dairy hand.[108] It suited everyone for Jennie to stay on. George was reassured by the fact that Jennie would continue as matron as 'she knows the workings of the Home'.[109] Austin, a young father of two small children whose wife was ill with tuberculosis and unable to fulfil the matron's role, was not able to manage alone. The Smiths had no savings, no home and children at school. They needed the money.

In December 1923 the Singleton home was closed. It was then sold and eventually demolished, the board relocating its function as a boys home to Kinchela near Kempsey. Jennie ceased contributing super-annuation in January 1922, which suggests she left the home at this time.[110] She joined George in Queensland and began a new role as a grandmother. Percy, returned from the war, set his parents up on his soldier settlement near Nambour, which they financed through their pensions. George established a dairy farm and continued working for the Anglican Synod. Both turned their backs on the missionary world.

Even so, Jennie ensured that George's work was acknowledged in his obituary 20 years later. He died in January 1940 and was buried in an unmarked grave. When Jennie died, seven years after him, in August 1947, she had arranged that his name be included on her gravestone.[111]

Notes

1. Retta Dixon Long writing about the Singleton home, *Our Aim*, February 1914, p. 7. *Our Aim*, begun in September 1907, was the Aborigines Inland Mission's monthly paper. In each edition missionaries from the field throughout New South Wales as well as the Singleton home contributed a report.
2. SJ Smith to Percy Smith, 9 August 1919, copy in possession of the author.
3. SJ Smith to Percy Smith, 3 August 1919. With the passing of the *Aborigines Protection Amending Act 1915* (NSW), the Aborigines Protection Board's officers gained power to remove children of mixed Aboriginal–white heritage from their families without recourse to a magistrate. This had a direct impact on the home's numbers. These began to rise from about 24 in the years immediately following the passing of the Act. From 1918 they hovered between 40 and 45, sometimes reaching 50.
4. Betty Dupleix, letter, 25 February 2003. Betty Dupleix is the Smiths' eldest grandchild.
5. Ellen Ross provides a good outline of family structure, values and role responsibilities for women of the lower middle classes — women of similar background to Jennie. See Ross, ch. 2.
6. A series of young, single women missionaries passed through the home. See *Our Aim*, 1907–20; also, '1905–1930 Missionary Roll, List of missionaries in service with the AIM', Australian Indigenous Ministries, Further Records, MLMSS 7244, Mitchell Library, Sydney.
7. Bryan Colton Brett, 'Recollections', unpublished manuscript, 1995, copy in possession of the author. 'Faith missionaries' were not to solicit for money, believing that God would provide the necessary money and accoutrements if it were his will that the work be sustained. An exponent and oft-cited example of this was George Muller, whose orphanages in Bristol, built solely from public funds acquired through prayer, were legendary. Muller's work was written up in the *Australian Christian World*, 26 January 1893. See Pierson.
8. At the annual general meeting of the Aborigines Inland Mission held in Newcastle in 1914, Jennie attended and sat on the dais alongside Aboriginal elders Charlotte and Billy Ridgeway of Karuah Mission near Newcastle. *Newcastle Morning Herald and Miner's Advocate*, 12 August 1914, p. 6.
9. My paternal grandmother, Tilda, once planned to become a missionary. She accompanied her mother to missionary meetings and taught Sunday School.

10. Donald Winnicott conceptualises the notion of transitional space, the playing space or cultural space 'in the potential space between the subjective object and the object objectively perceived, between me extensions and the not me'. Winnicott 1980 (1971), p. 118.

11. Williams, pp. 136–42.

12. Thanks to Reverend Trevor Leggott, whose generosity with his time enabled me to visit the AIM in May 1997. Together we opened boxes and files unaccessed for decades, and which are now located in the Mitchell Library as the records of the Australian Indigenous Ministries.

13. Jen Hibbard, one of the couple's grandchildren, citing Percy Smith. Jen Hibbard, letter, 7 January 1997.

14. Pansy Hickey, email, 25 February 2003.

15. Bryan Colton Brett, conversation with author, May 2003, in which he cited Tilda Smith's recollections. Her recollections are borne out by material in *Our Aim*; see August 1916, p. 7; October 1917, p. 7; August 1919, p. 7.

16. *Our Aim*, July 1909, p. 5.

17. Egerton Long, telephone conversation, 23 May 1997.

18. *Our Aim*, February 1908. A young woman, ME Watkins, was appointed but this was vetoed by the Missionary Council when it found she was not committed to the faith principles of the AIM. That the interviewers, including Retta Dixon Long, overlooked this matter initially indicates some eagerness to leave. ME Watkins, letter to Mrs Long, 4 April 1908, and Mr Smith, letter to Mrs Long c.1908, Australian Indigenous Ministries, Further Records, MLMSS 7244, Mitchell Library, Sydney.

19. *Our Aim*, August 1916, p. 7 & May 1919, p. 7.

20. *Our Aim*, May 1919, p. 7.

21. Pansy Hickey, telephone conversation, 9 June 2003. There is little evidence to show whether this was the practice of missionaries, and indeed *Our Aim*'s policy was to refer to the 'dark people'. The trend towards selection and definition of children on the basis of 'whiteness' was the board's practice. The missionaries appear to have acted on the basis of perceived destitution.

22. Pansy Hickey, telephone conversation, 9 June 2003. See also the account published in *Our Aim*, September 1909, of a group of people's reminiscences about old times and the loss of their culture.

23. McLeod, pp. 61–88.

24. George Colton Moore built 'The Colton Arms' in Greyhound Road, Fulham in 1836.

25. Betty Dupleix, letter, 25 February 2003.

26. Dyhouse.

27. Jen Hibbard, letter, 7 January 1997.

28. Recorded in *Our Aim*, February 1914, p. 5. George indicated that the girls would 'help their mother in their spare time'. Tilda, their elder daughter,

was 13, a common age for leaving school. She and Lou had a scholarship
to Maitland Girls' High School. Both she and her sister matriculated. Syd
and later Arthur also had scholarships, at Maitland Boys' High.

29. Daniel Matthews, 'Sixteenth report of the Maloga Mission, 1890-1', p. 46;
    West Middlesex Standard, 7 June 1891, Matthews Papers, press clipping
    no. 218, PRG 359/4/4, Mortlock Library, Adelaide. Matthews, who was
    soliciting funding at the time, may not have recognised that George was
    without means. But in the end, before departure, Matthews promised to
    support George 'for as long as he was with us'.
30. Betty Dupleix, letter, 9 February 1995, part of a series of letters to Bryan
    and Coral Brett, February–July 1995, in possession of BC Brett.
31. Daniel Matthews, 'Sixteenth report of the Maloga Mission, 1890-1', p. 56.
32. GC Smith to GE Ardill, 28 August 1892, Department of Education,
    Brewarrina (Mission) School 1876–1939, ref: 5/16718.4, Archives Office
    of NSW (AONSW), Sydney.
33. Undersecretary, Department of Public Instruction, to the secretary,
    Aborigines Protectorate Board, 9 September 1892, Brewarrina (Mission)
    School 1876–1939.
34. In fact George had been removed from the overseer's post at
    Warangesda as, according to the APA's Annual Report, he proved to have
    no farming skills. In my view this may have been a cover-up as George
    had lost the confidence of the Aboriginal people at Warangesda, along
    with the manager's wife, following the sudden death of a young girl,
    Daisy Brown, in the dormitories. The Aboriginal elders had demanded a
    coronial inquiry, which, although it found no evidence of cruelty and
    determined that her death was from pneumonia, suggests a considerable
    degree of distrust from the Wiradjuri people. See Manager's Diary,
    Warangesda Mission 1888–1897 (henceforth Warangesda Manager's
    Diary), entries 6–9 August 1892, MS 1791, National Library of Australia
    (henceforth NLA); '"Black: but comely," Being the Annual Report of the
    NSW Aborigines Protection Association for 1892', p. 4. From what I can
    gather, the arrival of Smith and Pridham (who would become the
    manager of Brewarrina) with Daniel Matthews in 1890 and their
    subsequent defection to the APA in January 1891 was a windfall for the
    APA, who were under much scrutiny following allegations of improper
    management by John Gribble. There was in inquiry conducted by John
    Treseder of the APA, who reported to Minister Parkes in July 1891. He
    investigated the conditions at Cumeroogunga and Warangesda and
    made recommendations for various appointments, including the
    overseer's post at Warangesda. GC Smith, who was at Cumeroogunga at
    the time, got the job. A letter from George to the APA's general secretary,
    George Ardill (August 1892), apologised for the non-arrival of Jennie,
    who was to take up a matron's post. It also referred to a suggestion of the
    post for George at Brewarrina which subsequently fell through. Indeed,

this particular letter was used by Ardill to support the proposal for that appointment at Brewarrina. The APA reports for 1892 and 1893 make much of the need for a married man after this, suggesting that Ardill made up the rule, or asserted it more particularly after this. Ardill, too, appears to have had a particular concern about morality which even his contemporaries remarked upon. He may also have felt a little more confident after the government inquiry and begun asserting his position more fully.

35. Betty Dupleix, conversation, 28 May 1999. At the time, single women were perceived as instrumental in the missionary effort: 'A work for the women of Australia', *Our Aim*, 21 October 1912, p. 5. The *Southern Cross*, 28 February 1890, published an item instructing women on how to form a missionary society. The *Australian Christian World* between 1890 and 1896 also wrote of the women missionaries of the China Inland Mission. The AIM and its sister organisation the Australian Aborigines Mission followed the principles and practices of the China Inland Mission by sending its missionaries to live in Aboriginal communities throughout New South Wales (see AIM, Further Records). See also Taylor. Retta Dixon had a vision of the AIM being staffed by single women missionaries along the lines of the China Inland Mission, which meant they could live among the Aborigines rather than gathering them together on settlements. She actually arranged for applicants to be interviewed by the CIM (see AIM, Further Records). The utilisation of young single women as missionaries was a matter which prompted the gentlemen of the board to intervene and insist that they were not to live 'alone' on the reserves, but in pairs. It was a debate that rumbled along between 1910 and 1920. *Sydney Morning Herald*, 27 January 1912.

36. Aborigines Protection Association, Annual Report 1885, pp. 3–7, Mitchell Library, Sydney.

37. Aborigines Protection Board, Annual Report 1896, Box 4, Aborigines, McClaren Collection, University of Melbourne.

38. Mary Anne Kennedy, manager Mr Pridham reported, was 'spoken to in relation to some unseemly remarks she had made to the Dormitory Matron which the latter had reported'. Perhaps the offence was much to do with Jennie's strict expectations of station within the servants' quarters and her conscientious view of doing a good job. There was a meeting, sorrow was confessed and the apology accepted (Warangesda Manager's Diary, 29 July 1896). Pridham had also come to Australia with Janet Matthews in late 1889. The Aboriginal men on the mission frequently argued with the manager about decisions they thought not in their interests, forcing the missionaries into a position of negotiation. (See, for example, Manager's Diary entry for 14 January 1891, where the younger men refused to work unless a separate hut was provided for them to eat their meals while working on the mission.)

39. It is not clear what he was doing, but it appears he gained some recognition as either a lay preacher or deacon in the Church of England, which enabled him to conduct limited church-related duties.

40. *Australian Christian World*, items regarding Myora Mission, 22 February 1894, p. 6 & 29 August 1894, p. 8.

41. Warangesda Manager's Diary, 25 August 1896. The couple's marriage certificate dated 11 September 1896 gives Jennie's address as Warangesda, Riverina, NSW.

42. Warangesda Manager's Diary, 26 September 1896.

43. Warangesda Manager's Diary, 10 October 1896.

44. The APA at this time was under the general secretaryship of George Edward Ardill. He took over in 1888 and remained in the post until 1897 when the APA amalgamated with the Aborigines Protection Board. Ardill then joined the Board. Ardill made it his mission to rescue young girls from the dangers of immorality. His network of homes, hospitals and orphanages catered to Aboriginal and white people. Stephen Gapps, 'Mr Ardill's scrapbook: alternative sources for biography', in Public History Review, vol. 2, 1993, pp. 99–107; the *Australian Christian World*, 31 August 1893, p. 1.

45. Daniel Matthews to the *Southern Cross*, 27 November 1897. The idea of a children's home at this time suggests that the couple were, early on, keen to take this path.

46. Betty Dupleix, 5 April 1995, letters to Bryan and Coral Brett.

47. Betty Dupleix, 9 February 1995, letters to Bryan and Coral Brett.

48. Dupleix, 9 February 2003.

49. GC Smith, postcard, 5 July 1899, included in Dorothy Smith, 'Of times and places' (an account of a journey undertaken by Dorothy and Percy Smith to the sites of Percy's childhood and his parents' work as missionaries), c. 1980. This has been distributed throughout the extended family. I have used the original now in possession of Betty Dupleix. A copy is in the Mitchell Library, MLMSS, uncatalogued.

50. Betty Dupleix. Tilda recalled 'some sort of promise' made by her father that led to the journey. See also Janet Matthews, 'The story of the Manunka Aborigines' Mission Home, 1905–6', p. 2, PRG 359/4/1, Mortlock Library, Adelaide.

51. Nancy Cato writes sympathetically of this event in *Mr Maloga*, Queensland University Press, Brisbane, 1993.

52. Janet Matthews noted in 1907 that a stone house was 'much needed for the overseer and his wife'. She noted that there was 'a tent in which orphan boys sleep, and a girls sleeping room' near the overseer's hut. Janet Matthews, 'The story of the Manunka Aborigines' Mission Home, 1906–7', p. 3, Matthews Papers, PRG 359/4/1, Mortlock Library, Adelaide.

53. On a visit to Walkers Flat in the late 1970s, Tilda reconstructed the Manunka site for her daughter. She also remembered visiting German

families who lived in stone houses on the hill above the Matthews house. Betty Dupleix to Bryan and Coral Brett, 21 May 1995.

54. Janet Matthews, 1906–7, p. 5.
55. Dorothy Smith, 'Of times and places'.
56. Rod Williams, Mannum Heritage Centre, Mannum, South Australia, has compiled this account of Jennie Christmas. There is a walkway in the main street of Mannum, 'Jennie Christmas Walk', with a plaque erected outlining how Jennie Christmas climbed the cliffs around the town to meet up with the women of the town, help their children and arrange for her children to go to school on Mrs Matthews' Mission. See also Bonita Ely, *Murray/Murrindi*, Experimental Art Foundation, Adelaide, 1980, an oral history providing an account of Jennie Christmas by her daughter, Dulcie Ely, unpaginated.
57. Betty Dupleix, 2 May 1995.
58. *Our Aim*, October 1917, p. 9.
59. At Warangesda, George had been astonished by the lack of Christianity and arranged for them to join the Scripture Union. He was bothered about 'drink', incurring the wrath of those on the mission who also liked drinking. Warangesda Mission, Manager's Diary, September 1891–August 1892. George Smith, cited in the *Christian*, 17 March 1892, press clipping, unnumbered, Matthews Papers, PRG 359/4/4, Mortlock Library, Adelaide.
60. Lovejoy, pp. 183–86. Russell McGregor's *Imagined destinies* outlines the influence of scientific racism on perceptions of intelligence in different racial groups in the late 19th and early 20th centuries.
61. Janet Matthews' evidence, Government of South Australia, 'Minutes of evidence of the Aborigines Royal Commission, Progress Report, 1912', South Australia, p. 57, Public Record Office Victoria. After the couple left, the mission was revoked when Janet Matthews retired in 1911. The events referred to concern a young missionary woman seeking advice about the people among whom the Smiths worked, possibly another missionary project.
62. Janet Matthews, 1908–9, p. 3; Betty Dupleix, conversation, 23 May 1999.
63. Percy Smith, written recollection, copy in my possession. Tilda, at seven, had also been sent away, but very quickly returned after developing whooping cough. Tilda told me about this incident just before she died in 1986. Betty Dupleix, letter, 7 May 1995.
64. GC Smith to Mr and Mrs Long, 26 March 1910, AIM, Further Records.
65. Betty Dupleix, letter, 7 May 1995.
66. Bryan Brett, conversation, 30 April 2003. This was a boast and point of identity for many Londoners born within the radius of Bow Bells. Like Jennie and George, missionary Charles Abel called himself a Cockney, although born in Wandsworth (see Wetherell, p. 1). The couple's origins were in the Fulham area.

67. Pansy Hickey, telephone conversation, 25 February 2003.
68. Historians of lower middle class British culture focus both on the upward mobility and the family centredness of these households. See Hammerton; Cullwick; Hall, *White, male and middle class*; Davidoff & Hall.
69. Matilda Brett, conversation, c. 1982. It is my memory of her reaction when, on the way to visit her, I was approached by an Aboriginal woman in the street asking for money. Tilda was concerned that the woman's begging was demeaning to her. I take this to be a reflection of Jennie's teaching and attitude.
70. The early missionaries came from diverse backgrounds. Some single woman missionaries recruited to the AIM had worked in menial jobs or in service prior to joining; others, such as Elsie Dietrich, who joined in 1914, and Amelia Partridge, who joined in 1915, were educated women from reasonably wealthy middle-class backgrounds. Still others, such as Mrs Bock, were widows. See AIM, Further Records.
71. *Our Aim*, June 1913, p. 3.
72. The AIM missionaries and other interested people also contributed to *Our Aim*, which promulgated the mission's purpose and public awareness of its cause to a readership which, by 1916, was based on a circulation of 2000. This does not include the exchanges and 'passing on' of the journal between family and friends.
73. *Our Aim*, February, 1913, p. 5.
74. *Our Aim*, January 1913, p. 7.
75. *Our Aim*, October 1913, p. 5.
76. *Our Aim*, February 1914, p. 6.
77. *Our Aim*, August 1910, p. 4.
78. *Our Aim* shows an interaction between the children, their parents and the home in the early years of the Smiths' tenure, which suggests the couple thought of the home as a refuge for the children according to their needs. These interactions diminished from 1915 onwards, presumably as the Board became more influential. *Our Aim*, February 1911, reported the visit of parents to the home; also, three girls returned to their mother who had only placed them in the home for 12 months; in January 1916 it mentions that 12 children with their parents met with the others for the evening service, 30 being present; February 1912, the death of a woman at St Clair, leaving behind her four children who were transferred to the Singleton home; August 1916, the departure of an older girl from St Clair to the home 'to finish her schooling and also to receive training in household duties which will fit her to take her place as a useful member of society'; September 1916, another boy received at the home to go to the public school; July 1914, the arrival of a 'wee half caste babe', and overcrowding prompting them to turn away a baby. *Our Aim* of October 1914 notes that: 'Three children have returned to their parents who were placed in the home temporarily.'

79. The handwriting on both cards is similar. The first, indistinctly post-marked 1912 and addressed to Tilda, dutifully describes the scene, the family she is working for. The second, unsigned, appears to have been sent in an envelope. It is more confiding, and private, the letter of an unhappy girl. Smith Family Collection, original with Betty Dupleix.
80. *Our Aim*, June 1914, p. 5.
81. *Our Aim*, May 1913, p. 5.
82. *Our Aim*, April 1913, p. 5.
83. *Our Aim*, June 1916, p. 7.
84. *Our Aim*, July 1916, p. 5.
85. GC Smith to Tommy Smith, July 1899. He remarked on the couple's delight in their son who enjoyed doing things for himself, at eight months old. Dorothy Smith, 'Of times and places'.
86. There is much literature on the mother–infant relationship. See for a starting point Stern and Pines.
87. *The Sydney Morning Herald* of 27 September 1912 published a summary of the APB's Annual Report in which it was stated both that the parental relationship should not be interfered with *and* that children should be removed from their surroundings 'as early as possible'. The researcher John Bowlby argues that to take a child from its mother is to disrupt continuity of being in the world, beginning in the earliest, preverbal stages of life. Separating a child from its mother, he said, is catastrophic for the child's internal psychic development. *Attachment*, 1994 (videorecording), scripted by John Bowlby & Anne Diack, BBC for Open University, London. His colleagues, James and Joyce Robertson, showed that childhood separation, when sensitively handled, need not be so damaging. James and Joyce Robertson, Tavistock Institute of Human Relations, London. Denis Brown, a psychoanalyst who has made a specialty of intercultural dynamics and change, notes that the 'good enough containing cultural frame', offering security and continuity to a sense of self, is essential. It is in the disruption of that life and culture, when the cultural envelope is also torn, that creates risk. Without it, the mind and self might disintegrate. Denis Brown, 'Transcultural group analysis: the foundation matrix and the stranger', introductory talk for workshop held in Melbourne, March 1996, unpublished manuscript in possession of the author. See also DG Brown, 'Group analysis, transcul-turality and ethics', *British Journal of Psychotherapy*, vol. 12, pp. 170–77. Peter Read takes up this point from a historian's perspective in his paper 'One hundred years of Aboriginality', presented at the Australian Psychoanalytical Society conference 2000, www. psychoanalysisdow-nunder.com.PADpapers/ papers3, accessed 22 July 2003.
88. *Our Aim*, January 1909.
89. GC Smith to Aborigines Protection Board, 27 March 1914, excerpt quoted in letter from the Board to Mrs Long, 30 March 1914, AIM, Further Records.

90. Letters from Secretary Beardsmore, Aborigines Protection Board, to Mrs Long, 30 March 1914, AIM, Further Records.

91. RT Donaldson, 'The Aborigines — past, present, future', *Proceedings of the Third Australasian Catholic Congress, 26 September–3 October 1909*, p. 485, AIATSIS Library, Canberra. By 1912 his position had hardened to argue that children should be removed as young as possible, even if their parents were legally married (*Sydney Morning Herald*, 14 May 1912, pp. 7 & 8). An item 'Dealing with halfcastes', published on 27 September 1912, summarised the Board's argument that the 'fullbloods should be provided for, and that children of mixed [A]boriginal white heritage should be removed from the reserves'. At this stage the board took the contradictory position that the relationship between parent and child should not be interfered with, but nevertheless for their proposals to work, children should be removed as early as possible. By 1915 the APB had met with the chief secretary to argue for increased centralisation of the board's power; viz., that the role of manager and teacher on the reserves should be combined, thus bringing the control of the teacher under the board. *Sydney Morning Herald*, 10 August 1915, p. 7.

92. Department of Education, *Course of Instruction for Aborigines Schools*, NP 371–97, 16EW, NLA.

93. A search of the Department of Education files where AIM missionaries were active shows that they actively advocated for the children's education. See, for example, the *Newcastle Morning Herald and Miner's Advocate*, 30 April 1902, p. 2, reporting on the exclusion of Aboriginal children from a school near Yass. Retta Dixon was involved, urging the minister to approve their return. The minister's response, alluding to the government's responsibility to the 'white' blood of the children, was a key factor in his support. In an editorial published in May 1919 Retta Long, a long-time supporter of Aboriginal children's educational abilities, took up the question of educational ability: whether Aboriginal people were genetically inferior. 'We are thankful that such erroneous ideas can be unquestionably discredited,' she wrote, 'not only by those who have given long years to the study of this people but for the colonists who without the intelligence and the sagacity of the blacks, could never have weathered the discouragements of early pioneering.' *Our Aim*, May 1917, p. 7.

94. *Our Aim*, April 1918, p. 6.

95. Retta Long's summary, *Our Aim*, May 1919, p. 7.

96. GC Smith to LW Long, 23 June 1920, AIM, Further Records.

97. Aborigines Protection Board, Annual Report 1918.

98. *Our Aim*, May 1919, p. 7.

99. GC Smith to LW Long, 14 June 1919, AIM, Further Records. Some years before, in 1913, an AIM missionary woman had held a dual appointment

as a subsidised teacher at St Clair. George thought they should be regarded in the same way.

100. GC Smith to secretary, Aborigines Protection Board, 29 August 1919, ref. 2/8350, AONSW, Sydney. The Board agreed to increase George's salary to 100 pounds a year and Jennie's to 30 pounds a year. Aborigines Protection Board salary register.

101. SJ Smith to Percy Smith, 9 November 1919, copy in possession of the author.

102. *Our Aim*, March 1916, p. 3. Tilda, too, benefited from Donaldson's 'friendship'. He encouraged her application to the board for a teaching position at Cumeroogunga, but his real plan was to interrupt the James family, who had held most of the teaching positions. A year later she was successful and, it is suspected through Donaldson's intervention, was paid an adult wage. Matilda Smith to Aborigines Protection Board, 9 February 1917, annotated by R Donaldson recommending her for a position (undated); Memo, Department of Education to Public Service Board, 7 March 1918; Department of Education, Cumeroogunga Aboriginal School 1910–39, ref: 5/15619A, AONSW, Sydney.

103. Wallis W Collins, hon. sec. Parents & Citizens Association, Singleton Public School, to the minister for education, 3 September 1918; Report of Miss Z Bockings, Singleton Public School, 20 September 1918; Thomas Austin, Special report to Inspector G Back re. Aboriginal children attending Singleton Public School, 23 September 1918; Memo: district inspector to chief inspector, Muswellbrook District, 'Question of exclusion of Aboriginal children from Singleton Public School', 28 September 1918; Peter Board, undersecretary, Department of Education, to J Fallick esq. MLA, Aborigines Protection Board, 9 October 1918. Board approved the exclusion of the home children from the school provided that alternative arrangements were made for their education. He suggested that a building from the school, which was refurbishing its premises, be transferred to the home's grounds. The renovations and removal took 18 months. Memo: inspector, Muswellbrook District to chief inspector, 4 May 1920; inquiries made 13 May 1920. Austin was appointed to the home and school as manager/teacher, accepting his appointment on 29 June 1920. Department of Education, Singleton Public School, ref: 5/17630B, AONSW, Sydney.

104. Aborigines Protection Board to Department of Education, 12 April 1920. Department of Education, Singleton Public School.

105. TH Austin, 9 June 1920, Department of Education, Singleton Aboriginal School, ref: 5/17632A, AONSW, Sydney. Austin refused to put up with the conditions — and penury — at the Singleton home and insisted upon repairs. It illustrates the severity of the conditions under which the Smiths operated.

106. Peter Board to Aborigines Protection Board, 5 May 1920. Department of Education, Cumeroogunga Aboriginal School, ref: 5/15619A, AONSW, Sydney.
107. Aborigines Protection Board Minutes, 2 June 1920, ref: 4/7128, AONSW, Sydney. The ward files show the transfer of a number of children from the home between 2 and 30 June 1920. Aborigines Protection Board ward registers, 1916–28, ref: 4/8533, AO reel 2793, AONSW.
108. George's dismissal was followed by an almost blanket lack of acknowledgment of the couple's existence in subsequent histories of the AIM: see Retta Long, c. 1950, *In the way of His steps*. Historians have also overlooked the home. Jeremy Long's seminal study *Aboriginal Settlements* documents Kinchela but not the Singleton home. In his 1996 submission to the National Inquiry into the Removal of Aboriginal and Torres Strait Islander Children, past president of the AIM Howard Miles pays cursory attention to the Singleton home, and neglects a second home opened at Homebush in 1924 in partnership with Elizabeth McKenzie Hatton. Peter Read, who drew attention to the phenomenon of the stolen children in *A rape of the soul so profound*, does not mention Singleton.
109. GC Smith to LW Long, 23 June 1920, AIM Further Records.
110. The Aborigines Protection Board salary register, 1917–1923, lists Jennie's superannuation contributions for the years between 1920 and 1921 when, inexplicably, she stopped contributing, ref: 2/8350, AONSW, Sydney.
111. George's obituary appeared in the *Nambour Chronicle*, 2 February 1940. Jennie died at Murwillumbah, New South Wales.

3. 'A devotion I hope I may fully repay'

Joan Kingsley-Strack

Victoria Haskins

In 1940, in a suburban household in Sydney, Joan Kingsley-Strack came across an article entitled 'Try an Abo apprentice' in the women's supplement of her newspaper. Quoting a happy female employer — '[X] has become one of the family and we have become very fond of her' — the article exhorted white housewives to avail themselves of indentured Aboriginal servants supplied by the New South Wales Aborigines Protection Board.[1] Joan Strack was outraged. For the past two years, as the enthusiastic secretary of the Aboriginal Citizenship Committee (which supported the Aborigines Progressive Association in the late 1930s), she had been actively assisting Aboriginal parents to retrieve their daughters from such apprenticeships, and to force the board to reimburse their wages.[2] She scrawled a derisory question mark against the statement that 'these wards of the State are placed in suitable homes which are selected by the Aborigines' Protection Board'. 'Nothing *like* it,' she wrote in exclamation to the claim the girls were educated to a 'fifth-class standard' before being sent out to work. And to the comment that the workers' wages were held in trust for them until being returned on their attaining maturity, 'Perhaps!' she snorted.[3]

Joan Strack could speak from personal experience. No less than three Aboriginal apprentices had worked for her in the past, and at the time of writing she was employing an ex-apprentice, previously indentured to her mother. As she recorded what happened to these women at the hands of the Aborigines Protection Board, her growing outrage hardened to such an extent that she joined the Aboriginal leaders of the Aborigines Progressive Association (APA), Pearl Gibbs (see Chapter 5) and Bill Ferguson, in calling for its abolition. Her story of activism in the late-1930s campaign for Aboriginal rights defies categorisation: a conservative, privileged woman in many ways typical of those to whom the board allocated apprentices, she found herself in the 'enemy camp', so to speak.[4] But Joan Strack herself saw no irony in her position. 'For generations my people have employed, have loved & understood the Aboriginals of N.S.W.,' she wrote to the Premier in 1938, appealing to him to meet an APA deputation. 'I myself have had them always in my home… & I know their dire need of just ordinary justice.'[5]

The granddaughter of successful English–Scottish selectors at Wallaga Lake on the Far South Coast of New South Wales, Joan in later years would tell people she too had been born there, but in fact she only ever visited. Her real birthplace, in 1892, was at her parents' home in the outer northern suburbs of Sydney, her father having been an engineer on the new railway line.[6]

As a wife and mother who lived most of her life in the comfortable suburbs of Sydney's North Shore, Joan Strack indeed personified the urban caste of 'well-heeled upper-middle-class ladies who took black domestics' in the 20th century.[7] Yet her outspoken opposition to this policy had arisen directly out of her personal relationships with her workers, and in this she was exceptional: the vast majority of white mistresses did *not* speak out against the system which in most cases worked in their own interests. What Joan Strack did was highly unusual, but it is an important story to tell, yielding a personal insight into a history of relationships between white and Aboriginal women that generations of repression and denial have obscured.

***

Joan Strack was my great-grandmother (better known as 'Ming' to family and myself). But her story was not passed down to me in the family oral tradition of memory; rather, it had, literally, been shut up and forgotten for nearly half a century. Like other women who did not follow the conventional scripts allotted to them, Ming's life was painful, the price high, the anxiety intense.[8] In 1942, after the birth of my father, Ming's fourth and final worker was committed to a mental asylum in a blatant attempt to silence both her and her voluble

Mary with Narrelle (the author's grandmother), 1923. Author's photo collection.

employer.[9] Ming, horrified, guilt-ridden, then embittered, concluded that 'all those wasted years' of campaigning for Aboriginal rights might best be forgotten. She put away her formidable archive attesting to the maltreatment of Aboriginal apprentices, and barely spoke of it again.

Many years later, in 1993, my grandmother (Ming's daughter) was showing me some of her treasured old photographs. One caught my attention: a hand-tinted snapshot of herself as a three-year-old, in the embrace of a uniformed Aboriginal nursemaid.

'Who's *this*?'

'Oh, yes,' said Gran, taking the photograph back from me. 'That was Mary. Dear old Mary. She was such a *beautiful* person. Do you know — she was more than my own mother to me.'

I looked again. Mary was smiling, shyly but proudly, the two of them beaming into the broad sunlight. Turning the photograph over, I read: 'Narrelle and Mary, East Kew'. I was intrigued. But my Gran was at a loss to explain how Mary had come to be with her. She suggested I might find the clue within the boxes that Ming had left behind, lying dusty and unopened on the floor of my aunt's garage for the past decade.

In Ming's boxes I found more photographs of Mary, glimpses through a lens of Ming's view of their relationship. Alone it seems of Ming's servants, Mary was photographed by Ming across the years she worked for her: Mary on the beach, in the backyard, on the verandah; sometimes serious, sometimes smiling; always with one or more of the Strack children, reflecting the fact that her relationship with Ming revolved around the care of the other woman's young children. A captivating pair of images shows Ming and Mary in identical positions on the beach with the children, taking turns at play. On the one hand it is an image of a feminine friendship idyll; on the other, there are no images of the two women actually together, and the contrast between the trim, fashionably dressed white woman and the plump and softly-bundled black woman is, disturbingly, redolent of the 'Old Slave South'.

Today, these images speak of colonialist nostalgia, and to our eyes mark Ming as unambiguously complicit in the Aboriginal child removal policy. Indeed, Ming would not take issue with Aborigines Protection Board policy for many years after Mary's departure (removed from her charge by the board after the birth of Mary's illegitimate child). And the fact that the board would obligingly supply her with a further two apprentices shows that she was not seen by the authorities as subversive in any way.

Ming's relationship with Mary was the most akin to slavery of any relationship she had with an Aboriginal person, servant or otherwise, the one most clearly structured as possession and exploitation. But as I ordered Ming's jumble of papers into a comprehensible narrative, an intriguing and paradoxical explanation for her eventual engagement in Aboriginal politics began to emerge. No wonder she found the 1940 article so offensive, with its happy employer saying that her apprentice was 'just like one of the family'. For what galvanised Ming to take political action was her inability under the bureaucratic regime of the Aborigines Protection Board to play that familial role of kindly white mistress to devoted black servant. And it was her failure to fulfil this ideal in her intensely emotional relationship with Mary — the woman my gran described as being 'more than my own mother to me' — that was of the most fundamental and far-reaching significance for Ming. Her efforts in support of Aboriginal rights, I came to realise, were ultimately redemptive.

It was with no small sense of relief that I set about recovering this hidden history, so clearly my own. When I found Ming's papers, I had been floundering for some time with the issues of writing Aboriginal history as a white Australian scholar. Mindful of critiques by Indigenous historians, such as the conclusion that it was not appropriate for white historians to write Aboriginal history, I had taken the escape route chosen by many.[10] Instead of studying the 'nuts and bolts' history, I would study white Australians' popular-cultural representations of Aboriginal and white women's relationships. After a year of research in this area, despairingly convinced my work was destined to the wastebasket of postmodern trivialisation, I had decided to go back to my roots — little imagining, however, that I would find the history of Aboriginal oppression and resistance so directly embedded in my own family history. Within a year or so, the hearings of the stolen generations inquiry would begin. As I pieced together Ming's story against that heart-rending refrain, I was struck not only by the willingness of Aboriginal people to share their painful stories, but by the corresponding silence from those families where the stolen children were, in all but name, enslaved.[11]

My attempt has been to recover a white Australian testimony on this history, from the perspective of one who was intimately involved. In the process, however, I have realised the complexity of the endeavour. I have had to reconstruct aspects of the Aboriginal women's experiences, for these are integral to the story; a certain degree of speculation on *their* perspective is also required to complicate Ming's concerns, assumptions and silences. But while their stories may be illuminated to some degree by Ming's records, I cannot purport to provide an Aboriginal perspective. Their conversations with her, even their letters to her, are 'voices' that come to me only through that mask worn by black and colonised people everywhere.

I remain particularly concerned not to usurp the role of Aboriginal historians, nor to infringe upon the various families' rights to comment or remain silent: the stories of the Aboriginal women remain their own.[12] Tracing the families of the four women who worked for Ming,

I eventually found Mary's eldest grandson living with his wife in a small country town in New South Wales, and went out to visit him. The welcome he and his wife gave me — they were especially happy to see photographs of Mary, who had died before any of her grandchildren were born — overcame my initial awkwardness. I felt I received a warm response from all the families, primarily — perhaps solely — because my own family was involved. As my personal connections to this history enlivened and transformed my research, I began to comprehend for the first time the bemusement with which many Aboriginal people view those who write the histories which are not their 'own'.[13]

Yet in finding that my link to Ming gave me the privilege to tell *her* story, I realised the limitations of my ability to interpret even Ming's motives and experiences. At the same time, I found that the story of her struggle would not exist were it not for her sense of connection with the women who worked for her. For it was Ming's personal engagement with her workers, and their experiences to which she bore witness, that drove her crusade. Just as personal and colonialist histories are interwoven, so too black and white lives are inseparably enmeshed in our past.

***

Ming was expecting her second child when she first entered into a contract to engage an Aboriginal apprentice. Recuperating from recent surgery, she wanted somebody to help her with the care of her three-year-old son during her convalescence. Though she had not had a servant before, Ming was familiar with Aboriginal domestic labour, her maternal grandparents at Wallaga Lake having customarily utilised Aboriginal people from the adjacent reserve, including two married women to work in the house. Ming's assorted aunts (including Jean, who almost certainly arranged Mary's transfer to Ming), who had married in the rural districts, likewise relied upon local Aboriginal labour. This 'employment' (there is no evidence workers were paid in anything other than food) was apparently undertaken with an air of noblesse oblige, masking Ming's family's dependence on Aboriginal labour and their role in Aboriginal dispossession.[14]

Mary, for her part, experienced the harsher reality. She was the third generation in her family to be taken to work for whites, beginning with the kidnapping of her maternal grandfather during a massacre in Victoria's Gippsland.[15] But Mary's traumatic history was not known or comprehended by Ming, and must be retraced somewhere other than in Ming's papers. Not even Mary's own descendants knew this history; like the one other surviving photograph of Mary, a formal portrait of her standing solemn and alone in a hallway, it is held within government archives.[16]

In 1916, aged 15, Mary was among the first major haul of female children taken after the passage of the 1915 *Aborigines Protection Amending Act* (NSW).[17] She and her two younger sisters had earlier come to the attention of the Aborigines Protection Board, in 1914, when the manager of Brungle Station reported their presence on the outskirts of the town of Gundagai in New South Wales. The board concurred with his suggestion that the girls should be placed in its Cootamundra Domestic Training Home for Aboriginal Girls, but their mother's refusal to relinquish them confounded that plan.[18]

Mary's mother had been through the mill of indentured domestic service in Victoria — had seen her younger sisters go through it too — after her father, a man of fierce independence, had been compelled to bring his children on to a reserve. And she had already fought for and lost two daughters and a baby, consenting to a mission-arranged marriage in the hope (unrealised) of getting them back, before being widowed as the mother of another three girls. Perhaps by choosing to marry again, and moving with her new husband (an Aboriginal man) to his home state of New South Wales, she hoped these three children might escape a similar fate. But under the new 1915 amendments in that state, which gave the board powers to remove Aboriginal children without parental consent or a court finding of neglect, Mary's mother could do nothing to resist the board's intervention. Six months after her two older girls, Mary and Sarah, were taken, her death from heart failure was formally registered by the Cootamundra police sergeant who witnessed her burial on a paddock just south of the town. This unusual formality was because the board had secured control of the youngest daughter, who was committed that same day to Cootamundra Home by a court order. She joined her sister Sarah there. Mary had already left, two weeks earlier, to take up her first situation at Wahroonga.[19]

Three years later, Mary came to work for Ming. Ming's initial invalidism set the tone for their relationship, masking Mary's total disempowerment, for some years at least. Ming had been traumatised by an operation, undertaken against her express wishes, to remove an ovary, her appendix, and 'some other part of the anatomy!' unknown to herself. Told by the doctor that 'the child must be removed', her distress was intensified by the absence of her husband, Norman, who was 'holidaying' and could not be located. Ming's description of this episode in her life reflects her sense of physical vulnerability as a woman, 'frantic with fear' and at the mercy of her own body as well as an errant husband and overbearing male doctors.[20]

In practical terms, Mary's support was vital. As well as assuming primary care of Ming's son, Mary would have taken over all the heavy housework (and much of the light). The unborn baby survived, and when Narrelle, my grandmother, was born five months later (premature and weighing a tiny three pounds) Ming would have depended even more on Mary — emotionally as well as physically.

A war bride who conceived virtually on her wedding night, Ming found that married life fell far short of her expectations. Not only were the couple ill-suited in temperament, but Norman, who had sustained serious head injuries during the war, found it difficult to settle down to supporting a wife and family. Ming wrote up her recollection of these early years of motherhood soon after Mary's arrival. Forced to take in piecework to keep them afloat, Ming had been unable to enjoy her baby son and was shamed by having to work, keeping it a closely guarded secret from her friends and family. Mary's arrival — an 'Aboriginal nurse girl came to me,' wrote Ming with evident relief, '...a dear soft eyed little soul, full of affection for us both' — marked the conclusion of this early phase of her married life.[21] Mary didn't just alleviate the private disappointments of Ming's life. With her crisp white nanny's apron and cap contrasted against her dark skin, marking her as Ming's human possession, she enabled Ming to present a public face of marital harmony and financial success.[22] As one of Ming's cousins reported approvingly after dinner with the Stracks in 1924: 'They seem happy.' She observed that they had a 'very nice' house, beautiful children, 'a car to use whenever they want it', and 'Joan still has the black girl & she adores the children...'[23]

But, despite a succession of moves interstate (first to Victoria, then back to Sydney, then to Queensland) and the birth of a third child, Helen, things between the couple did not improve. Norman was unable to retain a job, and borrowed heavily. In Brisbane, he succumbed to depression, and took to gazing silently at Ming while toying with his revolver. Ming went on 'holiday' without Norman, staying with the children and Mary at her parents' two-room shack at Davistown on the New South Wales Central Coast between February and May 1926. The one diary entry she made during the three months they were there, recording that she had contracted dengue fever and wanted her sister and mother to leave her alone with Mary, shows the extent to which Mary had become her sole female family support: 'Why don't they go home, there is nothing to do for me — & if there is Mary my old faithful will do it without fear or crossness. She is my one bright spot.'[24] This was also reflected in her rather paranoid claim on their return to the city in May that her mother and sister had 'told poor old Mary most wild things *about me*'.[25]

The Stracks' problems were not uncommon in the aftermath of the First World War, but Ming's sense of vulnerability and isolation, her fears of abandonment or worse by her husband, made her attachment to Mary the more intense.[26] For Ming, these were 'those dreadful years', through which Mary was 'faithful, gentle, always at hand to help or cheer me'.[27]

Constructing how Mary felt is more difficult as, unlike Ming, she left no private traces, only letters written with the knowledge that Ming would read them. The earliest surviving account of Mary's feelings is a letter she wrote when Ming was convalescing away from home during the time they lived in Melbourne, in the early 1920s. The tone of Mary's letter was tender. 'My Dear Mistress', she wrote:

> ...Just a few line to say that little Narrelle Peter are quite well and allso Mrs Commons [Ming's mother, visiting at the time] and Mr Strack all[so] myself. I do miss you very much. I am telling Mrs Commons all the nice thing about you, you are just like a mother to me when you are at home. No need to worry you self about the children ther quite all right...
>
> Well dear Mistres...have a good rest and dont worry so much about you little childrens the are quite all right...good by lot of love from us all Mary[28]

Perhaps Mary had indeed transferred her affections from her own mother to Ming. Elizabeth Clark-Lewis, in her study of African-American domestic workers' experiences in the 1920s and 1930s, however, noted workers' highly attuned awareness of their 'psychological value' to their mistresses, their sympathy for their lonely employers complicating the way in which the employers themselves thought of them as being 'just like family'.[29] The graceful way Mary let Ming know she had spoken of her to Ming's own mother certainly suggests that Mary recognised the complexity of her role with regard to Ming's difficult relationship with her own family. Ming delighted in the compliment, keeping Mary's letter with

Mary and Ming (Joan Strack) on the beach with the Strack children, Narrelle and Peter, 1922. Author's photo collection.

the notation on the envelope, 'Letter from my little Aboriginal girl "Mary"'. Together with Mary's naming of Ming as 'My Dear Mistress', these linguistic devices actually represent not intimacy but the rituals of deference and maternalism that underpin the domestic service relationship.[30] As such, they point to the framework of colonial dominance and subordination in which symmetry of dependence and attachment was impossible.

Ming's dependence, emotional and practical, on Mary was very real — her second child, even Ming herself, may not have survived without Mary — but for Ming, Mary was essentially replaceable. After all, there was always the availability of another of Mary's kind, another Aboriginal apprentice supplied by the state. For Mary, in contrast, her dependence on Ming was absolute. When the time came, and she needed Ming, this listing, this disparity in their relationship, would become stark. That time would come with the birth of Mary's own child, whose unexpected appearance demonstrated indisputably that Mary was a grown woman, with the potential to be a mother in her own right.

Mary's child, fathered by an unnamed white man, was apparently conceived during the three-month trip to Davistown. Ming did not mention Mary was expecting a child until Mary was about six months pregnant — possibly she had been unaware of it before then. She was curiously complacent, in her diary merely adding 'Mary's trouble' to the litany of catastrophes that afflicted her. Having again lost his job, Norman planned to move them all back to Sydney to escape their debts, and Ming secretly fantasised about leaving him. Ming's Aunt Jean wrote in commiseration: 'I am terribly sorry for you dear, & Norman, as well as Mary, *what* a thing to have happened just now — too dreadful when you are all needing her most...'[31] These attitudes highlight Mary's position: the significance of her pregnancy was not how it affected *her* life but how it impinged on the life of Ming and her family.

'I was almost distracted,' Ming recalled years later. '[I] put the matter in the hands of the police but they could do nothing. I brought her from Brisbane (as we were all coming to Sydney) and to the women's Hospital where her baby was born — a white child...'[32]

It seems Ming gave the name of the father of Mary's baby to the police, but there are no further clues as to what tragedy lay beyond that. One can only imagine how the impending birth of her child must have evoked for Mary memories of her own mother and of her enforced removal years earlier.

The Stracks, with Mary, arrived in Sydney in November 1926, and stayed with Ming's parents until they moved to a friend's cottage at Wahroonga. In early January, they had to leave that place. Ming took Mary, now eight months pregnant, into town to the Crown Street Women's Hospital, then she and the children went to stay at Davistown while Norman looked for work in Sydney.

Two days after her admission to hospital, Mary wrote to Ming. It was a lengthy, chatty letter, engaging Ming's focus on their own mother–daughter relationship. She told Ming of her difficulty sleeping: 'I could hear all the babies crying all night long, makes me think of dear little Helen. I do hope she will be good for you all. I am always thinking of you all.' Alluding obliquely both to the illegitimacy of her child and her own removal, and affectionately signing off

'Your fond girl', Mary pointed Ming to the fact that she had virtually no family and nobody other than her to turn to.[33]

In stamped envelopes Ming supplied, Mary sent letters of increasing urgency, telling her she was 'sick of the place' and anxiously reiterating her desire to 'get back home soon'.[34] The problem was that Ming did not yet have a 'home' as such (they had been staying at the house of a family friend) and Norman had not yet found a job. In her third letter Mary warned Ming against making her predicament known to the Aborigines Protection Board:

> One of the nurses was saying that there is a Home down at Bedfene [?] where you can go for three weeks or a fortnight with them and stay with them. Lots of white girls are doing that and going out to work again. If you tell Miss Lowe [the Protection Board 'Homefinder', who placed the apprentices in service] about it that means that I will not return back to you anymore. I am feeling worried about that, I think I had better write to Sarah [her sister, now living at Brungle Station] about it and get it over. I know you told all your people about me. So I suggest that I are to write to Sarah and tell her about it. I do hope I will not part from you and the children. I am feeling a bit upset about it. If you are down in town sometime, run out and see me. I would love to see you if you could fit it in. I do miss you and the children, thinking of you all every night. I give my love to Helen, Narrelle, Peter and Nean [Ming's sister] and I hope I will see them soon, if I am coming back to you all again...[35]

Mary had her baby, a girl, on 26 January 1927. She wrote a short note to Ming a few days later asking her to visit: 'I would like to have a talk to you.'[36] Her note reached Ming the day before the Stracks moved to a boarding house on the far western outskirts of Sydney. Two weeks later Mary wrote again, care of Ming's mother:

> Do try and come and get me. I am longing to get back to you if I could get someone to take baby, nurses are so nice to baby and I think one of the nurses said that I would be able to dop [adopt] baby if all goes well... Tell dear little Helen that I am coming home soon, if I am well. Love to you all, come in soon and take me to the home.[37]

According to Ming, Mary had 'implored' her to take her baby as well as herself, and this Ming 'had intended to do and said so', despite the board telling her that they would take charge of Mary's baby.[38] But at this point she was evidently not making her intentions clear to

Mary, and Mary's options were harshly constrained. It appears that Ming had not replied to the news of the baby's birth, and Mary's next letter, with her tentative suggestion that she give up her baby, took a full month to reach Ming. Five days after writing, Mary and her three-week-old baby were transferred from the hospital to the Ashfield Infants' Home, an institution for single mothers and their children utilised by the board for pregnant apprentices.[39]

Mary wrote again to Ming in May, care of Ming's mother, and again the following month, care of the Stracks' original address at Pymble.[40] These letters have not survived, and there is no way of knowing whether Ming replied. In July 1927 Mary and her baby were discharged from the Infants Home to the authority of the Aborigines Protection Board, transferred to Wallaga Lake Aboriginal Station, and thence interstate to Lake Tyers Station in Victoria.

In later years, Ming insisted that at the time she had been 'most anxious to have Mary again in my home'. The Aborigines Protection Board, she said, 'refused...to allow her to return to me'.[41] The records of both the board and the Infants Home suggest that the authorities may have been trying to locate Mary's stepfather, and may not have approached Ming at all.[42] Yet it appears that Ming herself had been in no great haste to have Mary back.

There are several reasons, apart from the evident confusion in the correspondence, why Ming may not have responded immediately to Mary's pleas to 'take me to the home'. With Norman unemployed, the Stracks were in fairly straitened circumstances — Ming supplemented their rent at the Penrith boarding house by serving in the kitchen — and so were not in a position to easily accommodate Mary and her new baby. Although Norman found work in May 1927, they may not have been in their own home until September, when they were renting at Lindfield. Ming was also preoccupied with the serious illness of three-year-old Helen, who came down with laryngeal diphtheria in June 1927. Ming contacted the board then to tell them that, due to Helen's illness, she 'would take Mary a little later'. This was presumably in response to Mary's last letter, and strongly suggests that the board had not actually 'refused' to allow Mary to go back to Ming at this stage.[43] But after a drunken doctor performed an emergency tracheotomy on the little girl at Ming's parents' home, Helen nearly died and was consequently rushed to hospital. The timing was terrible. The day before she was sent to Victoria, Mary made one last attempt to see Ming, coming out to Ming's parents alone, but Ming was not there, being at the hospital with Helen.

Despite these difficulties, Ming's failure to find some kind of emergency, stop-gap solution until she had a place for Mary implies that she assumed Mary could be collected at her convenience; that Mary somehow belonged to her. This belief can possibly be traced to a minor contest for Mary's services between Ming and the board back in early 1926.

It began when Mary applied for her trust monies held by the board, soon after her wages were raised to a fourth-year apprentice's rate (five shillings) in December 1925. The Stracks had been paying her wages to the board at a reduced rate, the third-year rate, since 1920: Mary had just turned 25 and had been working as an apprentice for close on ten years. Possibly the Stracks did not want to pay the wage rise, low as it was, and Mary may herself have offered to apply for her trust monies, when they all realised that her term of apprenticeship theoretically should have expired five years earlier. The board refused, agreeing only to remit five pounds on condition that Mary went for a 'holiday' at Brungle Station in the manager's care, in order, the board claimed, to afford her the opportunity to marry.[44]

In hindsight, Ming would interpret this, quite rightly, as a cynical reaction to Mary's claim on her trust monies, but at the time she was probably perplexed, having given no thought to the possibility of Mary ever leaving her, let alone marrying. She must have been very relieved when Mary returned to her in July, and while Mary's trust monies remained firmly in the board's grasp, Ming began paying her directly. She was probably not paying Mary much, if at all, given that Norman, the sole breadwinner, lost his job at the same time, but presumably she considered Mary to be beyond the authority of the board. Mary was under no such misconception, as her letter from the hospital shows, but Ming chose to disregard her warning.

***

If Mary felt betrayed by Ming we cannot know. They stayed in touch while Mary was at Lake Tyers Aboriginal Station in Victoria, and the correspondence they kept up throughout 1927 and 1928 appears to have been driven by Mary at least as much as by Ming. Mary sought her former mistress's advice regarding a solicitor to help get her trust monies back, as well as asking for monetary assistance (a 'loan') and for her clothes to be sent down. Although her tone remained friendly, if somewhat reserved, Mary addressed Ming now as 'My Dear Mrs Strack' and made no emotional appeals to her — at least not in the one letter that survives.[45] Instead, she wrote confidently and happily of having found relatives in Victoria, and of her 'dear little Baby'.

Finally receiving her trust funds from the NSW board after her marriage in 1928, Mary left the reserve with her daughter and her new husband. She apparently sent a letter to Ming as they left, but it was the last Ming would hear of her for some years.[46]

In February 1930 Ming thought she had found Mary, and wrote at once:

> My Dearest Old Mary
>
> At last I have found your address. I have written to you & sent parcels but have not had any letter from you since you left Lake Tyers. You poor old Mary! I was very sad to hear that you had lost your dear baby Mary. I *am* so sorry. How is the new little baby? Do write me a long letter, & Mary if you would like to come to me again, you can come whenever you like, just say, & I will send the money for your fare. You know that I will always love my old Mary & take care of you both.
>
> Am sending 10/- in this letter & a parcel of clothes. I heard from one of your people at Lake Illawarra (where we stayed for 3 weeks) that you had been very ill & got so thin. I do hope you are well. Just fancy your coming back to Wallaga Lake! What a long way, Mary. Were you trying to come to Sydney? If I had only known I could have helped you. I wrote letters to every place I could think of & at last wrote to Mr Bell at Lake Tyers, but he did not answer it, & then Mrs Mason at Lake Illawarra told me all about you & that your step-father had taken you to Brewarrina. Are you happy Mary? Do write soon.
>
> With love from Joan Strack[47]

Ming's information was incorrect (including the news that Mary's baby had died) and this letter was returned by the Brewarrina manager, who told her he knew of nobody by that name. But Ming herself had been unwell for some time as, unbeknownst to her, she had cervical cancer. Probably she had hoped to have Mary back to help her. At any rate, two months later Ming advertised for a nursemaid to look after the children while she underwent a complete hysterectomy. In many respects the situation was similar to when Mary came to her: once again Norman was away, and Ming ended up in hospital for eight weeks. But, in contrast to her feelings for Mary, Ming was obviously unhappy with the woman she had hired, describing her only once, abruptly, as 'a stranger, a woman I did not know'.[48] In 1931, Ming decided to go back to the board to acquire the services of another Aboriginal apprentice. She seemed to have given up seeking Mary.

Then, in May 1934, in the midst of a fierce battle with the board over her third Aboriginal apprentice, Del, Ming found Mary again. She was back at Brungle Station with her husband. By this time Ming's attitude towards the Aborigines Protection Board had undergone a profound change. She was now certain that the board had exiled Mary to avoid paying out her trust fund, and regretted that she hadn't taken the board to court herself, in Brisbane. Refusing to pay Del's wages to the board, in the hope of drawing them into a legal case and public exposure, she gave as her reason the board's reluctance to reimburse Mary. 'I wish the girl to have her earnings she is *not* a slave... Not one single penny will I pay to a Board which is so dishonorable.'[49] Almost certainly she tried to contact Mary to help her in her campaign against the board, especially as she had contacted Mary's solicitors at Bairnsdale at the same time.[50]

Mary's life had changed too. She had four children with her husband, as well as her first child who was still with her. The Depression was taking a deep hold everywhere — Norman's inability to find work now forced Ming to take the girls to live rent-free at her parents' Davistown place towards the end of the year — but for Aboriginal people, paid work was altogether impossible to find, and the pressure on the reserves increased dramatically.[51] Not surprisingly, the correspondence that now opened up between the two women revolved quite explicitly around Mary's needs. Significantly, Mary reverted to the use of the submissive 'My Dear Mistress', and made her more assertive requests through Ming's daughters rather than to Ming herself. 'Tell her to send me some old clothes and old shoes and hats', she instructed Narrelle. 'Tell her that I am running about with no shoes on and I don't like [it], makes my feet very sore.'[52]

This kind of one-directional giving of old clothes has been described as the 'ubiquitous expression of maternalism' in a domestic service relationship, a ritual serving to 'reify the differences between the women'.[53] Its continuation years after Mary's departure highlights the ongoing obligations that both women felt Ming owed Mary. For Ming, recoiling from what she had learned of the apprenticeship experience from Del, it may well have provided reassurance that *her* involvement in the system had not been 'dishonorable'. It reaffirmed those bonds that signified Ming as the caring mother–employer and Mary as the faithful daughter–servant.[54] Ming's emotional investment in this was all the more telling, given that she was hardly in a position to distribute largesse at this period in her life.[55]

For Mary, too, there seems to have been a genuine desire to re-establish the past. In her letters to both Narrelle and Helen, Mary suggested that she might visit them in Sydney: 'I would love to see you all again.'[56] When Ming was able to move back to Sydney at the end of January — Norman having found regular work — this suggestion became a tentative plan.[57] The outcome, however, depended on Ming's ability to assist financially, and she failed to make good her promise. Mary wrote:

> When I got this last letter from you I thought it was money [you] said that you was going to send me for my trip to Sydney. I was so disappointed when I opened the letter. I am getting two suitcases in town next week in case you send my fare this time. I would love to come down for a holiday just to see you all again... I am getting my clothes washed up [?] next week in case you send my fare. Try and send my fare if you can manage. Oh the last letter you wrote to [me] I thought it was the money when I see it R from Roseville I was glad you sent the money. Oh well I must stop now...[58]

But whether the offer of such a 'holiday' was genuine or not, Mary never did visit. Ming and Norman's marital problems spiralled extravagantly, wildly, out of control throughout the year, and it seems highly unlikely that Ming would have had Mary come to stay while in the throes of such domestic drama. The next year Mary's family moved from Brungle to Erambie Mission at Cowra, at around the same time as the Stracks also moved house, and once again the women lost touch with each other.[59]

They would never meet again. In January 1938 Ming received a letter from Mary's husband, William. 'Dear Mrs Strack,' he wrote, 'I received your letter today...'

> ...It came from Cowra mission. I am living in Yass with my sister-in-law Sarah Todd and also my six children. You will get such a shock when I tell you in my letter about my wife Mary, she is dead six month now and I gave all the children to her sister Sarah to care for them... Times are very hard these days to live. It takes a lot to keep six children although Sarah, my wife's sister, is very good to them and trying to rear them all up. I will bring my letter to a close...[60]

Ming *was* shocked. Mary had died, aged 38, of pneumonia. On the back of William's letter Ming wrote: 'My poor little faithful Mary died, neglected & starving & terribly ill, at the settlement at Cowra —

a *scandal* indeed, for she had done so much for me, & I could not trace her.'

The timing of this news had crucial implications for Ming's political trajectory. Ming had been attending the Parliamentary Select Committee Inquiry into the NSW Aborigines Protection Board since November 1937, intending to give evidence of the mistreatment and abuse of Aboriginal girls under the apprenticeship policy.[61] She had probably sought out Mary again in early 1938, as she had done in 1934, to seek reassurance that *their* relationship at least was not one of exploitation and abuse.[62] It is easy to imagine the intense shock and, indeed, guilt that Ming would have felt at the news of Mary's death.

In a furious letter to the newspaper shortly afterwards, Ming attacked the board, calling it 'a great poisonous fungus' and holding up Mary's experience as an example of its 'ghastly treatment' of Aboriginal girls. 'They have cared for my children with a devotion which I hope I may fully repay...' she wrote. 'They have been exploited long enough...'

> ...One girl worked for ten years at service, and after many months of legal battling the board was *persuaded* to pay her the munificent sum of £64.0.0.! ... 6 months ago this faithful and devoted little soul died, starved and neglected at one of the Board's Stations, when she was seriously ill.
>
> In all *our* illnesses this girl devoted herself, night & day to us, yet in *her* illness there was *not one* kindly *white* hand held out in sympathy or protection...[63]

The news of Mary's death galvanised Ming's determination to see the board exposed in the wake of the collapsed 1937 inquiry. Through the Aboriginal Citizenship Committee, which she joined a couple of months later, Ming pursued the board on behalf of individual domestic workers for their trust money.[64] She also announced her intention to establish a domestic workers club as a 'headquarters' from which to launch a call for an inquiry into the trust fund system. 'The girls are entitled to their money whenever they want it, but we claim that they have to wage a long and sometimes losing fight to get what is their own property,' she was reported as saying.[65] In some ways her activities foresaw the contemporary claims against state governments for the trust funds of Aboriginal workers, which in many cases were never paid out.[66] But there was a debt here than went far deeper than the missing cash, and one that could not so easily be repaid.

The relationship that had existed between Mary and Ming was based upon a fundamental inequity that Ming had both accepted and enjoyed. Clearly, Ming envisaged Mary as an eternally devoted and obedient daughter figure, her own life submerged in that of another woman. Yet Ming did not seem to realise how completely vulnerable, powerless and dependent on her goodwill Mary was; how her attachment to Ming — her 'devotion' — was imbricated by the frame-work of colonial dominance and subordination. Instead, Ming contrasted the love and affection she felt for Mary with the callousness of the government bureaucracy. Mary's poverty-stricken death was to Ming the most horrible evidence of this contrast, but in truth it was the inequality of race between the two women that was made suddenly, glaringly, grotesque by the way Mary died. The shock seemed to spur Ming out of her complacency. From this time on she not only campaigned against the board's apprenticeship policy, but also for the granting of full equality, through Aboriginal citizenship rights.[67]

***

Such documents as Ming left provide a powerful reply to the peculiar silence that envelops the history of the stolen generations: the silence of the white households into which the Aboriginal girls were placed. Of course, Ming envisaged her papers being read in the future — her very keeping of them is testimony to that. Insofar as she hoped that one day, if not in her lifetime, this history would be heard, she was also engaged in an internal dialogue, trying to order her experience in ways that might refute the accusation that she was party to a system of cruelty and racial oppression. (As her great-granddaughter, I too have a personal investment in the way I reconstruct her story.) But living her life according to a romantic notion of maternalism entailed real problems and contradictions, and beneath the sentimentality lay the anxieties and anguishes of an untenable situation.

And so, to return to that first, faded snapshot my gran showed me. Like all baby snaps it encoded a memory created not for the adult it depicted, nor for the adult who took it, but for the infant grown adult — for my gran. Leached of its political significance, its faded tints masking more unpleasant forgotten histories, it remains a memory left by Ming for her daughter, of a young Aboriginal woman who was taken from her own mother to become 'more than my own mother' to her. Here is the devotion that can never be fully repaid — the debt that cannot be redeemed.

Notes

1. 'Aboriginal domestics: try an Abo apprentice!', *Australian Women's Mirror*, 30 January 1940.
2. Haskins 2003.
3. Annotations against transcribed copy: Papers of Joan Kingsley-Strack (hereafter JKS Papers), Box 8, Folder 4, National Library of Australia, Canberra.
4. Horner 1994, pp. 110–11; see also Haskins 1998a.
5. Joan Kingsley-Strack (hereafter JKS) to Premier Stevens, c. Jan–Mar 1938 (draft, not known if sent), JKS Papers, 8, 6.
6. Jack Horner, letter, 19 September 1993, with enclosed notes from an interview with JKS, 3 March 1966; birth certificate of JKS.
7. Miller 1985, p. 148.
8. See Heilbrun 1998, pp. 39, 68.
9. See Haskins 2001, pp. 13–25.
10. See Aboriginal historians for the bicentennial history 1788–1988.
11. Human Rights and Equal Opportunity Commission 1997.
12. All the names of Aboriginal people in this chapter (except the public figures of the APA) have been changed to protect the privacy of their families. This article is published with the informed permission of Mary's descendants.
13. One's 'own' history in this context refers not to Aboriginal history in general, but to a specific identification with one's own family, community and place. This view has been expressed to me privately by a number of individuals, and was mentioned by Jackie Huggins in her unpublished paper presented at the State Library of NSW, 25 January 1995. See also Huggins 1990, p. 170; Huggins 1993, pp. 62–63; Sabbioni 1993, p. 8; and Aboriginal historians for the bicentennial history 1788–1988.
14. Mary was transferred to Ming directly from another situation in a nearby suburb, according to APB ward and salary registers. Jean was visiting Ming when she first fell ill, and had organised for a private nurse's services beforehand: Notes (n.d.), JKS Papers, 3, 11; diary entry (recollections), 12 December 1936, JKS Papers, 2, 12. Jean may well have known Mary's former employer personally.
15. Gardner 1993, 83. Mary's genealogy is covered in more detail in Haskins 1998, PhD thesis, University of Sydney.
16. Aborigines Protection Board photographs held at AIATSIS, Canberra.
17. Aborigines Protection Board Ward Register, 1916–1923.
18. APB Minutes, 29 October 1914, 5 November 1914.
19. APB Ward Register; APB Salary Register.
20. Notes (n.d.), JKS Papers, 3, 11; diary entry (recollections), 12 December 1936, JKS Papers, 2, 7-8
21. Notes, c. early 1920s and dated '1918', JKS Papers, 2, 2.

22. See Clark-Lewis 1994, pp. 113–17.
23. J Stobo to M Stobo, 19 December 1924, JKS Papers, 7, 1.
24. Diary entry, 28 February – 4 March 1926, JKS Papers, 2, 4.
25. Diary entry, 8–15 May 1926, JKS Papers, 2, 4.
26. See Evans 1992, p. 203.
27. Diary entry, 1 May 1934, JKS Papers, 2, 6.
28. Mary to JKS, c. early 1920s, addressed from East Kew, Melbourne, JKS Papers, 7, 1.
29. Clark-Lewis, pp. 109, 184–89.
30. See Rollins, p. 157.
31. Jean Magill to JKS, 21 October 1926, JKS Papers, 7, 1.
32. JKS to Rev. Morley, secretary of the Association for the Protection of Native Races, 31 [March 1934], Papers of AP Elkin, Box 69, Item 1/12/153, Fisher Archives, University of Sydney.
33. Mary to JKS, 9 January 1927, JKS Papers, 7, 1.
34. Mary to JKS, 9 January 1927; Mary to JKS c. 11 January 1927: JKS Papers, 7, 1.
35. Mary to JKS, 19 January 1927, JKS Papers, 7, 1. By 'Bedfene' Mary may have meant the Bethesda Salvation Army Home at Marrickville.
36. Mary to JKS, 30 January [1927], JKS Papers, 7, 1.
37. Mary to JKS, 13 February 1927, JKS Papers, 7, 1.
38. Diary entry, 8 June 1933, JKS Papers, 7, 3–5.
39. Ashfield Infants Home Admissions Book, 1924–1929 & Ashfield Infants Home Minutes, 1924–1927, 18 March 1927 (stating Mary's admission 18 February 1927), MLMSS 2983/47, Mitchell Library, Sydney.
40. Envelopes, addressed in Mary's handwriting, postmarked 17 February 1927 and 11 June 1927, JKS Papers 7, 1.
41. JKS to Morley, 31 [March 1934], Elkin Papers.
42. APB Ward Register; Ashfield Infants Home Admission Book 1924–1929. Both sets of records mention Mary's stepfather. The board had no Sydney address recorded for Ming, and as Ming's address was given in Mary's admission record at the Ashfield Infants' Home as the cottage at Wahroonga where the Stracks had originally stayed when they first arrived, we might guess that the authorities had no further information than that — although Mary knew her parents' address.
43. Envelope addressed in Mary's handwriting, postmarked 11 June 1927, JKS Papers, 7, 1. Letter has not survived.
44. JKS to Morley, 31[March 1934], Elkin Papers; APB Minutes, 14 May 1926, AONSW, Sydney.
45. Mary to JKS, 27 October 1927, JKS Papers, 7, 1. This is the only letter from Mary at Lake Tyers to survive, but from the content it is evident that this was not the first letter she had written to Ming from Victoria, and there are also four envelopes addressed by Mary and postmarked from Lake Tyers between November 1927 and December 1928: JKS Papers 7, 1. Ming

wrote of 'utterly heart-broken letters' she had received from Mary while Mary was in Victoria (fragment of a draft letter to the editor, 9 March 1938 (not known if sent), JKS Papers 6, 15; Jack Horner, letter, 10 September 1993 (enclosed copy)), and also of the 'many many times she wrote begging me to find out where her money was' (JKS to Morley, 31 [March 1934], Elkin Papers) but no such letters have been found in her papers.

46. Envelope, Mary's handwriting, postmarked 12 December 1928, JKS Papers 7, 1. Letter has not survived.

47. JKS to Mary, 13 February 1930 (returned 'not known at this address'), JKS Papers, 7, 1.

48. Diary entry, 12 December 1936, JKS Papers, 2, 7–8. Comment made in recollection: presumably the person hired was white.

49. JKS to Morley, 31[March 1934], Elkin Papers.

50. Diary entry, 1 May 1935, JKS Papers, 2, 7–8.

51. .See Goodall 1996, pp. 179–85; Miller 1985, p. 150.

52. Mary to Helen Strack, 2 January 1935; Mary to Narrelle Strack, 2 January 1935; Mary to JKS, 18 June [1935?], JKS Papers, 7, 1.

53. Rollins, pp. 189–91.

54. Diary entry, 9 March 1933 and JKS transcripts of conversation with Del, 20 & 23 April 1934, JKS Papers, 7, 3-5.

55. It is especially hard to imagine that Ming had an excess of wearable second-hand clothes since Del's departure in October 1934, when she was writing in her diary, 'We have all allowed ourselves to get into a deplorable state simply because there was never a farthing to spend on clothes.' Diary entry, 15 October 1934, JKS Papers, 2, 7–8.

56. Mary to Narrelle Strack, 2 January 1935.

57. Diary entries, 19 January 1935, 31 January 1935, 'March' [1935]: JKS Papers 2, 7–8.

58. Mary to JKS, 18 June [1935?], JKS Papers, 7, 1.

59. Envelope addressed to JKS from Mary, postmarked from Cowra, 13 May 1936, JKS Papers, 7, 1. The envelope was addressed C/O Ming's mother and forwarded to the Stracks' new place, suggesting that the women had lost touch for some time. The letter it enclosed has not survived. This represents the last surviving piece of correspondence from Mary in Ming's papers.

60. William to JKS, 13 January 1938, postmarked 21 January 1938, JKS Papers, 7, 1.

61. Diary entries 15 November 1937, 15 December 1937, 17 December 1937: JKS Papers, 2, 7–8.

62. Again, Ming had sent a parcel, but this had gone astray, as Mary's husband had 'never heard [of] or got the parcel you said you sent to Cowra for my poor wife' at the time of his reply: William to JKS, 13 January 1938: JKS Papers 7, 1.

63. JKS to the editor (draft, fragment), 9 March 1938 (not known if sent), JKS Papers, 6, 15; Horner 1993, letters to the author (enclosed copy).
64. Both Del and Jane (who worked for Ming's mother) successfully claimed their trust money in August 1938, almost certainly through Ming's activities. Letter, Del to JKS, c. mid- to late 1938, JKS Papers, 7, 3–5; Aborigines Protection Board Minutes, 3 August 1938; APB salary registers. It is likely that others she knew personally also were helped at this time.
65. Clipping, 'Relieve plight of Abo girls', *Labour Daily*, 10 May 1938, citing Mrs Strack, JKS Papers, 8, 9–10.
66. Doosey & Bull, personal communication, 1997; Simms, personal communication, 2 December 1997. See also Walden 1991, p. 92; Walden 1995, p. 200; Link-Up & Wilson, p. 238.
67. There is a sad postscript to this story. My gran recalled that in early 1941 Mary's widowed husband arrived on Ming's doorstep with Mary's first-born daughter and namesake (hereafter 'Mary Grace'), to ask Ming if she would take the girl in and look after her. The expectation that Ming would take in Mary's daughter indicates the enduring quality of her obligations to Mary, but again Ming was unable to meet these obligations. She already had Jane, her mother's former apprentice, working for her, and was embroiled in a court case. Norman and Peter were away at the war, but at home there was not only Helen, now a teenager, but also Narrelle, who was pregnant (with my father), and Narrelle's husband, Bruce. They were just about to move yet again, to a small flat where Ming was concerned that there would not be room for Jane. Following Mary Grace's return to Yass, her aunt Sarah wrote to Ming asking for the girl's date of birth, and told Ming that Mary Grace now had a baby son. Ming replied several months later, asking after Mary Grace and enclosing a 'small parcel of knitted baby clothes', promising to send more later. This letter is the last piece of Ming's surviving correspondence regarding Mary. The following month Jane would be committed to a mental asylum, an outcome so extreme and so unexpectedly unjust that Ming would withdraw from all political activities permanently, boxing up her papers and bundling them away. One might speculate that Ming felt very guilty about turning her back on Mary's child; nevertheless she did so. Notes, c. 1950s, on back of William to JKS, 13 January 1938; Narrelle Strack, conversation, 20 May 1993; Horner 1993 (notes from interview with Joan, 3 March 1966); Sarah Todd to JKS, 4 [October] 1941; JKS to Sarah Todd, 1 February [1942]: JKS Papers 7, 1.

Part 2

Shared struggle

4. 'Same bodies, different skin'

Ruth Heathcock

Karen Hughes

Ruth Heathcock (nee Rayney) was a South Australian nurse who worked with Aboriginal people suffering from leprosy in the Roper River and Gulf Country of the Northern Territory from 1930 to 1942. In treating their leprosy, she enabled her patients to continue living in their country and escape incarceration, which was usually for life, on the Channel Island lazaret off the coast of Darwin. Ruth demonstrated that she respected Aboriginal law above the recently imposed minority white laws that had resulted from colonisation, in spite of the fact that her husband was an official enforcer of those laws. A Northern Territory mounted constable, he was invested, as were all policemen in the Territory after 1920, with the power of Aboriginal 'protector'.[1] Ted Heathcock, however, was won over by Ruth and turned what she referred to as a 'blind eye' to the work she practised for over a decade while he was absent on patrols for up to six months at a time.

Eventually Ruth and Ted campaigned for a repeal of the Northern Territory Administration's *Ordinance for the Suppression of Leprosy 1928*, under which 'leprosy suspects' were detained. Ruth was well known as a skillful and courageous nurse and was awarded an MBE in 1951 for her bravery and initiative in the attempted rescue at Manangoora of wounded bushman Horace Foster. This involved travelling for more than 180 kilometres during the height of the monsoon season, through flooded rivers and the open sea, in a dugout canoe with four others.[2] She used the occasion, however, to make known the seminal role of Aboriginal people in the rescue 'without whom,' she maintained, 'I couldn't even have existed.'[3]

This essay focuses on Ruth Heathcock's work with leprosy during her period in Arnhem Land, and the critical role of Aboriginal women domestic workers in shaping the philosophy behind her professional activism. Her work was profoundly influenced by her lived experiences, including her socialisation as a child in the first two decades of the 20th century in the lower Murray region of South Australia. In her personal writings and interactions with non-Indigenous people, Ruth advanced the idea of Aboriginal women's autonomy, expert knowledges and ritual career status, which at the time were given little credence in either the popular imagination or the anthropological arena. Her participation in Aboriginal women's complex religious and spiritual life during her time at Roper River encouraged Ruth's later exploration of alternative areas of spirituality.

Much in Ruth's story has remained silent in all these years because of the clandestine nature of her work. Vic Hall's 1968 biography, *Sister Ruth*, limited by romanticism and the novelistic genre, suggests the need for a fresh exploration of this narrative in the light of current debates surrounding gender and cross-cultural friendships, and black–white relations from the 1930s to the early 1940s.[4]

Rich source material exists within the oral traditions of present-day Roper River community historians based at Ngukurr. Ruth Heathcock's presence continues to be memorialised there and her narrative is understood as an important historical signifier of cross-cultural relations that were outstandingly different to the dominant. Research for this chapter has evolved from new material recorded with the descendants of the house workers and other Indigenous historians within the Ngukurr, Numbulwar and Borroloola communities; from government records and archival sources; and from extensive conversations I had with Ruth Heathcock in Adelaide during the 1980s.[5]

***

In 1927 Dr Cecil Cook, the Chief Medical Officer of the Northern Territory from 1927 to 1939, published a report into the epidemiology of leprosy.[6] Cook concluded that leprosy had been introduced into the Northern Territory by Chinese indentured labourers in 1882, when the first known case was identified at the Pine Creek mines. Thereafter it spread progressively to Aboriginal communities as well as to a small number of the white population.[7] As the European population in the Northern Territory at the time of Cook's report was less than 1800, relatively few Europeans contracted leprosy in comparison to the much larger Indigenous population, in excess of 20 000.[8] This galvanised European perception of the endemic as an 'Aboriginal problem' from which whites needed to be protected if the north were to be 'won'.

Cook was unable to obtain funding for specialised medical treatment.[9] Instead, he advocated complete isolation, introducing a policy of segregation enforced through invasive surveillance, capture — via subterfuge if necessary — and compulsory detention at an offshore location, pathologising patients but rendering leprosy invisible. 'Non-European alien leprosy suspects' among Chinese, Malay and other indentured labourers were deported to their countries of origin under Cook's ordinance of 1928. Police patrols performed surprise raids to round up these 'suspects', often wrongfully diagnosed for transportation.[10]

Channel Island in Darwin Harbour, previously an offshore quarantine station, was converted to a leprosarium in 1930. The small island was without a permanent water supply and inmates suffered harsh physical conditions, segregated in unlined corrugated iron huts.[11] People of different clan, language and incompatible skin affiliations were forced together within the same locality, uprooted from their spiritual and cultural basis of country and community. At a time when 'the rest of the world was modifying its compulsory isolation laws, in Australia they were strengthened'.[12]

Driving the policies of public health in northern Australia during the inter-war years was the idea of making the tropics safe for the white person and thereby protecting Australia's northern border. As Warwick Anderson contends, 'framing disease, framing "environment", and framing "race" all were part of the same manoeuvre — with political and social consequences perhaps as profound as any military deployment'.[13] Alison Bashford likewise argues that 'there is no mistaking tropical medicine as part of the military and colonial enterprise'.[14] Compulsory isolation of diseased people was another facet of the concurrent draconian policies of separating Indigenous children from their families and removing Indigenous people from land. It was underscored by the same concepts of white anxiety: 'protection' and 'pollution'.[15]

The pathologising of bodies and the institutionalisation of disease was in conflict with an Indigenous approach to social medicine. People infected with 'the big sickness', as leprosy was known among northern Aboriginal people, were treated with love and inclusion.[16]

Integral to healing processes is the fundamental inter-connection between land and body, and their mutual enactment upon each other. 'Unlike [among] the white community,' Suzanne Saunders points out, Aboriginal people 'had no longstanding tradition of fear associated with leprosy. It was to them a new disease which they accommodated within an already developed understanding of the causes of illness generally...[and] it did not provoke rejection.'[17] Cook's policy arguably had a reverse effect on 'containment', increasing leprosy's spread in Aboriginal communities as people were forced into hiding, and infection went undiagnosed and untreated.[18]

Ruth Heathcock viewed the policy as a 'death sentence', and described her reaction to its implementation this way:

> Lepers they caught — caught — just like criminals. It was most inhuman and the beloved was on my side. Ted wrote to the administration, and the administration contacted Geneva, and spoke of the case of a leper travelling 150 miles from the coast down to me.
>
> So you can imagine why I wasn't going to have any of them reported and sent away. I would rather have gone to live with them.[19]

Ruth's initial activism remained in the private sphere. It was expressed through her personal actions and professional ethics, her relationships with Aboriginal people, and the education of other white people around her. She mediated between two laws and two ways of being in the world.

Ruth first encountered leprosy in 1930 when she was 29. She had recently arrived from Adelaide for a 12-month posting to run the Australian Inland Mission (AIM) hostel in the former tin mining town of Maranboy, 48 kilometres east of Katherine, along with fellow South Australian nursing sister Babs Sheridan. Ruth was sharing a meal with two Aboriginal women domestic workers at the hostel. She noticed a man sitting alone outside by the woodheap and asked the women to invite him to join them. The man, however, refused to enter the hostel. The women explained that this was because he had leprosy, and took the food outside to him.[20]

Leprosy was something Ruth associated with biblical times and she was initially shocked to find it at Maranboy. Her response was to acquire as much knowledge as possible about the disease's transmission and methods of treatment. She corresponded with her colleagues in Adelaide, principally Dr FS Hone, an Adelaide Hospital honorary physician and former Commonwealth quarantine officer under whom she had trained.[21] Ruth was satisfied that leprosy was not highly contagious — infection required prolonged contact and the transfer of 'live blood to live blood' — and could effectively be treated to arrest its spread in individual patients.[22] Isolation, a spatial response to contagion in highly populated European colonies such as India, was hardly necessary in sparsely populated northern Australia. Moreover, it was a shameful substitute for the provision of adequate health care.[23] Ruth was horrified when one day she glimpsed the bleak windowless train carriage heading from Mataranka to Darwin, transporting people for transfer on to Channel Island.[24]

As the local women at the hostel began to trust Ruth, they made her aware of significant numbers of leprosy sufferers hiding in the country along the Roper River, going without treatment for fear of being removed from their families and dying outside their country. Ruth was angry and especially disdainful of Cecil Cook's official neglect in disregarding the land-based cultural and spiritual dimensions of Aboriginal people's lives. She described incarceration as leading to a 'double death', spiritual as well as physical, in leprosy's so-called 'treatment', and she resolved to do something about it. Cook, ever the scientist, had no time for such views, which he regarded as rooted in superstition.[25]

Ruth had originally sought a career path rather than marriage as a framework for her life. At 16, she began instruction with the active unenclosed congregation Little Sisters of the Poor, which had opened in Adelaide five years earlier in 1912. Bound by perpetual vows of poverty, chastity and obedience, and the additional vow of hospitality, the sisters welcomed elderly destitute people into their homes as 'family members' on a permanent basis.[26] After two years Ruth felt constrained, as she had as a child, by what she regarded as inconsistencies and paradoxes within the dogma of institutionalised religion, and withdrew from the congregation prior to taking her final vows.[27] She changed her vocation to nursing, undertaking study at the Adelaide Hospital in 1921, and joined AIM in 1930.[28] She completed the equivalent of four years of medical training, graduating with triple certification in midwifery, medical and surgery electives.

Her aim to travel and work with Aboriginal people would satisfy a desire for social activism as well as an independent and adventurous spirit. These objectives were threatened, however, after she contracted a tuberculosis-related illness at the Torrens Island quarantine hospital.

Ruth's training was interrupted for a year, and she lost one of her lungs. Considered unsuitable for an inland posting because of her health, one of her first nursing appointments, in 1929, was close to her childhood home of Wellington, at the Point McLeay Mission on Lake Alexandrina south of Adelaide, working with Ngarrindjeri people (see Chapter 8). Ruth, however, kept up the pressure for an inland posting and AIM conceded, offering her a 12-month position at the Maranboy hostel, due for closure the following year.[29]

The AIM (not to be confused with the Aborigines Inland Mission) was established specifically by John Flynn to provide medical services to the white community in the colonising process of 'remote' Australia, and so can be seen as an imperial agent. Charles Duguid, on his first trip to Central Australia in 1934, was appalled at the racism that underscored this Australian icon, which he had assumed was:

> ...caring for Aborigines as well as whites. Instead it was accentuating the division, and when I returned to Adelaide I called on the Director of the AIM to discuss it with him. He was utterly frank. 'The AIM is only for white people', he told me. 'You are only wasting your time among so many damned dirty niggers'.[30]

But Ruth provided medical treatment to the Indigenous community on equal terms whenever it was needed as did several other AIM sisters.[31] She was able to reach out to Aboriginal people requiring medical attention through her relationships with the Aboriginal women employed as domestic servants at the hostel, who put her in touch with their communities beyond the boundaries of the AIM compound.

One of her patients at the Maranboy hostel was Edward (Ted) Heathcock, an English-born mounted constable who had been working in the Top End since the late 1910s. Ruth was interested in his extensive knowledge of and interest in Aboriginal peoples, and a friendship developed which led to their marriage at Mataranka in 1931. Unlike many who proceeded and followed him, who abused their considerable powers and, in particular, sexually exploited Aboriginal women, Ted Heathcock had a reputation in the Indigenous community for compassion, fairness and honesty.[32] Connie Bush described him as 'a very kind man but [he] would not let anyone break the law.'[33] Likewise, Val McGinness recalled: 'He was always very, very kind and gentle. I don't remember him arresting anybody.'[34]

After honeymooning at Elsey Station, the Heathcocks spent a brief time at Mataranka before moving to Roper Bar on the south-eastern border of Arnhem Land, considered (in non-Indigenous terms) the Territory's most isolated police station. Marriage to 'the beloved', as she called Ted, ensured Ruth's tenure in the Territory, allowing her to form a closer alliance with Aboriginal people. She was also able to continue her professional life as a medical nurse without the restrictions of working within an institutional structure. At Roper Bar she operated out of the police station as an independent nurse, with emergency back-up available from the Flying Doctor Service via peddle radio contact. She provided health care to the few local white cattle station owners, bushmen and travellers, and the much larger Aboriginal community.[35]

Ruth had Aboriginal people in her home assisting with the running of the police station, especially during the long periods Ted was away on patrol. These were often the wives of her husband's police trackers, their work contributing to an economy of exchange in which Ruth reciprocated, responding to social obligations within the local Aboriginal community, particularly in terms of medical care. Norah Wonamgai; Cara Thompson Nganjigee; Minnie George; Gypsy (Kykuri); Edna Nyuluk and her sister, Mundullullu (Alice Holtze); Nancy Burunbridj (from Rose River); Bluebell and her daughter Mareli (also known as Ruth); Priscilla Herbert (Milly); Nellie Huddlestone; Marie Roper; Missie; Big Polly; Little Polly; and Old Judy are among the women who worked with Ruth during her eight years at Roper Bar. Destabilising the classic colonial relationship of white mistress and Indigenous domestic worker, they became her closest friends, confidantes, teachers, extended family and valued co-workers, from whom she learned language, culture and aspects of women's law.[36]

Ruth came to understand that the knowledges, skills and resources of Aboriginal people underpinned not only her own existence but the existence of all white people in the Northern Territory. Ngukurr elder Rosalind Munur Baalwark, daughter of Cara Thompson Nganjigee and granddaughter of Norah Wonamgai, recalls that Ruth ate bush food and spoke words from Aboriginal languages, and that people considered her to be 'really relaxed just like an Aboriginal person'.[37] Norah Wonamgai and Old Judy adopted Ruth into their family and Norah named her 'Pitjiri', after the file snake (*Acrochordus javanicus*) which floats on the water in the wet

Ruth Heathcock and Edna Nyuluk, one of the women who worked with Ruth at Roper Bar in the 1930s, Ngukurr, 1984. Photography by Francois Perez from the documentary Pitjiri: the snake that will not sink.

season, when she observed that Ruth's body would not sink but 'bobbed up and down like a bottle' when they were diving for lily roots in a lagoon.[38] Norah Wonamgai's great-granddaughter, Audrey Bush Wulandja, interprets the unsinkable qualities implicit in Norah Wonamgai's choice of name metaphorically: 'If there was a sick person who needed her help it didn't matter how far away they were or if there was a fire or a flood, she would go straight through any obstacles to get to them.'[39]

At Roper Bar, people who had been living in the bush without treatment, fearing the ramifications of disclosure, began to come to Ruth through the mediation of the women domestic workers — always at carefully chosen times when her husband was away. They were mostly Alawa, Mara, Ngandi, Ngalakan, Warndarrang and Yukul people from the Roper River area. As trust grew that Ruth would not report them nor inform her husband of their whereabouts, others came from a wider radius, including from north-east and central Arnhem Land.[40]

During Ted's absences, the police station, isolated from the gaze of white society, became a different kind of gendered and cultured space, one governed largely by women's inter-cultural authority and knowledge. Through a shared understanding, the women worked together closely to establish what was essentially a covert operation to administer medical treatment to Indigenous people suffering from leprosy who were hiding in the Roper River hinterlands from missionaries (at nearby Roper River mission) and police. This meant that 'officially' there was no leprosy at Roper River. Between the first recorded instance in 1921 and Ruth's arrival in 1932 there had been a more or less steady increase in reported diagnoses in the Roper River district. After 1932 this tapered off almost completely, with only a single instance reported in 1933. It increased again in 1937, the year of Ruth's departure, to three recorded cases, and from then reported instances once more increased. But this increase wouldn't have been linked to Ruth's departure because of the covert nature of her work.[41] Rosalind Munur recalls the role of her parents, Cara Thompson Nganjigee and Pat Thompson Marranukum (also known as Paddy or Big Pat, who was employed as a police tracker) in guiding Ruth on foot or horseback to places where sick people were hiding. Cara made use of her expertise in eight Australian languages:

> There were sick people out in the bush and Ruth used to go with my mother and father for two or three days like that. They used to stay with old Sam's mother and father [Long Tom and Old Judy].[42] Some of the old men used to stay with Mr and Mrs Heathcock, they were really ill, no hands, no nothing.[43] They used to go and get them before the sickness might spread. A big group got away from Old Mission; they dug a hole under the fence and ran away — Ngungubuyu mob, from Rose River. Some Aborigines used to be afraid and run away but my mother used to talk with language and tell them not to be afraid and give them an understanding. A lot of work they used to do. Sister Ruth said, 'You don't have to be frightened. We're all the same, same body different skin.' She really understood our Aboriginal way. She understood Kriol and our language. People still understand that Mr and Mrs Heathcock been a big help here.[44]

Emergency surgery was sometimes needed on these bush trips. On one occasion a patient's bone was protruding from their arm, on which the flesh had been destroyed. Ruth was obliged to perform an amputation, improvising with horseshoe clippers.[45] In such situations, when the needs of a patient exceeded what her expertise or available instruments could adequately perform, Ruth claimed that she received spiritual help, often in the form of a pair of golden hands assisting with an operation. Local women accepted Ruth's experiences as congruent with Indigenous healing practices, embodying modes of interconnectedness and perception usually outside the experience of white women.[46] As Aileen Moreton-Robinson points out:

> Indigenous women perceive the world as organic and populated by spirits which connect places and people... Unlike white constructions of Christian spirituality, Indigenous spirituality encompasses the intersubstantiation of ancestral beings, humans and physiography. The spiritual world is immediately experienced because it is synonymous with the physiography of the land.[47]

Such commensurability served to deepen the bond between them and locate spirituality as an important site of resistance.[48] 'If I talked about all this down south,' Ruth would often say, in her characteristic down-to-earth manner, 'people would just think that I've got white ants in my head.'[49]

When it was learned that Ruth could be trusted with secrecy, more knowledge and responsibility were given to her. She was invited to participate in women's ceremonial life, the inner details of which she could not speak about. While many of the trackers' wives were young women of around 16, Norah Wonamgai, who took responsibility in instructing Ruth, was a senior woman of 45 or more. She was regarded as a clever-woman, an elder of high degree, a law woman and a ceremonial leader. She was born on the Roper River, before the coming of white people to her country. Indeed, as Rosalind Munur recalls, her first impressions were of the sightings of the first missionaries arriving along the Roper in 1908, when her brother Pilot Bob gave them permission to stop there: 'My granny was angry. "I don't like *mununa*," she said, "but I just have to carry on."'[50] Norah, remembered by Ruth as quietly spoken, independent, forthright and commandeering, was perhaps the single most influential person in Ruth Heathcock's life. In Ruth's later years there was rarely a conversation where she wasn't mentioned, where some knowledge that Norah had taught her was not referred to and invoked. Norah used her position as erstwhile domestic worker and goatherd to influence and educate Ruth, her role evolving into that of cultural consultant, diplomat, mentor, educator and friend. Norah and Ruth established an alternative kind of cross-cultural exchange to that practised on the Roper River Mission, 35 kilometres away, where the primary goal of the Europeans was to convert. It was a relationship of mutual respect involving consultation, negotiation, reciprocity, and the acknowledgment of Aboriginal sovereignty and its spiritual basis in the land.

Norah's role as an Aboriginal doctor complemented Ruth's as a white 'doctor' and midwife, furthering their interconnectedness. Norah assumed the senior position of classificatory grandmother in passing on knowledge.[51] Phillip Roberts, in *I the Aboriginal*, alludes to such mentoring exchange and its integral role in Indigenous women's cultural practice in the Roper Valley: 'One woman gives her trust to another, who thus becomes her guide, mentor, a point of reference — the figure of symbolic relations between her and the world.'[52] Ruth recalled how Norah would employ the metonymic relationship of her reflection in the mirror when attempting to impart the basis of telepathic communication, or 'travelling langa head': 'She'd take me in front of the mirror and she'd be cross, too. "See *you*," Norah would say, "well, *you* in that looking glass and *you* here. See, that spirit belanga you can travel anywhere."'[53]

***

In 1935 Ruth received a visit from a delegation of nine male elders, requesting that she accompany them to Burunju, where a large number of people suffering from leprosy were living in hiding. Because of the length and ruggedness of the five-day horseback journey, Ruth informed her husband, who insisted on accompanying them. On reaching Burunju, she was taken into a cave by the elders, where recognition of her healing was formalised in what appears to have been a doctor-making ceremony. Following this, Cara Thompson and Nancy Burunbridj led Ruth to a rock shelter nearby where a significant number of people who had contracted leprosy were hidden. Together, the women treated them over several hours. The elders proposed a plan for a 'dispensary' camp to be established at a concealed location close to the police station, enabling patients to safely receive continuing medical treatment from Ruth in addition to a regular supply of rations. They emphasised that no one but Ruth, Nancy or Cara should visit the camp.[54]

Oral histories from Ngukurr elders indicate that Ruth Heathcock's life narrative was understood within the context of the creation cycle of Kunapipi. This is a widespread and highly secret-sacred female-centred Dreaming narrative and ceremonial cycle (though not confined exclusively to women) which begins at the mouth of the Roper River and travels through Burunju to other parts of Arnhem Land.[55] Dennis Daniels, a former male ceremonial elder for Kunapipi ('my mother ceremony') outlined certain 'outer' or public aspects of this association when Ruth was on a visit to Ngukurr in 1984 (aged 83), during which the Kunapipi, suppressed throughout mission times, was performed as part of an initiation cycle:[56]

> She went to Ruined City and went from Ruined City to Roper Bar on horseback. Tom Costello [Daniels's grandfather], Ngalaikan and Ngandi tribe, knew that area well. She asked what totem had made Ruined City. He told her Catfish. She went into a cave at Ruined City and saw the sea turtle rock and canoe alongside and rope on the canoe and harpoon and paddle. She asked the old people, 'How did the canoe get here and the sea turtle?' They told her the canoe came with the old Catfish, Nguru. Nguru brought the canoe and the harpoon and the rocks and things from the sea. He started to come from Low Rock an island seven miles out. The name of that rock is called Magandoola. He went to Wiyakiba with canoe and sea turtle. When he got to Wiyakiba he said to the others, 'I'm taking one canoe and harpoon, rope and one turtle and the rest of you I'll leave you here at Wiyakiba.' He took Dugong as well, he had a rope around his neck and took them to Wanmurri, and another kind of catfish, Warama. Took Nguru, Warama, turtle, canoe, Dugong, harpoon and a rope and paddle. At Wanmurri he left one Nguru there and took the others to Kurrukul. All Catfish, leave salt water behind. He kept going to Ruined City. When they got there they all stayed in one cave had a meeting, had a ceremony, the Kunapipi ceremony.[57]

It cannot be seen as merely coincidental that a large number of the women who worked with Ruth had associations with and responsibilities for Burunju. Burunju, or Ruined City, is a sacred site in central Arnhem Land where a number of significant Dreaming narratives intersect — including in the cave near where the sufferers of leprosy were hidden, which is an important part of the Kunapipi business.[58] Cara Thompson, Mundullullu (Alice Holtze), Edna Nyuluk, Minnie George and Nellie Huddlestone all had primary ownership of or ceremonial responsibilities to Burunju, while Norah Wonamgai was a

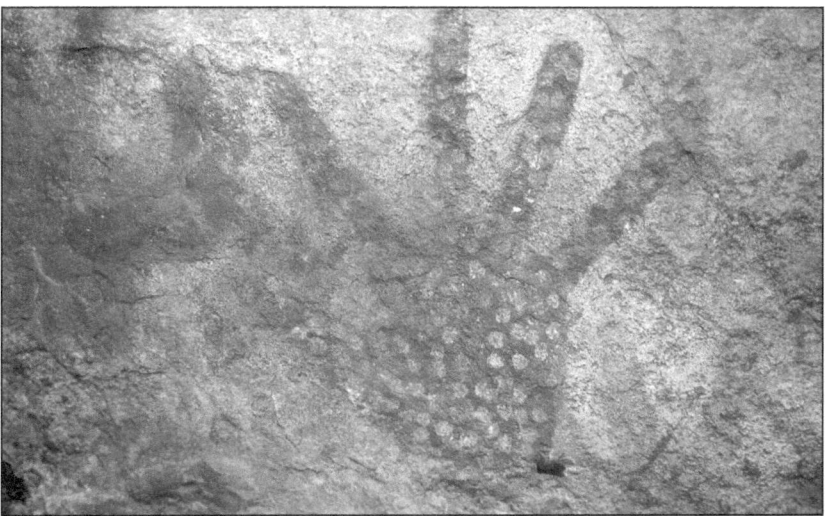

Ochre painting of hands covered in white spots, known as 'the bite of the native cat', the symptoms of leprosy, on the wall of the rock shelter where people suffering from leprosy hid from authorities during the 1930s and 1940s, near Burunju, Arnhem Land. Photography by Karen Hughes, 2003.

senior traditional owner for Murlinbahwah (Roper River). Minnie George and Nellie Huddlestone were both wives of Old (David) Walker, a senior traditional owner — *minininggi* — for Burunju, whereas Old Judy's husband, Long Tom, was *djungaiyi*.[59] Ruth's classificatory skin relationship to Norah as 'granddaughter' thus connected her to a web of relationships and responsibilities that enabled her to visit this sacred space.[60] (Cara, Norah's daughter, was also an important *minininggi* for Burunju, a position now held by her own daughter, Rosalind Munur. Cara's totem was Nguru the Catfish, and after her passing, Rosalind Munur has explained, her mother was transformed into one of the three Catfish tors that guard Burunju's entrance. The rock is known by Cara's Aboriginal name, Nganjigee, and is her totemic dwelling place.)[61]

In working for Ruth, these women were utilising their specialised knowledges in a range of innovative and complex ways, exercising their cultural obligations to country and community within a frontier space. While assuming the cover of a seemingly docile role within the colonial project as 'domestic workers', one imitative of white values expressing gender and racialised hierarchies, the domestic workers at the Roper River police station were in fact expertly subverting their positions so as to be active agents in cultural assertion. By inviting Ruth to participate at the interface of an Indigenous knowledge system, they coopted their 'mistress' into an astute strategy of tacit resistance to the imposed non-Indigenous values that attempted to separate people from country. The women's efficacy within this situation was partially because (unlike most Indigenous Australian domestic workers, particularly those in the southern states, who were strategically removed from their families) they were still living in their country, sustained by continued participation in familial, community, educational and ceremonial life while simultaneously participating in a European economy.[62] Their role as house workers was an extension of their role within the community rather than a disruption of it.

Ruth as 'white woman' could remain largely invisible because of the passivity ascribed to her gender and race, and an apparent 'legitimated' status within the dominant regime as 'nurse' and 'policeman's wife'. As James Scott notes: 'Resistance is often of a covert nature and therefore hidden from the presence of the elites and hence does not become apparent in their documents.'[63]

The freedom and independence enjoyed by these Indigenous women led Ruth to think of Roper River societies, such as Alawa and Warndarrang, as 'matriarchal': a description in stark contrast to prevailing views in both anthropology and popular opinion in which Aboriginal women were 'typically portrayed as downtrodden slaves of the men'.[64]

The elders sanctioned Ruth's work. Dawson Daniels, whose grandfather was Tom Costello, one of the elders who accompanied Ruth Heathcock to Burunju in 1935, locates her incorporation within an Indigenous knowledge system through the context of an earlier dream prophecy he was told of:

> Old people, my grandfather and his father had a dream, a good dream that someone would come out to them, to look after our sick people and take them to a better place. We believe that person was Sister Ruth and that dream apparently came true.[65]

In April 1937, Yee-eepinny (also known as Smiler), a cousin-brother of Pat Thompson who had worked for Ted ten years earlier, was brought to the police station (during Ted's absence on patrol) suffering severe peripheral nerve damage, including paralysis in the legs and the loss of toes and fingers, as a result of leprosy.[66] He had been carried on the shoulders of his aunt (Bukumurra) and uncle

(Kankubina) for nine months as they made their way to Ruth from Caledon Bay, 386 kilometres to the north.[67] On his return, Ted was visibly upset at Yee-eepinny's condition and deeply moved by his family's devotion. For Ted this marked a turning point. He felt he could no longer remain silent, and to Ruth's great relief decided to take a stand, something Ruth wished he had done much earlier.[68] In correspondence, Ted Heathcock appealed directly to the newly appointed Northern Territory Administrator, CLA Abbott, on human-itarian grounds. Abbott, however, consulted the Chief Protector of Aborigines, Cecil Cook, on the matter, resulting in Yee-eepinny's immediate removal to Channel Island.[69]

Smiler's incarceration was the last straw as far as Ted was concerned. With Abbott's support he initiated a petition to the League of Nations, outlining the mental and spiritual as well as physical suffering that enforced removal entailed. In speaking out against incarceration policies, Ted was not only risking his career but also imprisonment. Kankubina and Bukumurra's epic journey and their dedication to Smiler were reported in both the national and international press, drawing widespread attention to the inhumanity of Australia's questionable isolation policy. The Anti-Slavery and Aborigines' Protection Society in Australia and London lobbied the Australian Government for the awarding of the Albert medal for bravery to Kankubina.[70] In the interim, Ruth was given 'special dispensation' by the Territory administrator to treat leprosy patients in her area, although war interceded. Eventually, in the 1950s, mobile leprosy clinics were established in the Northern Territory.[71] Cecil Cook's period of power in the Territory was coming to a close. He and Abbott disagreed on almost everything. Two years later, 'against his personal wishes', Cook left for Sydney.[72]

Later in 1937 Ted was transferred to Borroloola, in Yanyuwa country, south along the Gulf of Carpentaria, and remained there until his secondment in 1942 to Alice Springs as a commander in the war effort, during which time Ruth was appointed a coast guard at Borroloola by the War Office.[73] 'My last home in the territory', Ruth was to inscribe with deep regret on the back of a photograph of the Borroloola police station.[74]

Leaving their daughter Ivy in Norah's care, and their newborn baby Rosalind with Old Judy and Long Tom at Roper River Mission, Cara and Pat Thompson accompanied the Heathcocks to Borroloola on the supply boat *Leisha*. Ruth was also assisted by a capable young Yanyuwa woman, Bessie Marshall Kithibula. Like Cara, who later became the first Aboriginal nurse at Roper River Mission, Bessie rapidly acquired excellent nursing skills. She was one of those who travelled with Ruth in the dugout canoe on the hazardous journey in 1941 for which Ruth later received the MBE.[75]

It is not clear exactly how Ruth maintained contact with her Roper River patients during these years but it would seem that Cara and Pat Thompson were integral to that process. In February 1942, during the Second World War Japanese air raid on Darwin, the Channel Island leprosarium was bombed. Patients made their way to the mainland by whatever means they could, some dying in the process.[76] Twice dispossessed, many found their way to Ruth at Borroloola.[77]

Ruth refused a request from the War Office to evacuate to Adelaide. Her strong nursing ethos would not allow her to leave her patients vulnerable. She had to be forcibly evacuated, under warrant, in late 1943. The War Office, however, conceded to her insistence that the leprosy patients she was treating travel with her to Adelaide, remaining under her professional care for the war's duration. Dr FS Hone, by now a towering figure in the South Australian medical establishment and a long-time supporter of Ruth's work, took charge of their placements in Adelaide hospitals.[78] Prior to the war's conclusion, Ruth recalled: 'I had to take them back by plane to Camooweal in the Territory to take over the hospital there for a while. Then I came back to South Australia where I have been ever since.'[79] Clearly this white woman did not wish, in the words of Lynn Riddett, to fade.[80] 'They [Ruth and Ted] were pushed out because they were too good,' remembered Yanyuwa elder Tommy Peter Jayalarri, a young man at the time of the Heathcocks' departure from Borroloola, 'and army came.'[81]

Ruth never saw Ted again. He died in Alice Springs in 1944, the result of complications from injuries he'd sustained during the First World War, where he'd served with the 2nd Light Horse Regiment.[82] No longer the wife of a police officer, Ruth was left without home or employment. It demonstrated the extraordinarily fragile nature of white women's agency and independence, tied as it was to marital status — and, in Ruth's case, supported by Ted's unusually progressive pro-Aboriginal stance.

Now, as a widow without independent means, her choices were more limited. Ruth assisted her younger sister, Marie Rayney, in caring for their elderly mother and resumed nursing at the Adelaide

Rosalind Munur, daughter of Cara Thompson Nganjigee; and Sammy Bulabl, son of Nancy Burunbridj, Roper Valley Station, September 2003. Photograph by Karen Hughes.

Hospital's Magill wards, working until the age of 65. For a while she was employed as a housekeeper on a station at Mount Druitt in the Western Desert at the time of the British nuclear tests at Maralinga in 1956. In 1988 she was named Marion Council 'citizen of the year'.[83] She continued to pursue her spiritual interests outside of the conventions of orthodox religion, joining the Rosicrucian order and practising Transcendental Meditation. She kept an 'open house', as she had in Arnhem Land, where people and stray cats were always welcomed and fed, and such matters were discussed. It seemed that her dominant spiritual insights, however, were informed by her Aboriginal influences, particularly Norah Wonamgai's specialised knowledges. In 1993 Yanyuwa elder Hilda Muir visited Ruth from Darwin with a blanket she had made for her. Forcibly abducted to Darwin's brutal Kahlin Compound (another legacy of Cook's eugenicist experiment) as a child of eight, Hilda Muir vividly recalled a time in 1932 when Ruth and Ted were appointed relief super-intendents — and how starkly this contrasted to the cruelty and deprivation she experienced before and after they were there: 'She was beautiful. I never remembered anyone so kind. [Ruth and her husband] were the only people that ever showed any compassion. We were the children of theirs.'[84] She described how Ruth made cotton frocks to replace the children's jute rompers and, with Ted, took them on excursions to the beach.[85]

Despite the early warnings of delicate health, Ruth enjoyed a long, healthy and productive old age, passing away peacefully at the age of 94 in May 1995. Ruth never saw her lived experiences as extraordinary. She thought her responses an integral part of being human and, in that sense, her life as ordinary. In her later years, she felt she was just beginning to understand the things that had happened to her in the Territory.[86]

It is interesting to reflect on Ruth's childhood to see what may have set her apart. Perhaps her attitude to the Indigenous people with whom she shared the country was shaped by her childhood peers and playmates at Wellington, South Australia, where she was born and grew up. Perhaps an understanding grew out of sustained social relations with women deeply embedded in her early childhood.

Ruth Rayney was the daughter of Irish immigrants Emily and John. Her father, a gentle, softly spoken, educated man, worked as an engineer on the railway line that supplemented the Murray River trade; her mother Emily was compassionate and supportive of her daughters' independence.[87] The Rayneys had six children, three older boys, followed by Ruth and her sisters, Marie and Fay. John Rayney died when Ruth was six and her mother was reliant on the labour of her sons (until they were enlisted to fight in World War II) in raising her daughters. Tragically, all of Ruth's brothers died in action.

Ruth was a tomboy, running up and down the metal roads, able to outrun her brothers. Independent, confident, used to responsibility, she felt secure growing up in a female-headed household. She attended Wellington District Primary School with a group of local Ngarrindjeri children whose families had left the segregation of the Point McLeay Mission, across Lake Alexandrina at Raukkan, after winning a fight to 'reclaim' and farm portions of their clan estates.[88] These childhood friendships and the rich interactions they opened with the broader Ngarrindjeri community around Wellington profoundly influenced her thinking, showing alternative ways of being in the world that laid the foundation for a cross-cultural understanding and pro-Aboriginal activism that was to shape her future work and life.

In Ngarrindjeri country, women were perceived to hold equivalent power to men. Always sceptical of authority, the only figure of it Ruth recognised outside the family structure was Ngarrindjeri elder Louisa

Karpeny, who made an indelible impression on Ruth's consciousness when she was a child. Louisa Karpeny was close to 100 years of age. As a young woman she had hidden in the rushes, petrified, when the British explorer Sturt and his party entered her country. Louisa was bicultural and bridged two worlds. She used her power as an ambassador and formed an important liaison with the district's most powerful European immigrant at that time, policeman and sub-protector George Mason. She was a woman of status and knowledge in her community, a skilled weaver and important healer and sorcerer, a *putari* who kept the *maraldi* bones.

'Everyone feared Great-Nanna [Louisa Karpeny] because she was one of the sorcerers with the *maraldi* bones,' says Daisy Rankine.[89] As a child, Ruth understood Louisa's power and thought of her as 'Queen of the Lakes':[90]

> My word she was severe when we used to go out there to fish as children on the Murray... Dear old thing, when I knew her she was elderly. She wore a blanket over her head. Her head was bald like an egg and there was one white curl. Did she ever have a voice! And she'd pick up a stick like this and we were scared stiff![91]

Louisa Karpeny was to foreshadow the influence of other Aboriginal women in Ruth's life, most notably that of the gifted clever-woman Norah Wonamgai in Arnhem Land. Karpeny's presence around Wellington symbolised an overarching authority that spoke of women's knowledge and of land. She remained a dominant figure in Ruth's childhood and helped frame her understanding of the potentiality of Aboriginal women's power and law and the gendered nature of country.

Unlike other non-Indigenous women who professed cross-cultural friendships and an understanding of Indigenous knowledges — Katherine Langloh Parker and Jeannie Gunn for example — Ruth was neither a landholder's daughter nor wife.[92] She had no vested interest in processes of dispossession, and in fact remained essentially true to the initial vows of poverty and hospitality she had taken as a teenager with Little Sisters of the Poor. Ruth Heathcock's lived experiences, dominated by relationships with powerful Aboriginal women, enabled her to express alternative notions of inter-subjectivity, deploying her white privilege to redress Indigenous disadvantage from a standpoint of friendship and equality.

Notes

1. See Austin 1997.
2. CLA Abbott to the Secretary, Department of the Interior, Canberra, 23 January 1946. For a detailed account see Ruth Heathcock, *The rescue*, unpublished manuscript, n.d., copy in possession of the author; Hall 1968; Hughes 1986; and Roberts 2003. See also Hill 1945; Jose 2002, pp. 139–42.
3. Hughes 1986; Heathcock, *The rescue*.
4. Hall 1968.
5. I am especially grateful to Rosalind Munur, elder of the Ngukurr community, for research advice and to the many other community members at Ngukurr, Roper Valley, Darwin and Borroloola who shared their knowledge and generously participated in the research process. I wish also to acknowledge the staff at the Northern Territory Archives Service for their helpfulness beyond the call of duty. This research was supported in part by the Northern Territory Government through the NT History Grants Program and through an AIATSIS grant as part of a larger research project on the lives of the domestic workers.
6. Cook was both Chief Medical Officer and Chief Protector of Aborigines.
7. Cook 1927; Hargrave 1980, pp. 25, 28.
8. Report on the administration of the Northern Territory for 1944–45 to the Parliament of the Commonwealth of Australia, Northern Territory Archives Service (NTAS), Darwin. Indigenous population figures are an estimate extrapolated from Hargrave 1980, pp. 3, 9.
9. Davidson 1978.
10. Saunders 1989.
11. Saunders 1989, pp. 33–36.
12. 'Statement of heritage value', *Heritage Register*, Northern Territory Government Gazette, no. S5; see also Saunders 1990, pp. 168–81.
13. Anderson 1996, p. 63.
14. Bashford, p. 252; see also Anderson 1996.
15. See for example Anderson 2002 and McGregor 1997.
16. It was known also as *Aragundagunda* in south-east Arnhem Land. Hargrave 1980, p. 202.
17. Saunders 1990, p. 171.
18. See Hargrave 1980, p. 29; Saunders 1989, pp. 15–16; Saunders 1990, p. 181, Thoneman 1949, pp. 168–70.
19. Hughes 1986.
20. Ruth Heathcock, personal communication, May 1984.
21. Woodruff 1951.
22. Ruth Heathcock, personal communication, May 1984.
23. Kettle, p. 136.

24. Ruth Heathcock, personal communication, May 1984. Leprosy suspects were usually transported in converted cattle carriages similar to the one illustrated in Saunders 1990.
25. Colin McCarthy, personal communication, 16 July 2003; see McGregor 1997; see also Hargrave 1980, p. 203 for discussion of Indigenous attitudes to leprosy.
26. Catholic online encyclopedia 2003, viewed 6 June 2004, <www. newadvent. org>.
27. Ruth Heathcock, personal communication, May 1984.
28. The hospital became known after 1962 as the Royal Adelaide Hospital.
29. Ruth Heathcock, personal communication, May 1984.
30. Duguid 1972, p. 100. It is ironic to note that the original AIM, the Aborigines Inland Mission, was founded by a white woman, Mrs Retta Long, who 'told me that she called on John Flynn not to cause confusion by using the same initials when the Australian Inland Mission began work but he refused to change them'.
31. See Riddett 1991 & Riddett 1993, p. 80, re. AIM sisters' resistance to contemporary eugenicist views.
32. See for example Hilda Muir, oral history interview by Francis Good, TS 793, NTAS, tape 1, 1993; Valentine Bynoe McGinness, oral history interview by Janet Dickson TS 532, TP 521, NTAS tape 3, 1984; Connie Bush, personal communication 1996.
33. Connie Bush, personal communication 1996.
34. Valentine Bynoe McGinness, Norther Territory Records Series (NTRS) 2266, oral history interviews TS 532, Northern Territory Archives Service, Darwin.
35. Hall 1968; Heathcock 1983 oral history interview, NTRS 226, oral history interview TS 240, NTAS, Darwin. The Aboriginal reserve of Arnhem Land was to the north of the police station at Roper Bar. To the south stretched large pastoral properties such as Urapunga, Roper Valley Station, Hodgson Downs, Elsey Station, St Vidgeons Station and Nutwood Downs. Many were formerly owned by the London-based Eastern and African Cold Storage Company during the violent period in the 1880s and 1890s known as 'the killing times'. These properties now had passed into individual ownership during a period of relative harmony in which Aboriginal people were able to coexist. See Morphy 1984; Harris 1993.
36. See for example Haskins 1998b, generally; Moreton-Robinson, pp. 21–31; Riddett 1993, generally.
37. Rosalind Munur, personal communication, January 2003.
38. Ruth Heathcock, personal communication, May 1984.
39. Audrey Bush, personal communication, July 2000.

40. Ruth Heathcock, personal communication, May 1984; Rosalind Munur, telephone interview, 1 August 2003.
41. See Hargrave 1980, pp. 287–92, for table of diagnoses recorded in the Northern Territory. It includes a map on p. 44 showing a complete retreat of contagion at Roper River from 1926–40, whereas leprosy either remained constant or spread rapidly in other parts of the Top End at this time.
42. By 'old Sam', Rosalind means Sam Thompson. Long Tom and Old Judy were also the parents of Pat Thompson. Another of their children, Matthew Thompson, was taken to Channel Island in the late 1940s.
43. Rosalind Munur is referring here to the home of Mr and Mrs Heathcock behind the Roper River police station. The sick people only stayed there while Ted Heathcock was away, otherwise he would have been forced to report them to Cecil Cook.
44. Rosalind Munur, personal communication, June 1984. Kriol is now the first language for most speakers in this region and is the language taught at school (see Harris 1993).
45. Ruth Heathcock, May 1984; Hughes 1986.
46. Hughes 1986; Hall 1968, generally; Moreton-Robinson, p. 18.
47. Moreton-Robinson, pp. 18–19.
48. See Paisley 2000, pp. 17–18, for comment on the connection between spiritual beliefs and personal politics in relation to the activist and theosophist Bessie Rischbieth.
49. Hughes 1986.
50. For information on the missionary service see Harris 1998; *mununa* is a generic south-east Arnhem Land term for white people; Rosalind Munur, personal communication, February 1997.
51. Colin McCarthy, personal communication, 16 July 2003.
52. Lockwood.
53. Hughes 1986.
54. Ruth Heathcock, personal communication, September 1984; Rosalind Munur, personal communication, June 1984; Hall 1968, pp. 47–48.
55. See for example Peggy Grove, 'Myths, glyphs, and rituals of a living goddess tradition' in *ReVision*, vol. 21 i3, p. 6 (1), 1999; R Berndt, *Kunapipi: a study of an Australian Aboriginal religious cult*, FW Cheshire, Melbourne, 1951.
56. Ruth Heathcock accompanied the author to Ngukurr, as well as Burunju, in September 1984 for the filming of the documentary *Pitjiri: the snake that will not sink*. She had also made a visit in the 1960s with Colin McCarthy and again in the late 1970s.
57. Dennis Daniels, personal communication, September 1984; see Capell 1960; Bush 1990.
58. Dennis Daniels, personal communication, September 1984; see also Capell 1960.

59. *Minininggi* translates as traditional owner, while *djungaiyi* translates to ceremonial guardian.
60. Rosalind Munur, personal communication, March 1997.
61. Rosalind Munur, personal communication, September 1984, March 1997; see also Hughes 1986.
62. See for example Haskins 1998; Haebich 2000; Read 1999; Human Rights and Equal Opportunities Commission, *Bringing them home*.
63. Scott 1985, pp. 284–89.
64. Little serious attention (apart from Phyllis Kaberry's *Aboriginal woman: the sacred and profane* and some of the unpublished fieldwork of Ursula McConnell) was given to Indigenous Australian women's autonomy and religious life until Diane Bell's 1970s fieldwork and the resultant publication *Daughters of the Dreaming*. See also Bell 1987; Cheater 1993; Evans et al. 2003; Austin 1990, p. 15.
65. Dawson Daniels, Ngukurr, September 1984, in Hughes 1986. See generally Sansom 2001 for a discussion on the powerfully interactive presence of Dreaming beings, forces and Law within the seemingly 'everyday'. See also Hughes 2001.
66. Rosalind Munur, personal communication, August 2003.
67. National Archives of Australia (NAA): Ted Heathcock to Cecil Cook, 7 October 1937, F1 37/580 Darwin, and 'Witchdoctor's long trip' in the *Western Australian*, 31 May 1937, F1 37/580; Gibson 1992, 'Kancubina-Kiang-oo-panny'.
68. Colin McCarthy, personal communication, 16 July 2003.
69. NAA: 'Witchdoctor's long trip', F1 37/580.
70. NAA: John Harris, secretary, Anti-Slavery and Aborigines' Protection Society, to the Rt Hon. SM Bruce, high commissioner for the Commonwealth of Australia, Darwin.
71. Grant; Hughes 1986.
72. Saunders 1989, p. 36. Cook once said of Abbott: 'I didn't find him difficult at all. I simply didn't know of his existence. He never consulted me, never told me anything.' Cecil Cook, oral history interview, NTRS 226, TS 179, p. 13, NTAS, Darwin.
73. Colin McCarthy, personal communication, 16 July 2003. Records of Ted Heathcock's involvement in the war effort are in commissioner of police F77 correspondence files, 1935–58, File 41/43, NTAS, Darwin.
74. Ruth Heathcock, personal photographs, private collection of Sandra Fishloch.
75. For Bessie Marshall Kithibula's recollections of the 1941 rescue, see Bessie Marshall a-Kithibula 1992, 'The death of Horace Foster at Manangoora'.
76. Saunders 1989, p. 32; Connie Bush, personal communication, June 1995. Connie Bush's mother, Norah Roberts, was a patient on Channel Island. Left without care, she died in the days following the 1942 bombing. For more on this see also Phillip Roberts's account in Lockwood.

77. Ruth Heathcock, oral history interview by Dallas Cooper, May 1983, NTRS 226 TS 240, side B, tape 1, NTAS, Darwin.
78. See Woodruff.
79. Heathcock, oral history interview, 1983, NTRS 226 TS 240, side B, tape 1, NTAS, Darwin.
80. Riddett 1993.
81. Tommy Peter Jayalarri 1984, unpublished oral history transcript recorded by John Bradley, 4 June 1984.
82. Ted emigrated to Australia in 1912. He joined the Queensland 2nd Light Horse Regiment in 1914 and served at Gallipoli. Tom F Heathcock to the commander, Northern Territory Mounted Police, commissioner of police F77 correspondence files, 132/45, Northern Territory Archives Service, Darwin.
83. Grant 1992, p. 93
84. For eugenics and Aboriginal people see Austin 1990; Austin 1993; McGregor 1997, pp. 161–72. Hilda Muir's recollections: Joel Magarey, '40 years on, Ruth's kindness is remembered', the *Advertiser*, 28 January 1993.
85. Magarey, '40 years on...'; Hilda Muir, oral history interview by Francis Good, NTAS, 1993; Hilda Muir, telephone conversation, 2 September 2003; Hilda Muir, *'Very big journey': my life as I remember it*, Aboriginal Studies Press, Canberra, forthcoming; Hall 1968, p. 159.
86. Hughes 1986.
87. The early journals of George Taplin show that Ruth's father paid a visit to the Point McLeay Mission, though we do not know what for. See Taplin, journals, 28 October 1878.
88. Jenkin, pp. 229–31
89. Bell 1998, p. 337.
90. Hughes 1986; Hughes, 'Pioneer for humanity', the *Advertiser*, 3 June 1995, pp. 6–7.
91. Ruth Heathcock, personal communication, August 1987.
92. See Ellinghaus; Evans et al. 2003.

5. 'Never forgotten'
Pearl Gibbs (Gambanyi)

Stephanie Gilbert

Few people can claim a political life akin to that of Pearl Gibbs. First drawing public attention in defence of other Aboriginal people in the 1920s, she only stepped away from her activist platform with her death in 1983. Her legacy lives on. Gibbs knew and worked with almost every major Aboriginal activist in 20th-century Australia. These include her mentor, William Ferguson, as well as William Cooper, Jack Patten, Margaret Tucker, Joe McGinness and Charles Perkins. She could also claim to have worked with other major rights activists, including Jessie Street, Faith Bandler, Michael Sawtell and many, many more. Her sphere of contact included prime ministers, attorneys-general, numerous members of parliament in New South Wales, waterfront and other unions, feminist groups, women's groups, and members of the media. She was the first Aboriginal woman to speak on Australian radio and the first to present a scripted radio show.[1]

Gibbs worked across the racial divide to draw together those who had never worked with one another. Many non-Aboriginal Australians had never considered the situation of the Indigenous people of their country until challenged by Gibbs to do so. Media accounts of Pearl Gibbs time and again confirmed her impact on the lives of Australians, whether they were from the conservative or leftist side of politics. Pearl knew and called upon Australians of all kinds, from all rungs of society.

Many stories about Pearl Gibbs describe her as 'half-caste', a label that belies her stature as one of Australia's most prolific and effective Aboriginal leaders, and a tireless worker for the Aboriginal cause. Gibbs set a benchmark for commitment and networking, using her ability to draw in allies of all persuasions as they were required. These networks included the non-Indigenous women and organisations so crucial to Gibbs' activism. At all times Gibbs represented the Aboriginal people with honour, and with her Aboriginal identity at the core of her imagining, her methods and her presence.

***

Gibbs was born Pearl Mary Brown in 1901 to an Aboriginal mother, Margaret Brown, and white father, David Barry. Her older sister, Olga, was two years old at the time. In 1910, her mother married Richard (Dick) Murray, an Aboriginal man, from Brewarrina like herself.

Much of Gibbs' early schooling was undertaken in Yass. Her mother had earlier tried to enrol her in Cowra but was told no blacks were allowed there. It was at Cowra and in Yass that Gibbs had her first encounters with racial discrimination. Aboriginal children had been banned from attending the public school in Yass since 1897 so, with the other Aboriginal children, Gibbs attended the Mount Carmel Convent School run by the Sisters of Mercy. The family moved out closer to Bourke and Brewarrina in 1910 to take up work on a sheep station.[2]

In 1917, Pearl and Olga moved to Sydney to work as domestics — positions that may have been organised by their parents' employer. They were fortunate to gain work in the wealthy area of Potts Point. Gibbs continued to work as a maid and cook throughout the 1920s, and during those years married an English sailor. Although she and her husband later separated, the marriage produced a daughter and two sons, one of whom later joined the Australian Navy.[3]

Gibbs' political education grew when she met other young women and girls apprenticed as domestics by the Aborigines Protection Board. During the 1920s, Gibbs assisted a number of these young women to negotiate with the board. She was deeply concerned by their working conditions and the stories they told of being taken from their families. She decided she would make representations on their behalf to the board. It is said that she was deeply moved and remembered for a long time the reaction she got from the staff when she visited the board's offices.[4]

In the 1930s, with the Great Depression in full swing, Gibbs lost her job and was forced to live in the Unemployed Workers' Camp at La Perouse. After some time spent living with her mother in the camp, they moved to Nowra to work on seasonal pea-picking. During this time, Gibbs came to know and associate with Aboriginal people from Wallaga Lake. She was so angered and disgusted with the cruel and unfair practices on the Aboriginal reserve, as well as with Aborigines Protection Board policies generally, that she helped organise protests against some of the management decisions. In one instance, she undermined a community manager's order that the women only shop while he was present by encouraging them to purchase underwear. In another, she organised protests by the pea-pickers for better industrial conditions. These experiences increased her distrust of the board's officials but also created her first links to political bodies and ministers in the New South Wales Parliament, including Jack Beale, the first environment minister in a New South Wales government.[5]

It was in 1937, in response to a call from William (Bill) Ferguson, that Gibbs visited Sydney to help form the Aborigines Progressive Association (APA). At this point, her political and ideological development grew exponentially. Gibbs became one of the early members of the association and spent the rest of her life politically aligned with Ferguson, its leader. Her first public speech was in Sydney when the APA was created. She had accompanied Bill Ferguson and Michael Sawtell to the Domain and, after they spoke, she stood on their ladder and addressed the crowd. At a time when it was rare for women to express themselves publicly, she spoke with fluency and passion and attracted a large crowd. She later recalled: 'I shook and I shivered and the ladder was rocking... I was so fighting mad, I didn't know what to say first because there were so many things... They had to get me down on the ground and then I started.'[6]

Bill Ferguson and the APA's president at that time, Jack Patten, believed Gibbs was the APA member best equipped to speak to the women of Australia on matters affecting Aboriginal women and girls. Gibbs spent the next several years addressing groups where women were the dominant audience members. Her activities, however, were not restricted to these groups alone. In mid-1937, at Ferguson's request, Gibbs went to Brewarrina Aboriginal Station to investigate claims about sexual abuse of the dormitory girls. Ferguson wanted to present this and other evidence of maltreatment at a parliamentary inquiry into the conditions of Aboriginal people in New South Wales. Although this inquiry went ahead on 17 November 1937, it was prematurely dissolved and Gibbs' evidence was never given. She did attend, however, as a representative of the Sydney Feminist Club, as she had recently struck up a friendship with fellow member Joan Kingsley-Strack through a chance invitation to a tea party Strack had hosted for Aboriginal domestic workers.[7]

***

Australia's 1938 sesquicentenary celebrations provided the perfect opportunity for activists to draw the public's attention to the situation of Aboriginal people in Australia. William Cooper from the Victorian-based Australian Aborigines' League (AAL) proposed a Day of Mourning, which he encouraged the APA to co-organise. The Day of Mourning and Protest would coincide with the 26 January 'celebrations' but would be for Aboriginal people only. Prior to the day, the APA issued a press release, saying:

> The 26th of January 1938 is not a day of rejoicing for Australia's Aborigines; it is a day of mourning. This festival of 150 years' so-called 'progress' in Australia commemorates also 150 years of misery and degradation imposed upon the original native inhabitants by the white invaders of this country.[8]

The Day of Mourning and Protest Conference was held at the Australian Hall in Elizabeth Street, Sydney after the sesquicentennial street procession. The celebrations included a re-enactment of Governor Philip's landing. Aboriginal people had been brought from Menindee and Brewarrina to take part, and were housed at the Redfern police barracks. Ironically, the barracks' horse-breaker and tracker was Helen Grosvenor's father, Ike. Helen, Gibbs, Ferguson and Jack Patten were the main organisers of the day, which centralised Gibbs' position in Australian politics. Helen fed information to Bill Ferguson about the presence of the Aboriginal people at the barracks and the plan was to persuade them to boycott the re-enactment. Ferguson, however, was unable to get to them as they were banned from receiving visitors.[9]

Much planning went into the Day of Mourning, including many posters and handbills sent west, north and south to as many pockets of Aboriginal people as possible, inviting them to attend. Patten travelled into the country to deliver the handbills to reserves. As history shows, the conference was attended by many great Aboriginal activists of the time, including those who had been agitating for more than ten years for a change to the policies of the Aborigines Protection Board. A common theme ran among the speakers of the day: equality, recognition and the right to be Aboriginal people alongside the equality, responsibility and quality of being an Australian citizen. Ferguson said: 'We do not want an [A]boriginal member of Parliament. We want ordinary citizen rights, not any special rights such as that.'[10]

Patten said: 'We, as [A]borigines, have no reason to rejoice on Australia's 150th birthday. This land belonged to our forefathers 150 years ago, but today we are being pushed further into the background. Aborigines throughout Australia are literally being starved to death.'[11]

As well as the Day of Mourning's instigator, William Cooper, other notable Aboriginal people in attendance were Douglas Nicholls, former AFL footballer, and Margaret Tucker, who had been indentured under the NSW Aborigines Protection Board. Margaret had moved to Melbourne in 1925 and was associated with the Communist Party of Australia. She was not recognised widely as an activist at that time, but gained notoriety after her involvement in the Cumeroogunga strike in 1939. Margaret Tucker went on to represent Aboriginal people on the Victorian Aborigines Welfare Board.[12] Her contact with Gibbs remained sporadic but their concerns and personal experiences of service bound them. Later both were involved with the fight for the 1967 referendum and the project to make the documentary *Lousy little sixpence*.[13]

The only non-Aboriginal people in the audience that day were two members of the press, although earlier in the month Mary Montgomery Bennett, a non-Indigenous activist, had applied to attend (see Chapter 6). At the time, Bennett was a teacher at the United Aborigines Mission Station at Mount Margaret, 160 kilometres from Kalgoorlie. She was making her way to Sydney to attend the conference when she was quoted as saying 'the aim in Western Australia and the Northern Territory is to let the [A]borigines die out as quickly as possible'. She also wished to urge that throughout Australia Aboriginal people be granted the 'franchise and educational and working conditions equal to that of white citizens'.[14] It is unknown what she did when she learned of her inability to attend, although she had previously been in written contact with William Ferguson and William Cooper.

Shortly after the Day of Mourning Gibbs, at last, was presented with an opportunity to speak on her experiences at Brewarrina, which she had been unable to share with the earlier parliamentary committee. Gibbs became renowned for the words she spoke as part of a delegation from the conference that met with Prime Minister Lyons. The *Daily Telegraph* reported that the Aboriginal women in the party presented their positions in an eloquent and forthright manner.[15] Gibbs reportedly said, 'I am more proud of my Aboriginal blood than of my white blood.'[16] This statement made a big impression on Mrs Lyons, who would quote it in 1966 to Gibbs' colleague Jack Horner.

***

Later in April 1938, Jack Patten, who had spent time growing up in the highly politicised camp at Salt Pan Creek near Peakhurst in south-western Sydney, had a dispute with Ferguson that led to a split in the APA. Ferguson and Gibbs ended up representing the western New South Wales communities, and Patten the coastal dwelling peoples.

Meanwhile, Gibbs continued to generate a deal of news coverage. In February 1938 she addressed the Housewives' Progressive Association, saying:

> You white people awoke on Anniversary Day with a feeling of pride at what you had done during those 150 years, but did you think of the [A]borigines' broken hearts, and that for them it was a day of mourning? What has any white man or woman done in this country to help my people, the [A]borigines? The [A]borigines are now taking up the matter for themselves, and asking for citizenship. It is not ridiculous or silly for them to ask for citizenship in a country that is their own.[17]

This perspective of a right to citizenship led to Ferguson, Gibbs and the APA's push to create the Committee for Aboriginal Citizenship, formed in March. At its helm was long-term ally Michael Sawtell. Joan Kingsley-Strack (see Chapter 3) was appointed secretary. Kingsley-Strack and Gibbs had known each other since the previous year through their mutual concerns about the treatment of Aboriginal girls in service. It was Gibbs who took Kingsley-Strack to her first public protest meeting. Gibbs' involvement derived from her own history of service in the 1920s and her contact with other young women in the same situation; Strack's from wanting to assist the young women in her service and in the homes of her acquaintances. It is hard to imagine any commonality between these two women from such different spheres of Australian life, yet they shared a desire to see equality for Aboriginal people and to reduce the control of so-called experts.[18]

In the late 1930s the state government promised a revamped system for the management of New South Wales' Aboriginal people, and the lobbying began over who would join the new governing body, the Aborigines Welfare Board. The APA relied heavily on its allies, including left-leaning Christians, progressive feminist groups, leftist unionists and the Communist Party of Australia, to support its position. The APA's relationships with its allies were complex, especially given that Patten had different allies to Ferguson and Gibbs.[19] The APA advocated an end to white control of Aboriginal lives and wanted to represent Aboriginal people themselves, but it faced opposition from some anthropologists, who increasingly claimed a superior knowledge of Aboriginal issues. The anthropologists argued for their own place on the board on the grounds that they understood the traditional and cultural knowledge of the 'primitive' Aborigines. Politically, the APA could not acknowledge anthropologists' understanding of 'cultural knowledge' because this would imply they supported the idea that anthropologists should have control over Aboriginal people.

Kingsley-Strack and Gibbs, the only Aboriginal member of the Committee for Aboriginal Citizenship, worked for two years to get the organised women's movement to support citizenship rights as perceived by Aboriginal people and not anthropologists. Many women's groups at the time leaned towards a maternal approach to Aboriginal women, and clearly an argument for Aboriginal autonomy challenged their position. In the move towards a new Aboriginal Welfare Board, many women's groups firmly supported the role of anthropologists in the management of Aboriginal people; hence, they supported the inclusion on the board of female anthropologist Caroline Kelly, a protégé of AP Elkin. Kingsley-Strack had been one of those who supported Elkin, but after her involvement with Gibbs and the committee she came to adopt the APA's position.

It was around this time that Jessie Street came into Gibbs' political life. As president of the United Associations of Women (UAW), Street supported the nomination of Caroline Kelly. The UAW believed that Kelly fulfilled perfectly their desire to have women and anthropologists on the board.[20] Street became an important person in Gibbs' activism, as will be discussed later in the chapter.

Victoria Haskins has documented how Kingsley-Strack's perceptions changed from the maternalistic to the collegial as she spent more and more time working with Aboriginal activists during her time on the committee.[21] In aligning herself with the call for citizenship for all Aborigines, she alienated herself, to some extent, from the women's movements she had previously been central to. Kingsley-Strack's class and connections were of benefit in the APA struggles with the board on behalf of apprentices, but she also proved useful in other ways. In 1937, she wrote to the Premier of New South Wales asking him to accept a deputation from the APA. She also wrote to the newspapers regularly:

> As one who *knows* — not of the actual massacres — but the hopeless and heart-breaking degradation and slow starvation and generally ghastly treatment that has been meted out to *their* children by the so-called 'Protection' Board of N.S.W. which is and always has been a great poisonous 'fungus' which has lived and is still living upon the very life-blood of the Aboriginals and half-castes in this State, I feel that I *must* say here, a little of what I intended to say in evidence, at the late 'deceased' Enquiry into the Board's administration of the affairs and funds of the 'Pampered' Aborigines![22]

Gibbs' opinion was also frequently reported in the newspapers, her words illustrating her passion for the plight of Aboriginal people. Indeed, the two women appear to have been a formidable team. On 4 August 1938, Gibbs told the United Associations of Women: 'I cannot think that the government intends anything else but slow death for the Aborigines, for they are being slowly starved to death. They live from day to day on the promises of the Government.'[23]

During the split of the APA and the fight over the following two years until the new Aborigines Welfare Board was established, Gibbs and Kingsley-Strack fought for the representation of Aboriginal people and for their citizenship rights. The APA spent much time talking to its supporters and attempting to recruit more. During this time Gibbs addressed the International Women's Day conference of the Housewives' Association, the School of Modern Writers, the Fellowship of Australian Writers, and the Radiant Health Club, to name a few. In one instance, Gibbs and Strack went to a gathering of the Oxford Group, which opposed the Hitler movement in Europe. Here, according to Jack Horner, 'people could find their own peaceful answers to perplexity through their candid exchange of good, earnest, anxious and dedicated wishes'.[24] After dinner, the group gathered and, after a general discussion, listened to Gibbs. She described life on government reserves, including the managers that came with them. She described the poverty and the living conditions that led to influenza, trachoma or venereal disease. Gibbs' audience was appalled at what they heard and ashamed that this was happening in their own backyard.[25] Once again, she had passionately drawn Australia's attention to the plight of Aboriginal people.

***

On 30 July 1938, the state conference of the APA was held in Dubbo. It had been called by Bill Ferguson in response to the politicking of Jack Patten in Sydney, who had become 'president' of his own faction at a meeting held at La Perouse the previous Easter. Ferguson was duly elected president at the Dubbo conference and Gibbs its secretary. They decided to make their base in Dubbo and passed the requisite motions through the floor. Yet Gibbs' position in the organisation soon brought its own complications. She was a woman to speak her mind with clarity, sometimes anger and certainly always passion. In 1939 she made some comments to Australia's new Attorney-General, RG Menzies, that raised the ire of Ferguson. Discussing capital punishment in the New South Wales penal code, Gibbs argued that Aboriginal people struggled with the concept of capital punishment because having been taught that God always forgives, their notions of personal restraint were dulled. Although the APA was opposed to capital punishment, Ferguson argued against Gibbs' position in what became known as the *Dubbo Dispatch*, saying that Gibbs had no right to represent her views as the APA's position on Aboriginal people and capital punishment.[26]

In 1939, the APA discovered that the new Aborigines Welfare Board wouldn't include Aboriginal people. In reaction, Michael Sawtell and Pearl Gibbs announced that the APA would run three of its members for parliamentary seats in the next election, with Gibbs standing in Parramatta. Via the *Dubbo Dispatch*, Ferguson contradicted this statement, arguing no decisions would be made about this idea before the next APA conference, scheduled for March. Jaded by Ferguson's rebukes and the lack of support for the cause, Gibbs chose to move back to the South Coast. Ferguson continued to garner support in western New South Wales, with a trip to Moree where he created a branch of the APA on 30 March 1939.[27]

After the new Aborigines Welfare Board legislation was passed in May 1940, Joan Kingsley-Strack resigned as secretary of the APA, disheartened by the lack of progress. The Committee for Aboriginal Citizenship continued its work on the proposal to get Aboriginal representation for a number of years after her resignation. Ferguson continued to lead the APA in Dubbo.

In 1941, Gibbs moved to Port Kembla. She was presented with the opportunity to broadcast a speech through 2WL in Wollongong, in which she eloquently addressed the issue of Aboriginal citizenship:[28]

> It is the first time in the history of Australia that an Aboriginal woman has broadcast an appeal for her people. I am more than happy to be that woman... My people have had 153 years of the white man's and white woman's cruelty and injustice and unchristian treatment imposed upon us... Our girls and boys are exploited ruthlessly. They are apprenticed out by the Aborigines Welfare Board at the shocking wage of a shilling to three and six per week pocket money and from two and six to six shillings per week is paid into a trust fund at the end of four years. This is done from 14 years to the age of 18. At the end of four years a girl would, with pocket money and money from the trust, have earned 60 pounds and a boy 90 pounds. Many girls have great difficulty in getting their trust money. Others say they have never been paid. Girls arrive home with white babies. I do not know of one case where the Aborigines Welfare Board has taken steps to compel the white father to support his child. The child has to grow up as an unwanted member of an apparently unwanted race. Aboriginal girls are no less human than my white sisters... The bad housing, poor water supply, appalling sanitary conditions and the lack of right food, together with unsympathetic managers, make life not worth living for my unfortunate people... Please remember, we don't want your pity, but practical help. This you can do by writing to the Hon. Chief Secretary Mr Baddeley, MLA, Parliament House, Sydney, and ask that our claims be granted as soon as possible... Remember we, the Aboriginal people are the creditors. Do not let it be said of you that we have asked in vain. Will my appeal for practical humanity be in vain? I leave the answer to each and every one of you.[29]

On 25 January 1941, at a meeting of the Committee for Aboriginal Citizenship called by Michael Sawtell, Gibbs welcomed the opportunity to speak with Mr Doug Nicholls, 'the leading Aborigine of Victoria'.[30] In that meeting, she argued that the land had been stolen from Aboriginal people and that sacred grounds had been desecrated and destroyed but Aboriginal people had received nothing in return.[31] Also at the meeting was the Archdeacon RBS Hammond, president of the Fellowship of Australian Writers, secretary of the Howard League for Prison Reform and secretary of the Official Labor Party (a splinter group of Labor opposed to the policies of Jack Lang). A resolution was passed:

...that this Public Meeting of good Australian Citizens urges all other good Australians to support in their various ways, the granting of full citizenship rights and status to the Aborigines. We also urge all Australian governments to do their duty in helping the Aborigines to fit themselves for citizenship, especially in the matter of education.[32]

While Gibbs had ceased to be secretary of the APA, she had not slowed in her never-ending activism.

In 1942, Gibbs contributed a series of well-received articles to the *Nowra Leader* discussing the 1940 legislation. Aboriginal representation on the Aborigines Welfare Board was finally approved in 1943 and on 25 August 1944 Ferguson became one of two Aboriginal appointees. In 1944 the Post-war Reconstruction and Democratic Rights referendum proposed to alter Commonwealth powers in a number of areas, one of which was authority over 'the people of Aboriginal race'. The federal government wanted to take over responsibility for Aboriginal affairs, which currently resided with the states. Many Aboriginal people and their supporters believed this was the only clear path to civil rights for Indigenous Australians. To the dismay of Gibbs and others on the citizenship committee, the referendum was lost. Ferguson believed this to be a sure sign of the ignorance of a large number of the Australian people about those of other heritages.[33]

Gibbs remained on the South Coast with her parents until the end of the Second World War. During that time, her stepfather passed away. It is unclear in which year Gibbs moved to Dubbo with her widowed mother and sister. Some reports claim it was 1945, although in 1949 she wrote a letter to the *Sydney Morning Herald* addressed from Port Kembla, in which she discussed the restriction of liquor to Aborigines:

We are taking an equal part in the community life and are thoroughly welcomed, accepted, and liked by the white residents. It seems that someone has suddenly decided that we are to be treated different from, and inferior to, our white brothers, as persons having no rights whatever. We realize that the State and Federal Governments' policy of assimilation is biologically sound, but we fail to see how it can be a success if we who have assimilated ourselves into the social and economic life are to be deprived of civil rights. Those of us who have acquired education have been taught that democracy has a Christian basis, on moral standards of honesty, unselfishness, and love. We claim that these standards of democracy do not apply where we Aborigines are concerned. Signed Pearl Gibbs, Secretary, Aborigines' Advancement Association.[34]

When Gibbs and her family arrived in Dubbo, they stayed with the Fergusons and then the Carneys, where the first Aborigines Progressive Association executive meeting had been held in 1937. Gibbs became re-enchanted with the Ferguson goal and began to work with him again. She focused some of her attention on establishing a Dubbo branch of the Australian Aborigines' League (AAL) and served as vice president. This organisation for the first time linked Aboriginal bodies across state boundaries.[35]

In 1950 Ferguson died, and his seat on the Aborigines Welfare Board was taken up by Herbert (Bert) Groves. Despite the death of this APA stalwart and mentor, Gibbs pushed the organisation to continue its work. The writer and activist Len Fox said of Gibbs at that time:

> She persisted in every way she knew. She wrote to the papers — she had a scrapbook jammed with scores of these impassioned pleas for her people's rights — she spoke out, she interviewed people, she worried people, she annoyed people, she became a damned nuisance. She persisted and still persisted.[36]

Gibbs served as secretary of the Dubbo APA until it lapsed later in the 1950s. The post-war years were difficult times for Aboriginal people as prejudice and lack of employment continued to have an impact on family and community life. Gibbs remained focused on Ferguson's goals, which had become so much her own, and continued to run many social activities, like dances, to raise funds for the visits she made to the Aboriginal communities in western New South Wales. The networks she had established earlier in her activism strengthened throughout this time.[37]

Gibbs was widely envied for her networking and organisational skills. For example, in September 1949 she successfully managed the quick organisation of a going away gathering for the renowned Aboriginal tenor Harold Blair, who was on his way to North America to study. The gathering was held at the Palms Hall, La Perouse.[38] Meanwhile, the struggle for citizenship continued. The Council for Aboriginal Rights was created in 1951 in Melbourne and established a presence in Dubbo in 1953. Under its banner, Gibbs was again in contact with the powers that be, showing her incredible ability to pull in the contacts she needed. She instigated discussions, for instance, about whether the *National Service Act 1951* (Cth) included the obligatory service of Aboriginal people. Through her local member and the relevant minister, as secretary of the Council for Aboriginal

Rights she was able to confirm that Aboriginal people were not required to perform either national service or the training.

In 1953, she wrote to the acting premier to inquire whether Aboriginal people were, in fact, able to be served in cafes and other places. He responded that 'if any business person or concern refused to see good to or provide service of accommodation for an [A]borigine, the latter would have the same rights of redress as any other member of the community might have in similar circumstances'.[39] In eliciting a response like this from a minister, Gibbs continued to chip away at the structures that supported discrimination.

When the Sydney branch of the Council for Aboriginal Rights held a conference on 4–5 March 1953, Gibbs was one of the main speakers. Again, she reaffirmed her goals of citizenship rights and equal representation on the Aborigines Welfare Board.[40] The following year she moved closer to this goal when she became the only woman ever elected to the board.

There were two positions on the board for Indigenous Australians: one for 'full-blood' Aboriginal people and the other, which Gibbs filled, for 'mixed-blood' Aboriginal people. The 'full-blood' position had been vacant for five years prior to Gibbs' appointment. The 1947 census had put the number of remaining 'full-bloods' at 900.[41]

Gibbs' appointment was welcomed by Aboriginal and non-Aboriginal people alike. She received letters from across the state and the breadth of political persuasion, often espousing the same paternalism she had fought against for so long. Dr J Wearn, a dental surgeon of Sydney, wrote to Gibbs offering his congratulations, saying that he had worked in the far west children's health scheme for 25 years and he had a 'full blooded girl Ella Wanaweena with us at home. She has worked with us for years'.[42] Dr E Kent-Hughes from Armidale also offered his congratulations, arguing 'reserves should be kept for those who cannot manage to live unaided'.[43] Gibbs responded to each of these letters but the contents of her replies are unknown.

Gibbs' contacts with women's groups also continued, with the League of Women Voters inviting her to an end of year party as the guest of honour upon her appointment to the board.[44]

Gibbs aimed through her appointment to work on better lives for Aboriginal people but found her ability to influence major decisions was severely limited. She felt many decisions were made in the public bar, where, as an Aboriginal woman, she was unable to go. Added to those restrictions, she was still denied access to the very communities she wanted to represent. She was not invited to go with officers to the missions, and her own financial position was difficult. She was still living in Dubbo at the time and caring for her mother, by then a woman of 80. Gibbs managed to fulfil her responsibilities to the board while living on a widow's pension, although she did receive a daily allowance, and conveyance costs were covered by the board. She was nevertheless extremely frustrated by the limitations placed on her ability to help her people, and resigned in 1957. She summed it up neatly a couple of years later when she said: 'Aborigines want more than Board reports... They want action, not words.'[45]

A large part of the problem faced by Aboriginal people, Gibbs believed, was racism itself. With that in mind, in March 1956 she encouraged a new player into the field. Faith Bandler, the daughter of a South Sea Islander brought from Vanuatu to work on the Queensland canefields, became a founder of an organisation designed on similar lines to the Committee for Aboriginal Citizenship, known as the Aboriginal–Australian Fellowship (AAF). Its aims were to have Aboriginal and non-Aboriginal people work together on equal terms for the betterment of both, including the repeal of discriminatory laws. While Bandler would play a central role in Aboriginal politics both at state and federal level for the next 12 years, Len Fox describes Gibbs as the main influence in the founding of the fellowship. He says she was so committed that she attended all the meetings, deputations, demonstrations and conferences she could get to.[46]

Back in 1951, Bandler had attended, along with other Australian delegates, the World Youth Festival. In that group of delegates was Ray Peckham, who later played a major part in the Aboriginal rights movement. Standing on the dock to see them off was Pearl Gibbs, who had earlier introduced them to each other.

Gibbs encouraged Bandler to draw on her many contacts to the benefit of the fellowship. It was the beginning of a working relationship that reached its pinnacle in 1967 with the successful referendum. They could not have known, when they brought together about 12 concerned people in March 1956 to organise an initial meeting the following July, that the AAF would become the force it did in Aboriginal affairs over the next 13 years. It led to the nationalising of Aboriginal interests as never before.

Central to the AAF was the ability to draw in all manner of people. The group first met at the home of poets Muir Holburn and Marg Pizer, and then at the flat of Gibbs' friend, the feminist and unionist

Lucy Woodcock.[47] The first public meeting of the AAF was held in the United Associations of Women's rooms in Market Street, Sydney. Although Gibbs put a lot of work into the creation of the AAF, Bert Groves was voted in as president, with Gibbs as vice president and Bandler as secretary. Early members of the Aborigines Progressive Association also became foundation members. Gibbs resigned from the vice-presidency after 12 months but continued to be an active member. She went back on to the executive in 1961. In 1962, both Bert Groves and Pearl Gibbs were voted into life membership of the AAF.[48] The AAF ceased its work in 1969. Bert Groves passed on late the following year.

Initially, the AAF believed its role was 'to assist, defend, and promote the Aboriginal cause'.[49] It sought to 'foster greater social and economic opportunities'.[50] However, it was also integral to the 1967 achievement of citizenship rights. Historian Sue Taffe identifies three campaigns during the 1950s and 1960s that led to success in the 1967 referendum.[51] She describes them as the Aboriginal–Australian Fellowship campaign for a referendum in 1957, the national petition campaign in 1962–63, and the 'yes' vote in 1967. Bandler also sees the campaign as having being fought over a 10-year stretch.

One individual also integral to the cause was Lady Jessie Street. The AAF became involved with Street through Faith Bandler's friendship with her. Jessie Street had been living in London, and on her return to Sydney contacted Bandler. She had been pushing for the plight of Aboriginal people to be presented to the United Nations but was hampered by being based in London and denied entry to the United States of America, which housed the headquarters of United Nations. It was Street who drafted the original petition calling for a referendum and asked Bandler to present it to the AAF. She believed that more could be done from within Australia by a national interest group. Lady Jessie Street became a patron of the AAF, along with Dame Mary Gilmore. At this point Street and Gibbs established a unique relationship bonded by a belief that women legitimately had a place in politics. Bandler argues that it was these two women who provided the impetus which lead to success in 1967.[52]

Street's petition calling for a referendum was presented to an audience of around 1500 people at the Sydney Town Hall in April 1957. The audience included hundreds of Aboriginal people brought together through Gibbs' extensive contacts. Harold Blair entertained the audience and Doug Nicholls chaired the meeting. Although many journalists attended the event, there was no press or radio coverage.

The following year saw another landmark in Aboriginal politics. In February 1958, 12 representatives from all the mainland states gathered in Adelaide at the Federal Conference of Aboriginal Organisations to discuss the formation of a national representative group, which they called the Federal Council for Aboriginal Advancement. This new group articulated its goal as 'helping the Aboriginal people of Australia become self-reliant, self-supporting members of the community'.[53] Bert Groves, President of the Aboriginal–Australian Fellowship, attended from Sydney, thus entwining the fellowship's political agenda with that of the Federal Council. The AAF had already collected around 10 000 signatures from people supporting a call for a referendum to change the constitution. Leslie Haylen, Member for Parkes, presented this petition to the federal parliament on 14 May 1967.

The 1960 meeting of the Federal Council, held in Newport, Sydney at the Workers Educational Association summer school site, featured an amazing mixture of people, including members of parliament Gough Whitlam, Gordon Bryant and Don Dunstan; Dr Charles Duguid; members of the Aborigines Welfare Board; and Aboriginal delegates from around the country, including Gibbs. When they next met, in 1961, delegates adopted the resolution: 'We must abolish apartheid in our own country before the next Commonwealth Prime Ministers' conference or we could find ourselves in the same position as South Africa found itself at this year's conference.'[54] Pearl Gibbs also attended that conference. Once again, she was able to contribute to the history of Aboriginal activism in Australia. Joe McGinness, who passed on in 2003, attended and became the president of FCAA at that conference. He would remain so until the end of FCAATSI in 1978. The conference was also attended by Charlie (Lester) Leon, who was president of the AAF for many years.[55]

In 1962, the Aborigines Progressive Association was again reignited into existence. Bert Groves was voted in as president by a new generation of activists that included Charles Perkins and Chicka Dixon. This served to join earlier activists with the new order. Bert Groves, Charlie Leon and Pearl Gibbs also served as links between activists and the advancement organisations.

***

After Gibbs resigned from the Aborigines Welfare Board in 1957 she established the first hostel in New South Wales designed to serve the needs of rural Aborigines requiring hospital treatment. Based in

Dubbo near the hospital, the hostel was established through funds Gibbs had secured from the Sydney branch of the Waterside Workers Union and, later, through the Aborigines Welfare Board. The board employed her as the warden of the hostel, although this never curbed her activism, even against the board itself. After the hostel closed, she was allowed to stay on as a tenant by the Aboriginal Lands Trust of New South Wales, who managed the premises at that time. It is unclear when her mother passed away, although it is known that she was still alive in 1966, aged over 90, when Jack Horner, a fellow member of the AAF and FCAA, visited Gibbs. Gibbs herself lived in that hostel at Bembrose Lane, North Dubbo until her death.

Before the 1965 Aboriginal–Australian Fellowship conference Gibbs, along with Ken Brindle and Ray Peckham, travelled through the north-west of New South Wales encouraging Aboriginal people to attend. She was aged 60. She would remain active as long as her health allowed her. Even when restricted to life in Dubbo, she kept her finger on the Australian political pulse. Heather Goodall, who collected stories from Gibbs in 1981, recalls that whenever Gibbs talked about her earlier work her passion showed. Speaking about the hiring out of young girls she said: 'The girls were told not to mix with Aboriginal people, sent to strange places, separated from all their relations. And they wholly and solely belonged to whoever employed them — and I call that slavery!'[56]

Jack Horner describes Gibbs' public statements as veering between careful criticisms and pure vitriol. 'She was never guilty of flattery,' he says. In her private life, though, she tended to more gentle, her jocular, penetrating discussions including the encouragement of younger Aboriginal people in their political development. She 'taught us not to admit defeat', Jack says.[57]

To the very end, Gibbs agitated for better conditions for Aboriginal people. Her last newspaper interview was in late January 1983, just three months before her death. Again, she spoke her mind about the place of Aboriginal people in Australia:

> Pearl believes land rights for Aborigines is one of the answers to the problems facing the black and white communities. 'Something must be done,' she said. 'There's no good saying: "Give Australia back to the Aborigines." That's not the answer. Certain portions of land should be returned to Aborigines. It will be many years before we get land rights and for states like NSW there will be a tough time ahead.'[58]

Pearl Gibbs passed away on 28 April 1983, aged 81, ending a life of influence inconceivable in its greatness. Her achievements were many and included the ability to bring people from everywhere and every walk of life to fight for the rights of Aboriginal people. She lived reconciliation before it was ever conceived of as part of Australia's political life. At all times her thinking remained influenced by and loyal to her mentor Bill Ferguson and her absolute passion and commitment to her Aboriginality. Gibbs was central to Aboriginal activism, a great intellect, teacher and colleague. In his tribute to her, Kevin Gilbert wrote: 'Throughout history, wherever there has been massacre, genocide, deprivation of human right — wherever tyranny ruled — the human spirit objected, often rising to heroic proportion. One such spirit was Pearl Gibbs...she held one course: justice, humanity, honour within this country.'[59]

Goodall leaves us with a message from Gibbs for the future: 'I don't think colour or creed makes much difference. Let us put in our time for human rights and let us live toward that... This is what I want people to remember.'[60]

Notes

1. Horner 1994, p. 117.
2. Horner 1994; Goodall 1983.
3. Goodall 1988a, p. 211.
4. Horner 1974; Horner 1983; Goodall 1988a.
5. Horner 1983.
6. Goodall 1983, p. 21.
7. Horner 1994, p. 106; Haskins 1998a.
8. Patten & Ferguson, p. 3.
9. Horner & Langton.
10. 'Aborigines Day of Mourning: emphatic protests', *Sydney Morning Herald*, 27 January 1938, p. 6.
11. 'Aborigines Day of Mourning', *Sydney Morning Herald*, 27 January 1938, p. 6.
12. Horner 1994, p. 64.
13. Jones 2000.
14. 'Treatment of the Aborigines: missionary school-teacher's protest', *Sydney Morning Herald*, 10 January 1938, p. 6.
15. 'Report of the Lyons deputation', *Daily Telegraph*, 1 February 1938, p. 17.
16. Horner 1994, p. 70.
17. 'Treatment of the Aborigines', *Sydney Morning Herald*, 12 February 1938, p. 20.
18. Haskins 1998a.
19. Goodall 1986.

20. Haskins 1998a.

21. Haskins 1998a.

22. Joan Kingsley-Strack, letter to the *Sydney Morning Herald*, 9 March 1938, in 'The life and times of Bill Ferguson, 1965–1970', MS 4112, Australian Institute of Aboriginal and Torres Strait Islander Studies, Canberra.

23. The *Sun*, 4 August 1938, quoted in 'The life and times of Bill Ferguson, 1965–1970', MS 4112, Australian Institute of Aboriginal and Torres Strait Islander Studies, Canberra.

24. Horner 1974, p. 111.

25. Horner 1974.

26. Horner 1974, p. 82.

27. Horner 1974.

28. Full text appears in Gilbert 1983, pp. 13–17

29. Gilbert 1983, pp. 7–8.

30. Michael Sawtell, Chairman, the Committee for Aboriginal Citizenship, calling for a meeting upon the need for Aboriginal citizenship on 25 January 1941 at 3.00 p.m., Joan Kingsley-Strack Papers 1941+, MSAcc01/35, National Library of Australia, Canberra.

31. Committee for Aboriginal Citizenship, 'Report of meeting', Joan Kingsley-Strack Papers 1941+, MSAcc01/35, National Library of Australia, Canberra, p. 2.

32. Committee for Aboriginal Citizenship, Joan Kingsley-Strack Papers 1941+, MSAcc01/35, National Library of Australia, Canberra, p. 4.

33. Horner 1994, p. 133.

34. Pearl Gibbs, 'Aborigines' rights', *Sydney Morning Herald*, 19 August 1949, p. 2.

35. Horner 1983, p. 16.

36. Fox 1983, p. 41.

37. Horner 1983.

38. Horner 1994, p. 171.

39. G Kelly to CG Robertson, 25 June 1953, Pearl Gibbs Collection, MLmss 6922 1 (8), Mitchell Library, Sydney.

40. Horner 1983, p. 17.

41. 'New board member: first woman elected', *Dawn*, 1 July 1954, p. 18.

42. Dr J Wearn to Pearl Gibbs, 26 August 1954, Pearl Gibbs Collection, MLmss 6922 1 (8), Mitchell Library, Sydney.

43. Dr E Kent-Hughes to Pearl Gibbs, 17 August 1954, Pearl Gibbs Collection, MLmss 6922 1 (8), Mitchell Library, Sydney.

44. Honourable Secretary Booker to P Gibbs, 26 November 1954, 'Invitation from League of Women Voters of New South Wales to end-of-year party as guest of honour', Pearl Gibbs Collection, MLmss 6922 1 (8), Mitchell Library, Sydney.

45. Quoted in Bandler 1989, p. 7; Horner 1983.

46. Fox, p. 43.

47. Marilyn Lake, 'Radical daughters', *Age*, 8 March 2001, p. 1–2.

48. Bandler & Fox; Horner 1983.

49. Bandler & Fox 1983, p. 33.

50. Bandler & Fox 1983, p. 34.

51. Taffe 2001, p. 1–7.

52. Lake 2001, pp. 272–73; Bandler 1989, p. 72.

53. Taffe 2001, p. 10.

54. 'Protest on racial policy', *Sydney Morning Herald*, 3 April 1961, p. 6. South Africa was forced to withdraw from the Commonwealth after the prime ministers' conference in question.

55. Bandler & Fox.

56. Goodall 1983, p. 21.

57. Horner 1983, p. 19.

58. Heather Jeffrey, 'Pearl has been breaking down 20th century's racial barriers', *Dubbo Weekend Liberal*, 29–30 January 1983, p. 82, Pearl Gibbs Collection, MLmss 6922 1 (8), Mitchell Library, Sydney.

59. Gilbert 1983, p. 6.

60. Goodall 1983, pp. 21–22.

Part 3
Public lives

6. 'Whatever her race, a woman is not a chattel'

Mary Montgomery Bennett

Alison Holland

> There can be no reasonable objection to mixed marriages. Some of the greatest servants of the human race were children of mixed marriages: Timothy, St David, Elizabeth Barrett Browning, Booker Washington and many more. The objection is to prostitution and robbing children of their right to a father's love as well as a mother's.[1]

In presenting evidence before the Moseley Royal Commission into the treatment and condition of Aboriginal people in Western Australia, leading Aboriginal rights activist and mission teacher Mary Bennett called for the banning of polygamy in the settled districts.[2] Prior to this she had helped drive a feminist campaign for 'an honourable native policy', which included a call for Aboriginal people to free themselves from 'undesirable customs', such as polygamy, and Aboriginal women to freely choose a marriage partner. On Bennett's urging, the leading feminist group in the state, the Women's Service Guilds, called for an end to all forms of 'marriage bondage' and 'domestic slavery'.[3]

Neither of these requests fared well. While Bennett's demand was dismissed as out of step with contemporary administration, there was little direct engagement by the all-male inquiry with the particular feminist requests. Pursuing its own agenda on Aboriginal marriages, the administration ignored them. Being primarily concerned to control and monitor all 'half-caste' marriages, it was not concerned with polygamy because it was a practice it identified with 'full-blooded' Aboriginal people. Indeed, it saw Bennett's demands as unfashionably interventionist. Yet, for Bennett, polygamy was not an outmoded 'tribal' custom. She argued that on the male-dominated Australian frontier it had been preserved, even though conditions no longer sanctioned its use. It was, according to her, a distinctive feature of culture contact maintained to facilitate a sexual economy between white and black men. She argued that such conditions enslaved Aboriginal women. While the feminist agenda ultimately focused elsewhere after its 'defeat', Bennett continued to push her anti-slavery campaign, believing that there was ultimately much more at stake. She argued that on Aboriginal women's marital status rested the Aboriginal future.

This fascinating aspect of Mary Bennett's humanitarian agenda has received little historiographical attention to date, despite a growing body of work in this field.[4] Bennett was one of a number of non-Aboriginal inter-war humanitarians, male and female, who were deeply concerned about the condition of Aboriginal people and, more particularly, about the direction of policy. Among them there was a concern about the historic mistreatment of Aboriginal people, a feeling that such injustices should not be replicated in the future, and a belief that an effort should be made to prevent Aboriginal people from merely dying out.[5] Most agreed on the need for a national approach, all were concerned by the role of the police, and most were calling for a reformed administration headed by scientists and humanitarians. I argue Bennett's critique was the most wide-ranging and unique. In particular, she spearheaded a gendered approach. She was not *only* concerned about the position of Aboriginal women but believed that it was the platform upon which all other reforms rested. In highlighting marriage she was emphasising the central importance of sex and gender to the native question and, more obliquely, to Australia's colonial inheritance.

Not surprisingly, it has been within feminist historiography that a closer assessment of Bennett has been made to date. Influenced by a growing body of work in the field of gender and imperialism, Australian feminist historians have analysed Bennett's contribution.[6] As part of this work, I have sought to emphasise the humanitarian (rather than purely feminist) links to Bennett's activism.[7] In the context of a burgeoning women's movement, feminist networks were very important in providing a forum and context within which to share and define concerns; however, it was her humanitarian links that continued to sustain Bennett on Aboriginal questions when she became marginalised from the broader feminist movement. What made her work distinctive was her often close association with Aboriginal individuals and communities. I argue that there was a closer link than previously thought between the demands of key women reformers, such as Bennett, and those of the Aboriginal activists.

Bennett was a classic example, being spurred to action by Anthony Martin Fernando, an Aboriginal activist whose lifelong concern with the condition of his people saw him travel the world in the first decades of the 20th century, publicising his concerns in an effort to find justice.[8] His passion eventually landed him in jail for a spell. When Bennett visited him there she was deeply impressed by his conviction and by his accusation that her own interest was driven by cant and hypocrisy. To some extent this meeting stirred her to practical action in Australia. Once there, a noticeable feature of her campaign was constant counsel with Aboriginal people. A mark of the respect and trust she commanded from the Aboriginal community was her life membership of the Australian Aborigines League, a prominent inter-war Aboriginal lobby group.

While much of the historiographical debate has focused on questions of interpretation and definition, all contributors have agreed on the Christian maternalism and imperial antecedents to the inter-war non-Aboriginal women's campaigning. There has been an emphasis on descriptions of the imperial context of humanitarianism and feminism, rather than a weaving of specific issues to imperial discourses. Bennett's critique of Aboriginal marriages and her discourse on slavery provide an opportunity to explore how the contents fitted the framework, particularly as the demands regarding polygamy and marriage bondage were so unique in these years. Apart from the feminists who supported her agenda, no one was raising this as an issue. What was it about and what does it tell us about Bennett? Was she being overly imperialistic and interventionist, maternalistic, or culturally relativist and radical in lobbying for Aboriginal women's liberation? Why did she feel she could speak on Aboriginal women's behalf, and was there any basis to her view hat Aboriginal women were in fact seeking their freedom in this way?

One of the difficulties with analysing this part of Bennett's campaign is that it was intimately connected to a British feminist campaign, spearheaded by the St Joan's Social and Political Alliance, to free Indigenous women from what was perceived as their slave-like status, not only in the contact situation but also, more controversially, within their own cultures. Yet this particular campaign has not been the subject of historiographical attention, despite a keen interest by British and North American scholars in the British feminist campaign in India which included an attack on Indian marital practices.[9] In the light of contemporary historiographical interest in gender and colonialism, and in contemporary feminist politics concerning relations between Indigenous and non-Indigenous women, this is a significant gap.

So, how do we begin to interpret it? The question that seems pertinent to contemporary literature is whether this campaign was complicit with the fundamental tenets of empire at the time, or ran counter to the designs of Britain's paternalistic colonial bureaucracies. The campaign to make Britain's colonial subjects monogamous is in itself fascinating. On the face of it, it is rampant imperialism backed by Christian zealotry which targeted customary marriage practices with great severity from the late 19th century. Clearly, there is the question of just what Bennett and the feminists intended by freedom or slavery in this context. And there is also the question of how the targeted Indigenous populations reacted to this intervention. But there is a third point at issue: how such interventions were received at the time. Were they considered to be aiding or hindering the imperial project? Did native administrators welcome this initiative in the inter-war years as something that furthered their programs for 'their' Indigenous populations, or was it an annoying and troublesome [white female] intervention?

According to HF Morris, a historian of British colonial policy and practice, the interventions of the St Joan's Social and Political Alliance certainly complicated the issue and were not welcomed by an administration under siege on the question of Indigenous marriages.[10] In the Australian context, Mary Bennett argued that demands for the abolition of polygamy were antithetical to the administration's aims in Western Australia. She believed that the mission's insistence on monogamy protected Aboriginal women caught in the vulnerable state of culture contact; hence, it preserved Aboriginal society from what amounted to state-sanctioned extermination.

This chapter will look at this intriguing and culturally specific dimension of Bennett's campaign to explore how one white woman conceived of Aboriginal women's rights in inter-war Australia against a backdrop of a consolidating empire and increased interest in Indigenous races both nationally and internationally. But before exploring the particularity of Bennett's agenda in Australia, we need to have the important background context within which to understand it.

The imperial context

When Bennett came to Australia in 1930 to settle and investigate Aboriginal conditions first-hand she was 50 years of age, childless and of independent means. She had lived in England most of her life, although she was born and raised in north-west Queensland on her father's pastoral station. Aboriginal people had been part of her life from birth, her father having employed them on the station and earned himself the despised reputation of benevolence towards 'the blacks'. This meant that Aboriginal people were Mary's 'childhood friends'. Like many women of her class and background, Bennett finished her education in England, before marrying and settling there. Nevertheless, it seems from her writings that she had long nurtured a deep intellectual interest in Aboriginal matters. In her biography of her father, published in 1927, she offers a detailed appraisal of Aboriginal policy and practice which demonstrates a firm grasp of the history as well as the contemporary policies.[11] Her research shows engagement with the colonial newspapers and broadsheets, and with leading Australian ethnographies. It also demonstrates a keen reading of contemporary imperial discourses concerned with native policy.

Bennett's active participation in the humanitarian movement followed the death of her husband in 1927. It seems that her widowhood provided the opportunity to engage in something she had cared about most of her life. Adopting the Aboriginal cause provided not only a legitimate female intellectual outlet but a life purpose and meaning. While her publication of *The Dalleburra Tribe of Northern Queensland* (1927) suggests a prior ethnographical interest, her humanitarianism found expression in the context of an inter-war British culture deeply emersed in matters of colonial policy and practice.[12] This was the high point of British imperialism in Africa, but it was also a time of anxiety regarding potential threats to a fragile world peace. The First World War had strengthened concern that racial conflict might present such a possibility in the future. While maintaining a hold on their colonial dependencies, British administrators were keen to contain this potential threat from 'within'.

Colonial policy was therefore a hot and exciting topic of theoretical debate among the educated elites, as demonstrated in a number of public inquiries, newspaper coverage and special conferences devoted to it. Included here was a greater imperial interest in Australian conditions. As in Britain, native policy in Australia had become a keen area of concern by the late 1920s, largely because of a number of sensational cases of injustice in the north and north-west. These revealed an alarming state of interracial unrest and unjust treatment of Aboriginal people. The cases were also notable for generating a strong humanitarian outcry in the southern cities. Many of the organisations and groups formed at this time saw themselves as part of a broader empire-wide humanitarian agenda strongly influenced by the work of the prestigious Anti-Slavery and Aborigines' Protection Society (Anti-Slavery Society). This organisation had long been interested in the position of the native races of empire but its work was considerably revived in these years.

The League of Nations and Britain's pre-eminent role within it had much to do with this humanitarian revival. The League generated a new international concern with the fate of native races, which resulted in recommendations concerning their protection and governance. Defining native races as 'a sacred trust of civilisation', articles 22 and 23 of the League's Covenant called for fair and humane conditions of labour, just treatment, a voice in government, and land. This created for the Anti-Slavery Society a more sympathetic environment in which to do its work, and it seized the opportunity provided. It quickly became a centre for the discussion and dissemination of information regarding imperial policy. In 1926 it pressured the League to adopt the Slavery Convention and, by 1932, an international expert was commissioned to exert pressure on member nations to abolish all forms of slavery.

Bennett was greatly energised by this imperial milieu. It provided a receptive environment in which to launch her Aboriginal rights agenda. She became a member of the Anti-Slavery Society in 1927 at the behest of her friend and fellow humanitarian Constance Cooke, an Australian feminist whose involvement in the Aboriginal cause saw her lobbying powerful allies in London. This precipitated a correspondence with the leading figures of the society which was to last for the rest of her life. She also began publishing articles on the 'Australian Aboriginal problem' in the *Manchester Guardian*, becoming something of an Australian authority in England and earning herself the reputation of a 'champion of the blacks'. But it was not just within humanitarian circles that she found a platform for her concerns. By the 1930s Bennett had witnessed the rise of feminist politics. Being based in England for the formative years of her womanhood, she saw the radical potential of feminist activism — an activism that had been concerning itself with women's status in the outposts of empire for some time, and which was greatly energised by this new international context.

Slavery and the feminist agenda

The renewed emphasis on an international anti-slavery agenda was particularly pertinent to a feminist community long concerned with the slavery of women. Up until the late 1920s this concern centred on Western and Eastern practices considered antithetical to women's freedom, such as trafficking in women for the purposes of prostitution (the white slave trade), or cultural practices like *devadasi* in India and the *mui-tsai* system in China and Hong Kong, which were understood to enslave girl children.[13] From the end of that decade, however, feminists increasingly turned their attention to the position of native women within tribal marriages. A view prevailed that native women were treated as slaves because they were living in marital arrangements, such as polygamy and child marriage, which made them the property of their men.

The feminist community's focus on Indigenous women in these years says as much about their own positions as it does about the lives of Indigenous women. A number of historians have pointed to the centrality of slavery to the development of Western feminism.[14] Carole Pateman has shown how, in order to articulate and comprehend the subjection of women in patriarchal societies, slavery has been a persistent theme in feminist discourse since the 17th century.[15] Of relevance to Bennett's specific campaign is Peggy Pascoe's analysis of late 19th-century women's missionary and rescue work on the American frontier. She argues that representations of women in culturally and religiously sanctioned forms of marital and domestic slavery—the Chinese 'slave girl', the Mormon woman 'subjected' to polygamous marriage, and Indian women 'consigned' at birth to polygamous men to whom they became 'slave drudges and maltreated wives'—helped shape a critique of female powerlessness that supported an ideology of white, middle-class, Protestant female authority in the American West.[16]

The 'enslaved' Indigenous woman of the inter-war years was similarly invoked to support an ideology of white, middle-class female authority. The inter-war years saw a very robust international feminist community pleased with the momentum of change and confident about its future. This had as much to do with a conception of modernity and their role within it as it did with actual feminist gains. By the late 1920s a number of women had achieved national enfranchisement but the League of Nations generated a conception of (Western) women as international citizens too; hence, inter-war feminists saw themselves as the new citizens of a new civilisation, one that was itself understood to be emerging from the 'customs and prejudices of the patriarchal age'.[17] This gave British women a whole new purpose. As new citizens, feminists were members of the 'advanced races' and were required to dispense a duty of care to their 'less forward' compatriots.

Nowhere was this demonstrated more clearly than in the British Commonwealth League, a powerful network of women representing Britain and the various member countries, established in 1925 to work for gender equality in the British Commonwealth.[18] It was through organisations such as this that British and Australian women were to see themselves as politically active in the important questions of the day. The league defined its mission as 'building up a strong woman's empire political power to be used for good'. It affiliated to the Anti-Slavery Society and sent representatives to League of Nations conferences. From the outset, it emphasised the moral responsibility of white settlers to members of the 'less advanced races' in their midst, particularly in relation to the protection of women and girls. It established a 'less forward races' committee and at one of its first annual conferences addressed the specific issue of the social condition of women of 'other than British race' governed under the British flag.

In her study of the British Commonwealth League, Angela Woollacott has argued that what feminists sought was a sibling relationship with Indigenous women, whom they regarded as their younger sisters.[19] Wanting to share their 'light', feminists characterised Indigenous women as still living in states of patriarchal darkness. But it was more than this. If, as Antoinette Burton has shown, British feminists had earlier used the symbol of the entrapped Indian woman to authorise their own claim to suffrage and legitimate their role in empire, in the vibrant new international context of the inter-war years, the entrapped Indigenous woman became a symbol of feminist might.[20] Working for her liberation became a means of flexing their citizen muscles. They no longer needed Indigenous women to help define their status so much as to realise it.[21] How successful they were would be a litmus test of their own advancement. Through organisations like the British Commonwealth League, white 'Anglo' feminists celebrated their liberated condition and demonstrated their advanced race status. They also legitimised their intervention in the private lives of their less forward sisters.

Central to Western feminist understanding of women's advancement and freedom was the liberty to dispose of oneself in marriage. Monogamy was synonymous with civilisation and women's freedom. The problem with polygamy, as the feminists defined it, was that it was based on infant betrothal or bestowal: young girls were promised by their parents to older men, whose camps they entered as pubescent women. Not only were they understood to lack choice but tribal marriage was thought to be associated with other practices, such as vaginal laceration or introcision. This had particular resonance in inter-war Britain because of India's *Child Marriage Restraint Act* of 1929, which followed much public debate on the issue. An example was the publication of Katharine Mayo's propagandist tract *Mother India* in 1927, which depicted the physical devastation that early marriage and motherhood had imposed on Indian women.[22] It was in this context and under the influence of the new slavery discourse that the international feminist community became more concerned to free native women from polygamy and other tribal practices considered to be antithetical to their freedom.

Symptomatic of this was the campaign of the National Women Citizens' Movement and the St Joan's Social and Political Alliance, launched at the British Commonwealth League in 1930 following the publication of the new Slavery Convention. The convention defined slavery as 'the status of a person over whom all or any of the powers attaching to the right of ownership are exercised'. The representative of the National Women Citizens' Movement, Nina Boyle, argued that the convention opened the way for the progressive abolition of customs that made native women the property of their men. She used the opportunity to launch a campaign before the British Commonwealth League for the liberation of native women from the conditions of slavery in which they lived. At a conference of the league in 1932, the theme of which was 'Marriage from the Imperial

Standpoint', a resolution was adopted on Boyle's recommendation: '…in view of the breaches of the Slavery Convention involved in the maintenance and protection of marriage customs which sanctioned the sale or purchase of women, the conference urge Governments to recognise that woman is not a chattel to be sold by her father but that women should have the right of consent in the disposal of their persons.'

In her appeals Boyle made the point that this was a feminist issue because of the male establishment's reluctance to intervene on the matter. Indeed, at an earlier league conference, Mr John Harris, representative of the Anti-Slavery Society, pointed out why this was so. He maintained that a serious difficulty in the 'uplift' of native women was that they nearly always represented an asset of a varying and disposable value to their communities.[23] He suggested that anti-slavery work on their behalf was hampered by British administrators' recognition of the 'delicacy of interference'. Certainly Morris has shown how, under indirect rule, administrators were loath to intervene in traditional marital relations.[24] While district officers might condemn practices such as child betrothal or the cruel treatment of a wife by a husband, when it came to family matters they preferred to leave it to customary law. He nevertheless points out that it was on this issue, more than any other, that administrators and missionaries clashed. He suggests that the interventions of the St Joan's Alliance added a special dynamism to the controversy concerning marriage among Africans in the inter-war period.[25]

Part of this dynamism was that feminist concerns were matched by a new international morality on this question. This was particularly evident in the early to mid-1930s when the status of native women was raised at the League of Nations. Women representatives called for the Permanent Slavery Committee of the League to work for their liberation, pointing out that issues such as polygamy, infant betrothal, child marriage and wife exchange should be subject to League scrutiny via either the Mandates, Traffic in Women and Children, or Slavery commissions. Pushing Boyle's line, women emphasised the gendered nature of the slavery debate, arguing that there should be no sex discrimination in the application of the Slavery Convention.

As a result of these recommendations, the League of Nations concluded that the direction of a common native policy should be the breakdown of all forms of 'domestic slavery' and 'marriage bondage', and that in the process of 'assimilating Western white civilisation', the Indigenous mind should be enlightened as to the 'true value of human freedom' as it related to women. It was urged that the admini-stration of native affairs should lead to the progressive abolition of all customs that bordered on slavery: all customs that permitted the purchase, sale and barter of women and children, and thus denied their human rights. In a remarkable imperial gesture, the British Commonwealth League argued that policy direction should be towards encouraging Aboriginal men to stop thinking of their women in terms of tribal law, and for all such laws to be gradually eradicated. They requested all affiliates to promote the idea that 'whatever her race, a woman was not a chattel to be sold to a polygamist or anyone else'. By 1935, the International Alliance of Women was calling for governments to abolish polygamy by law.

As good Commonwealth citizens with their fingers on the international pulse, Australian feminists concerned with this issue incorporated this wording in their submission to the Moseley Royal Commission. For her part, Bennett stressed the missionary line: that the few 'uncontaminated' tribes be left alone; that rather than give their extra wives up, native men should be prevented from appropriating any more; and that in the settled areas the property status of human beings be declared illegal, with one law — the law of the land — operable for black and white women.

Mary Bennett and slavery in Australia

The feminist recommendations owe much to Bennett's articulation of 'the problem' in Australia, which was only intelligible within this imperial context. Before her return to Australia, Bennett gave a paper to the British Commonwealth League on the condition of Aboriginal people in federal territories. In particular, she was concerned to show how, despite protective legislation, Aboriginal men, women and children were not protected because many features of the legislation were not adequately policed — a theme she would return to. On the question of protection she specifically requested that feminists familiarise themselves with the position of Aboriginal women. In the following year her book *The Australian Aboriginal as a human being* (1930) was published, in which she called for the application of international standards to Australian conditions, particularly in Central and Northern Australia, where she believed an honourable settlement with Aboriginal people could yet be made.

In 1930 Bennett joined Cooke in delivering an anti-slavery appeal to the British Commonwealth League. Like Boyle, they seized the opportunity that the Slavery Convention provided to publicise their concerns about native policy in Australia. They felt particularly justified in their position because of the publication of the Bleakley Report, a federal government–sponsored investigation into the status and condition of Aboriginal people in the centre and north of the country. This had confirmed the 'slavery' of Aboriginal women on the frontiers. Cooke had previously informed the league of the vulnerable status of Aboriginal women in the face of white intrusion.[26] Because of this, she argued, they had an anomalous legal status: subject to tribal law yet living in British territory under British law without access to its protections. She also suggested that while tribal marriage laws were designed to maintain the health and strength of the race, women were subjected to cruel and revolting practices in connection with these marital rights. For her part, Bennett used the Slavery Convention to highlight the economic dimensions of colonialism, suggesting that Australia was breaking the Slavery Convention by using forced Aboriginal labour for private profit, refusing to pay Aboriginal people and removing them from tribes and families to work for white people in Darwin.

It was not until after her self-funded year-long investigation along the north-west coast of Australia in 1931 that the marriage between slavery and the position of Aboriginal women was made explicit in Bennett's discourse. During this time she visited a number of mission stations. She was particularly impressed with the Presbyterian mission at Kunmunya (in the Kimberley), run by Reverend Love. Indeed, this mission became her model of a sound administration. What impressed her most was that Love did not seek to destroy the essence of Aboriginal culture. As she informed the Women's Service Guilds: 'He sought to conserve the "good" of native culture while creating conditions for the eradication of "undesirable customs".'[27]

It was the positive example set by Love that gave Bennett the confidence and determination to launch her anti-slavery appeal, publicising sensational newspaper pieces in the following year regarding 'conditions akin to slavery' in Australia. Alluding to the *Child Marriage Restraint Act* in India, she called on Australian women to do for Aboriginal women what British women had done for the women of India. Slave-like conditions existed, she argued, because Aboriginal people were treated as something other than human — men as unpaid and frequently coerced labourers or 'serfs', and women as the traded merchandise of black and white men. Central to her anti-slavery agenda was a critique of tribal practices such as polygamy and infant betrothal, which she argued provided the justification for the abuse of Aboriginal women and which, because of the high level of disease attendant on these practices, ultimately hastened the process of racial extinction.[28]

But her critique was more subtle still. While colonialism had left Aboriginal families impoverished via dispossession and consequent starvation, Aboriginal women were doubly disadvantaged. Originally the property of their Aboriginal husbands under polygamy, they could be sold, bought or exchanged to white men for sexual purposes. She was most concerned about what she defined as the 'recrudescence' of polygamy for prostitution. She argued that although they had lost their land, and their culture had been destroyed, polygamy had been revived and the introduction of Western influences into tribal life had serious repercussions on the status of women.

It is, of course, debatable whether polygamy had ever died away. Anthropologists certainly give some weight to Bennett's view. Diane Bell has pointed to the advice of anthropologists in the 1930s who observed that polygamy was being dropped and monogamy taken up as a result of changing economic circumstances and influences, particularly in the wake of white occupation.[29] Diane Barwick has shown how this trend occurred much earlier in the south-east, a view that is supported by Aboriginal evidence.[30] But it also had particular relevance in the area of the Mt Margaret Mission in Western Australia where Bennett worked. Located on the eastern goldfields, the area had been settled by whites for some 40 years, and the Aboriginal people of the region had suffered great economic upheaval through dispossession, the discovery of gold and drought.

If Bennett's assessment was right, her feminist appeal was particularly pertinent. An outdated tribal custom that was hard on women had been revived for prostitution. While she was certainly critical of the Aboriginal patriarchy, she was equally critical of the white man, whom she believed capitalised on the property status of Aboriginal women and commercialised the practice of polygamy for personal gain: 'In the North-West white men barter with the old native men for the unpaid labour of the young men and for the old men's surplus property in wives and a British and (supposedly) Christian public takes up the catchword and rivets the fetters of 'white slavery' on black women.'[31]

This left Aboriginal women in an incredibly vulnerable state, particularly as mothers, because with no standing before the law they were subjected to the removal of their children. It was also racist because Aboriginal women were being subjected to a system that would not be tolerated for white women. In line with her push for equality before the law, Bennett urged the feminist community in Australia to lobby for the sanctity of Aboriginal women's bodies. It was on her recommendation that at the British Commonwealth League conference in 1932, where marriage was the theme, Australian feminists launched their honourable native policy. A key recommendation was that native and 'half-caste' girls and women who wished to free themselves from 'the polygamy and prostitution of the commercialised patriarchal system, be allowed to invoke the protection of the law of the land, and exercise their own free will in the choice of their husbands, and...not be handed over to claimants as property'.[32]

At that same conference Edith Jones, a close colleague and friend of Bennett and a member of the Anti-Slavery Society, went so far as to suggest that the Commonwealth Government should produce a national policy on child marriage, 'sometimes to old polygamous men', and whether Aboriginal women could choose their husbands.

In the following year, 1933, Bennett and Jones were particularly energised by the festivities in London surrounding the centenary of the abolition of slavery. Jones used the occasion to request Australian women to 'rouse sympathy for the freeing of their native sisters' from conditions which, restricting the liberty of their persons, constituted a form of slavery as recognised by the League of Nations. At the same time, it was the allegations of slavery made by Bennett at the British Commonwealth League, and splashed across the London dailies that year, that partly led to the appointment of the Moseley Royal Commission. Her evidence of polygamy in the settled districts was strongly influenced by her experience on the Mt Margaret Mission.

Polygamy and the missions

By the time she was requesting Commissioner Moseley to ban polygamy in the settled districts, Bennett had been employed as a self-trained teacher on the Mt Margaret Mission in Western Australia for two years. Established in 1921 by Rod Schenk under the auspices of the United Aborigines Mission, it was not subsidised by the government but supported as a ration depot for indigent natives. Aboriginal people came to the mission for food, clothing, medicine and employment. Coming from New South Wales, Schenk was alarmed by the poor physical condition of the Aboriginal people in the west, particularly the women, whom he described as commodities

Mary Bennett with Dunawa and Jimma in the Small Girls' Cooking Class, Mt Margaret Mission. Education was central to Bennett's rescue of Aboriginal girls and one of her weapons against what she saw as their eventual enslavement in prostitution. Joan Kingsley-Strack Papers (Series 8, item 8, MS9551), National Library of Australia.

sold by 'old polygamists' to white men for flour, tea, sugar and tobacco. Mysie, Rod's wife, was anxious for this practice to cease. Their attack on polygamy was part of the missionary effort of conversion. As a practical step, Mysie established a raffia room on the mission where the women could make baskets to sell. This they regarded as an alternative to earning their living in white men's camps.

Like missionaries worldwide, the Schenks shared an abhorrence of traditional Aboriginal marital practices because of what they perceived as the domination of old men (gerontocracy) and the servility of women. Women were always cast as victims of patriarchal disposal: there were no female polygamists in their schema. They also shared the belief that Aboriginal women were more open to change or conversion; conservatism was the preserve of men. Bennett spoke of Aboriginal women's 'instinctive passion for purity and innate desire for chastity'.[33] Referring to the three young Aboriginal women who were her first recruits, Mysie reflected how they 'braved their husbands' wrath to commence work, paving the way for the rest'.[34] Bennett reflected how not one of the girls had been 'set free' without a battle with the missionaries.[35]

While monogamy was, as Bell has noted, one way of transforming a nomadic culture to a sedentary one, Tony Scanlon argues that the mission attack on Aboriginal marriages was an overall strategy to weaken the power of the senior men by allowing younger men to marry before their allotted time.[36] This was certainly the concern of the Schenks and Bennett. As humanitarians they were preservationists; they wanted to see the Aboriginal race survive and prosper. It was their view that polygamy contributed to racial decline for a number of reasons: because the old men monopolised the young women; because it was associated with initiatory practices such as subincision, which they argued prevented conception; and because the young girl was frequently repulsed by the union. Once the women were 'sold' to white men, disease further complicated the matter. Furthermore, Bennett and the Schenks believed that polygamy was the cause of inter-tribal violence. If prohibited, Bennett told the royal commission, it would stop a number of other abuses, such as vicarious killing and injury, wife lending as social obligation, wife exchange, wife barter to white men, initiation mutilations, witchcraft rituals and child marriage.

Rod Schenk's long-term objective was to create settled Christian villages for Aboriginal people so that they could be self-supporting. He identified economic independence via work, wages and land, and the building of homes and monogamous Christian marriages as vital to the long-term viability of Aboriginal people. A key part of this strategy was to place Aboriginal and part-Aboriginal children (particularly girls) in special-purpose homes on the mission where they would receive a (Western) education. According to Mary Bennett, the homes had three specific purposes: to provide a home for children whose parents were unable to provide for them; to protect girls from old native men, who claimed them as extra wives; and to protect the children from white people who abused and exploited them.[37] In her evidence to the Moseley Royal Commission she pointed out how the homes were the start of the Christian villages Schenk hoped to achieve, 'where parents could keep their children and help to look after them'.[38]

In just three years, the number of girls in the mission homes nearly trebled, from 16 in 1928 to 40 in 1931.[39] According to Mysie Schenk, it was the mission's policy of keeping families intact that accounted for this rapid increase:

Mount Margaret policy was that children should stay in the homes only with the willing cooperation of the parents; that it was better for children to stay in their own country where parents had daily contact with them to nurse, cuddle and talk to them, and where they knew that they were being fed properly.[40]

It was also, according to the Schenks and Bennett, why Aboriginal people preferred it to Moore River, the government settlement north of Perth, where part-Aboriginal children were subjected to training and sent out to be assimilated in the white community. Mogumber, as the government settlement was known, was a feared and hated place primarily because of the way Aboriginal children were often forcibly removed to it, away from family and kin. It was so feared, Bennett told the royal commission, that mothers would blacken their part-white children with charcoal to avoid this fate. Indeed, some of the girls who escaped from the settlement were among the first children in the mission homes. They were also among the first to marry monogamously, according to Christian law.

Not that Christian marriages were a regular feature of mission life. The first marriages at Mt Margaret did not occur until 1932, some 11 years after the mission's inception. While the marriages were regarded as a watershed, it does not appear that they opened the floodgates. As Mysie and her daughter reflected, each wedding after these became a tussle.[41] Nevertheless, missionaries saw in these marriages affirmation of the rightness of their approach. Determining Aboriginal motivation is, of course, much more difficult. While there has been a burgeoning historiographical interest in the topic of interracial marriage, there has not been a corresponding interest in *intra*racial marriage, particularly of the monogamous kind.

In looking at the adoption of monogamous marriage by Aboriginal people in Central and Northern Australia, Bell argued that Christian ideology was less influential than economic changes in hunter-gatherer societies.[42] As polygamy was integral to land tenure, dispossession provided a climate within which monogamy became the norm. On the other hand, Scanlon and the Berndts have suggested that where monogamy was adopted, Christian ideology did play a role, that Aboriginal people accepted the arguments put to them about the 'advantages' of the system.[43] Yet, seemingly contradicting this assessment is Peggy Brock's view that although the United

Aborigines Mission succeeded in converting many of the people of Nepabunna in South Australia to Christianity, this did not extend to tribal marriages, which until the 1950s were performed in the traditional manner.[44]

Christine Choo reveals the complex layering of meaning in mission-arranged marriages, pointing out a native fear about the possible impact of tribally 'wrong' unions and yet a willingness in some to partake.[45] She maintains that extramarital sexual relations, elopement and wife-stealing were rife in Aboriginal society largely because of the impossibility, under gerontocratic rule, for young people to marry. While not all women were passive in these arrangements, Choo argues, most became the focus of fights between men, and many suffered violence, including death. In her reconstruction of mission marriages she shows how mission intervention in tribal arrangements in fact exacerbated this brutality. Nevertheless, she points out that for the women involved, mission marriages were generally happy affairs that resulted in security and safety, and that in accepting the mission way these women were not necessarily relinquishing their tribal ways. Yet these were not without criticism. Reflecting on the violence associated with polygamy, one of Choo's female Aboriginal informants admitted 'womans was like a slavegirl'.[46]

Choo also points to the tension between the administration in Western Australia, which did not condone missionary intervention, and missionaries for whom monogamous Christian marriages represented the basis of future Christian Aboriginal communities.

Polygamy and the administration

As in the African context, Aboriginal marriages became a site of contestation between administrators and missionaries, particularly in Western Australia where the Chief Protector, AO Neville, wanted total control of Aboriginal marriages to put into effect his policy of absorption. Although he had given his consent for the young girls to stay in the homes, Neville preferred that they be sent to Moore River. This was particularly true of part-Aboriginal children, whom he wanted to see removed from the influence of the camps altogether. This became even more important following the inter-governmental decision on absorption in 1937, when a conference of administrators from the various states agreed that the direction of policy would be 'the absorption of the natives of Aboriginal origin, but not of full-blood, into the white population'.[47]

Aboriginal marriages had long occupied the attentions of administrators. However, the focus was sharpened in the context of what was
identified as a growing 'half-caste' population. In a massive exercise
of social engineering, administrators orchestrated the assimilation
of the 'half-castes' into the white population largely via separation
from their people, training in institutions and marriage in the white
community. All marital relationships were vetted by the chief
protector/commissioner.

It was Neville who strongly influenced the conference to adopt such
a policy. He proudly advertised his state's attempts at addressing '
the half-caste problem', enshrined in the passing of a new West
Australian *Native Administration Act* in 1936. Neville informed the
conference that while marriage was important, so too was the fate of
children. He boasted his ability, under the new legislation, to act in
loco parentis to all Aboriginal children. This meant he could take
them from their mothers at any stage of their lives. Marriage was
important, he said, in order to 'prevent the return of the half-castes,
who are nearly white, to the black'.[48]

There was a strong sense, in the report of the conference, that what
concerned administrators most was the self-perpetuation of the
Aboriginal community, the result of which was characterised as a
potential swamping of the white. Professor Cleland from South
Australia pointed out that 'half-castes' were increasing not as a result
of additional white blood but via intermarriage among themselves.[49]
Neville maintained that his control of 'half-caste' marriages was not
to vet interracial marriage but intraracial marriage. Under his law,
Neville informed the conference, 'no half-caste need be allowed
to marry a full-blooded [A]boriginal if it is possible to avoid it'.[50]
Furthermore, he could prevent the missions from allowing 'half-
castes' to marry whom they liked with a consequent increase in
population.

Customary law in relation to the Aboriginal family didn't seem to
be a problem to any of the administrators. To Bennett's allegations,
prior to this conference, of polygamy and white men's treatment of
Aboriginal women as property, Neville argued that it had never been
departmental practice to interfere with traditional customs.[51] He also
argued that trafficking in women hardly occurred in the settled
districts. Indeed, discussion of tribal marriage only entered the debate
obliquely as tribal practices that were, according to Neville, going to
spell the end of the 'full-blooded' Aboriginal people. Chief Protector

Cook from the Northern Territory suggested that a policy of laissez-faire would probably see the Aboriginal population extinct within 50 years through female sterility (caused by gonorrhea), disease and starvation. Neville argued that the 'problem' would eventually solve itself through starvation and the perpetuation of tribal practices. According to this logic, it was in the administrations' interests to leave tribal practices alone.

In their account of the Mt Margaret Mission, the Schenks make the point that the absorption resolution clarified the growing resentment they had felt from the administration.[52] The mission had antagonised the administration over a number of years on a number of fronts: they wanted more land for the mission, they refused to send girls out into domestic service, and they insisted on the payment of wages for their Aboriginal labourers. However, marriage remained one of the stronger sticking points between the two. For Bennett, absorption merely exacerbated the vulnerable status of Aboriginal women. Neville had said: 'Our policy is to send them [Aboriginal and half-caste girls] out into the white community, and if a girl comes back pregnant our rule is to keep her for two years. The child is then taken away from the mother...the mother goes back into service.' Bennett argued that this put a premium on the abuse of women and ultimately resulted in state-sanctioned prostitution.[53]

Anxious to implement the absorption decision and put a halt to mission marriages, Neville moved to license the missionaries. Although the move failed, it fanned the flames considerably, with Bennett bringing forward specific cases to show the impact of Neville's arbitrary power on the lives of Aboriginal people. She even accused him of the suicide death of one 'half-caste' man who was unable to marry the girl of his choice.[54]

By the late 1930s Bennett also saw this issue as part of a broader denial of Aboriginal civil rights, as administrators assumed more and more control over their Aboriginal populations under repressive legislation. In this respect, she joined a burgeoning Aboriginal civil rights movement which was vociferously arguing the case for equality with the white race. Among them were a number of Aboriginal women who were requesting, among other things, the right to marry partners of choice.[55]

Conclusion

The contest over Aboriginal women's bodies in the inter-war years, of which this campaign is but one example, reveals the complexity of the imperial project in Australia and the difficulty of analysis. Bennett's interventions were well and truly cast within an imperial paradigm. It empowered her to speak, while lending credibility to her demands. It also ensured her position of authority over Aboriginal people. The humanitarian rhetoric harnessed the discourse of progress that underpinned imperial domination. Not only was the campaign for the liberation of Indigenous women defined as white, advanced races uplifting black, less advanced races, it was in itself an example of progressive humanitarianism. Furthermore, if monogamy was central to civilisation as the feminists defined it, then it was also necessary to imperialism. Far from expressing a cultural relativism, then, the campaign to abolish polygamy exposes imperialism of the maternalist brand. Yet it also exposes the intransigence of paternalist imperialism. As a litmus test of Western women's advanced race status it failed. Imperialism, it seems, provided yet another context for the battle of the (non-Indigenous) sexes.

Nowhere was this more clearly the case than in inter-war Australia, where feminist demands on this question fared incredibly poorly. On every effort to improve (in their terms) the lives of Aboriginal women, they failed. Indeed, despite the centrality of slavery and the anti-polygamy line taken by Australian feminists in these years there was very little real engagement with it. Neville scoffed at Bennett's tirades as groundless and irrational, while Moseley dismissed all allegations of slavery. Even the feminists were not particularly engaged. Despite incorporating the latest international ethics into their programs and platforms on this question, there is little evidence that they embraced it as any more than rhetoric. Unlike Bennett, they were quick to drop it after the findings of the Royal Commission had determined that all slavery allegations were baseless. The anti-slavery agenda was ultimately the preserve of Mary Bennett who, with the support of Constance Cooke and Edith Jones, had launched it in 1930 in the British context and continued to argue it long after.

Bennett's campaign sat more comfortably in the British context, where it was far less radical. Unlike in Australia, humanitarianism in inter-war Britain was central to the development of the imperial agenda. It was a deeply embedded and accepted part of the culture of empire. Indeed, acknowledging the role of empire in colonial contexts provided justification for more careful control of Indigenous populations. In Australia, on the other hand, there was intransigence towards accepting the humanitarian critique. Indeed, it could be argued that one of the important outcomes of the 1937 conference of administrators in Australia was that it marginalised it. The problem, or even the potential threat, was not a colonised people but an Indigenous people.

On one reading, Bennett's campaign was steeped in irony. If we understand polygamy to be integral to the maintenance of Aboriginal society, then advocating its abolition was attacking the very thing she was trying to protect. However, Bennett had many friends, allies and informants within the Aboriginal community. Further, as a missionary teacher her activism was conceived in colonialism, yet what made her critique radical was its application in the Australian context. Unlike her British counterparts, Bennett was drawing a clear connection between the so-called slavery of Aboriginal women and colonialism, which had forever changed their lives. Her critique was not about Aboriginal women in their own cultures as such. It was about Aboriginal women caught in the net of culture contact. If colonisation had never occurred, Aboriginal women's lives would have gone on much the same as they had before, which Bennett maintained was better than the lives of women in British slums.[56]

What made Bennett's critique unique for its time was the fact that she identified and linked the gendered and racialised outcomes of colonial rule. She saw the 'Aboriginal problem' as a feminist issue because, at its base, it was about the rights and status of women as human beings. But it was also about a profound racism. Aborigines — men and women — were seen as cheap labour to be used up at will. Inter-war feminists acknowledged gender as important too. Yet on the whole, despite their genuine concern with the position of Aboriginal women, Australian feminists were ultimately less willing to acknowledge, much less be critical of, Australia's colonial legacy. Sisterhood had its limits. It was left to the St Joan's Social and Political Alliance to take the position of Aboriginal women in Australia to the international arena in 1937, where they suggested that Aboriginal women suffered from a double bondage and a slave status.

The inter-war feminists were hardly out of step with their society. Australian governments did not have to acknowledge their colonial legacies until the 1990s, following the formal legal acknowledgment of native title. When Bennett was staking her claims it was widely thought that there was no colonial inheritance in Australia to answer to. In this context, and like her counterparts in the African context, Bennett's interventions remained an annoying and troublesome interference. Yet what was at stake, she believed, was the preservation of the race. In its crudest sense the fate of the Aboriginal race depended on the fate of its women. Australian governments had long been accustomed to understanding the pivotal role of women in the health and regeneration of the race, and enacting policies designed to sanctify motherhood. However, this was towards the preservation of the white race and, in inter-war Australia, there was little interest in the preservation of 'the black'.

Notes

1. Mary Bennett to William Morley, 26 February 1939, papers of the Association for the Protection of Aborigines, series 7, University of Sydney Archives.

2. *Royal Commission appointed to investigate, report and advise on matters in relation to the condition and treatment of Aborigines*, 1934, Acc 1934/2, transcripts of evidence, AN 537, Royal Commissions, Acc 2922, State Archives of Western Australia (hereafter SAWA).

3. AN 537, Acc 2922, transcripts of evidence, SAWA.

4. McGregor 1997; Markus 1990; Paisley 2000; Holland 1999; Holland 2001b; Holland 1995; Holland 2001a; Reynolds.

5. McGregor 1997; McGregor 1993.

6. See in particular Lake 1999; Lake 1993; Lake 1996; Lake 1998; Lake 1994; Paisley 2000; Fiona Paisley 1993; Paisley 1995; Paisley 1997b; Paisley 1997a.

7. Holland. See works cited above.

8. For further context see Heather Goodall 1998b.

9. Minault 1982; Lind 1988; Burton 1994; Ware 1992a; Procida 2002; Midgley 1998.

10. Morris, HF & J S Read.

11. Bennett 1927a.

12. Bennett 1927b.

13. *Devadasi* was a practice in India where girl children were dedicated to temple prostitution, and the *mui-tsai* system in China and Hong Kong saw young girls adopted into servitude, sexual and otherwise.

14. Pateman; Midgley 1992; Ware 1992a; Rich; Burton 1994, pp. 75–89; Pascoe.

15. Pateman, p. 124.

16. Pascoe, p. 69.

17. Sweet, p. 336.

18. For a good discussion of the league see Paisley 2000, pp. 33–69.

19. Woollacott 2001, p. 137.

20. Burton 1994.

21. Holland 1999, pp. 68–105.

22. Sinha 1998.

23. Harris 1927.

24. Morris & Read, pp. 214–15.

25. Such a controversy was sparked by the Marriage Ordinances, introduced in British territories in 1902 to provide for the registration of Christian marriages among the indigenes. Not only was the legal framework

unsatisfactory, but the ordinances were in many cases anomalous. They were subject to problems and criticisms from within the administration. At the same time, educated African women were questioning their status under the law, while outside Africa groups like the St Joan's Alliance were stirring public opinion on the rights of African women.

26. Constance Cooke 1927.

27. Lecture by Mary Bennett to Women's Service Guilds, 11 December 1931, Rischbieth Papers, MS 2004/12/235–303, National Library of Australia.

28. 'Allegations by Mrs Mary Bennett in regard to native slavery and traffic in native women', AN 1/7, Department of Native Affairs and Native Welfare, Acc 993, 116/1932, SAWA.

29. Bell 1988.

30. Barwick 1978. For the Aboriginal perspective see Pepper 1980.

31. Bennett, 'Allegations…in regard to slavery'.

32. 'A call to the women of Australia to demand an honourable Native Policy', Rischbieth Papers, MS 2004/12/162, National Library of Australia.

33. Bennett 1930, p. 113.

34. Morgan 1986, p. 58.

35. Bennett 1935.

36. Scanlon 1986, p. 90.

37. Bennett, Moseley Royal Commission (1934), transcripts of evidence.

38. Bennett, Moseley Royal Commission (1934), transcripts of evidence.

39. Morgan 1986, pp. 106, 124.

40. Morgan 1986, p. 107.

41. Morgan 1986, p. 131.

42. Bell 1988, p. 350.

43. Scanlon 1986, p. 95; Berndt 1951.

44. Brock 1993, pp. 150–51.

45. Choo, Chapter 7, pp. 186–243.

46. Choo, p. 219.

47. Australia, Parliament 1937, *Aboriginal Welfare. Initial Conference of Commonwealth and State Aboriginal Authorities*.

48. Australia, Parliament 1937, *Aboriginal Welfare*, p. 11.

49. Australia, Parliament 1937, *Aboriginal Welfare*, p. 10.

50. Australia, Parliament 1937, *Aboriginal Welfare*, p. 11.

51. June Kitson 1933, 'Allegations of slavery by Mary Bennett', AN 1/7, Department of Native Affairs and Native Welfare, Acc 993, 116/1932, SAWA.

52. Morgan 1986, pp. 213–14.

53. Australia, Parliament 1937, *Aboriginal Welfare*, p. 12.

54. Kitson, 'Allegations of slavery'.

55. Petition to the president and members of the Royal Commission at Broome from the Half-Castes of Broome, MN 393, Women's Service Guilds, Welfare of Aborigines, Feb–Nov 1937.

56. Bennett 1930.

7. 'Would have known it by the smell of it'
Ella Hiscocks

Anna Cole

When Ella Hiscocks visited the Cootamundra Home for Aboriginal Girls in the early 1940s she recalled 'I would have known it by the smell of it.'[1] She had been to the girls' home once before, escorting a young Aboriginal girl there, and had not been impressed. Yet when offered the position of matron at the home by the Chairman of the Aborigines Welfare Board in 1945, she took it, reluctantly, for three months. She was under threat of a transfer 'way outback' by the Department of Education and, being recently widowed, was without recourse to her husband's income or to the role of wife of a station manager.[2] Hiscocks would retire a little over 20 years later, a story in the *Cootamundra Herald* noting she had become the home's longest serving matron.[3]

The Cootamundra Domestic Training Home for Aboriginal Girls, as it was officially known, was set up in 1911 in an old hospital just out of Cootamundra, a country town 380 kilometres south-west of Sydney. It was established as a 'training institution' for Aboriginal girls too young to be 'apprenticed' out to domestic service. It ran from 1911 until 1967 under the regime of first the Aborigines Protection Board and later the Aborigines Welfare Board.

The Aborigines Welfare Board

In 1939 the Aborigines Protection Board, which had overseen the removal of Aboriginal children since 1909, was replaced by the

Aborigines Welfare Board. Its new Chairman was Mr Alfred Lipscombe, ex-superintendent of Dr Barnardo's Homes and the author of *Breeding and management of livestock*.[4] The objective of 'assimilation' was formally added to the board's first annual report in this year. To decide on policy and make rulings that affected the day-to-day lives of Aboriginal people across the state, this board, made up of 11 male, non-Aboriginal bureaucrats, met for two hours each month in a central office in Sydney.

The new policy and administrative guidelines for the Aborigines Welfare Board were set out in a Public Service Board report which stipulated a 'more detailed administration and an increase in staff to enact comprehensive techniques of surveillance'.[5] In answering criticisms of Aborigines Protection Board staff and conditions made by Aboriginal and some feminist and humanitarian lobby groups, the Public Service Board report stressed the need for more detailed methods of surveillance, both of Aborigines Welfare Board staff *and* Aboriginal people.

Previously, staff had been employed as ministerial employees under the sole direction of the board. Under the new board, the superintendent and other employees were to be subject to the provisions of the *Public Service Act 1922* (Cwlth). This formalised staff employment and began the long process of mainstreaming the board within pre-existing structures of administration. Thus the Aborigines Welfare Board, responsible for administering the new official policy of assimilation, marked a period of increased bureaucratic standardisation.

One of the most immediate consequences of this reconstitution of the Aborigines 'Protection' to the Aborigines 'Welfare' Board for Aboriginal people, particularly those living on government stations, was an increase in bureaucratic procedures associated with the surveillance of the domestic sphere.[6] Under this new bureaucracy the management and control of Aboriginal girls and women, specifically the control and surveillance of their domestic arrangements, was an integral part of the new 'standardised practices' of administration.[7] Moves to regulate the work of managers and matrons on board stations and institutions were part of such attempts at standardisation. In 1940 the duties of both manager and matron were codified in the *Manual of instructions to managers and matrons of Aboriginal stations and other field officers*, which was distributed across New South Wales.[8] New report forms, to be filled out by managers and matrons daily, weekly and monthly, were introduced with the manual. The manual contained specific directives that codified the role matrons were expected to play in surveying and reporting on women's and children's behaviour. It was the matron's responsibility to report to head office about school attendance; the cleanliness of homes and bodies; attitudes towards housework; 'baby care' aptitude; the diet of mothers and children; the amount of instruction in sewing and domestic work, and the number of girls who attended these classes; as well as on 'leisure activities' of station residents. Institutions such as Cootamundra played a central role in these bureaucratic attempts to deeply interfere with and shape Aboriginal girls' and young women's domestic lives.

In the decades that followed the Second World War, white women increasingly worked as matrons at the Aborigines Welfare Board's children's institutions around the state of New South Wales, and on Aboriginal stations as 'lady' welfare officers, as teachers and nurses, and, later, as witnesses and government representatives at a parliamentary inquiry in the late 1960s, which contributed to the end of the board. Assumptions about their special responsibility for socialising Aboriginal women and children, educating them in cleanliness and hygiene and regulating sexuality interacted closely with post-war racial policy and contributed to women's central and largely forgotten role in the administrative and symbolic world of the New South Wales Aborigines Welfare Board.

While the board was attempting a new level of surveillance and bureaucratic control, it simultaneously experienced a reduction in its budget during the Second World War, and in the post-war era.[9] One way to fill the gap between the extended policy and the shrinking budget was to increase the unpaid workload of female employees of the administration.[10] Thus these assumptions about the role that white women could play at what was considered the racial 'boundary' between Aboriginal and non-Aboriginal communities — training for assimilation by monitoring the domestic sphere of Aboriginal lives — interacted with an administrative stress on increased surveillance at a time of budgetary cutbacks.

Working women, such as Matron Hiscocks, did not leave collections of letters or journals for future historians, as did many of their better-off, middle-class reformist contemporaries. Their days were filled with attempts to 'fight dirt', order domestic environments, 'train' and educate Aboriginal women and children, and, in some instances, openly criticise the board's authority. But these women's historical traces, as left in the official record and in interviews, are particularly revealing of the different ways ideas about the mission of white femininity cross-cut with racial administration and the government's efforts to order the domestic worlds of Aboriginal families and communities.[11]

Matron Ella Hiscocks

Hundreds of Aboriginal girls and young women passed through the institution at Cootamundra under the authority of the Protection and Welfare boards. The home is remembered today with pain, grief and mixed emotions by many who were sent there.[12] Matron Ella Hiscocks' life and work for the board embodied some of the inherent contradictions in its policy and administration, and its attempts at increased bureaucratic control alongside a limited budget. This is reflected in her ambivalent memories of the place. Through Hiscocks' ambiguous position we can see how women's roles as board employees and their perceived special responsibility as 'protectors' and 'carers' were fundamentally irreconcilable. Played out unhappily in the life and work of Hiscocks is the essential incompatibility between her role as 'surrogate mother' to hundreds of Aboriginal girls and her wider role in a state-sanctioned policy of enforced 'assimilation' and the attempted destruction of Aboriginal family life. Reconstructing the working life of Hiscocks may help our understanding of the ideology and circumstances under which ordinary, 'good' women came to work for, and rationalise, what we know now to be extraordinarily brutal ends, with ongoing repercussions for Aboriginal families and communities today.

***

Ella Hiscocks was born in rural New South Wales in 1901 and began her career in 1922 as a teacher in the segregated school at the Pilliga Aboriginal Reserve, in the north-west of the state. She lived alone in town, riding out each day on a bicycle to the Aboriginal reserve. Her work at Pilliga as a young, unmarried woman gave her a lasting impression of conditions experienced on the Aborigines Protection Board reserves during the 1920s. Her memories of the people she met and worked with at that time recall the impoverishment and ill-health experienced by residents. She remembered that many of the Aboriginal people at the reserve were 'half-starved'. These first-hand impressions of conditions on Aboriginal reserves contributed in future years to her ambivalent relationship with the administration during the course of her career with the board.

From the Pilliga reserve school, she moved to an Aboriginal settlement near Lismore and was again put in charge of the school there. She married soon after. As she remembers, it was partly because of her influence that her husband, a farmer's son with little prior involvement with Aboriginal people and no formal training in book-keeping, became manager of an Aboriginal station south of Quirindi.[13] The employment of inexperienced and unqualified men like Hiscocks' husband reflected the idea held by the Protection and Welfare boards that white people possessed racialised skills for living which they could pass on to Aboriginal people. Ella became the station's matron: ironically, a position open to her exclusively because of her status as wife of the manager. The Aborigines Welfare Board at that time only employed women as station matrons if they were married to the manager. As an ex-matron from Brewarrina Station recalls: 'We were a package deal.'[14] Station matrons were paid for only three or four hours a day but were expected to be on call at all hours and overall received considerably less than their manager husbands.[15] In particular, matrons were expected to take special responsibility for monitoring and reporting on Aboriginal women and children in their homes, or 'dwellings' as they were more often referred to in board reports and correspondence.

From Quirindi the board moved the Hiscocks husband and wife team to Cumeroogunga, where they stayed for three years. When Ella's husband died prematurely from a ruptured appendix she returned to work as a teacher at the Aboriginal school in Lismore, the position of station matron no longer open to her as a single woman. Over the next few years, she taught at Aboriginal segregated schools in Lismore, Tuncester, Yass and Coraki.[16] It was during a visit Hiscocks made to the Cootamundra Girls' Home in 1945 that Alfred Lipscombe, the Chairman of the Aborigines Welfare Board, asked her to fill in at the home for three months.[17]

Working for the board

The welfare caused us so much loss and pain. When can we start our grieving? How long are we going to have to grieve? And sometimes I think about how they don't want to spend any money to put things right — but how much did they spend taking the kids away? How much did it cost them? How many of them got jobs and supported their families by taking ours away?[18]

The job of matron-in-charge at the board's Cootamundra Girls' Home was one of the most significant roles played by a non-Aboriginal woman working for the 'Aboriginal' administration. In recognition of her work among Aboriginal children, Matron Hiscocks was awarded an MBE at the end of her career.[19] Ex-inmates of the home remember her 'work among Aboriginal children' differently.[20] Many have mixed memories of Hiscocks, who acted partly as a 'surrogate mother' to hundreds of Aboriginal girls removed from their parents. Betty Ellis, in Cootamundra from the ages of three to 15, has 'good and bad' memories of Hiscocks: 'She was strict, very distant...didn't have much rapport with the girls. "I'm the Matron and you're the girls"... that sort of thing.' But, Ellis concluded, 'the only way to live is to forgive'. She attended Ella Hiscocks' funeral in 1998 and estimated that about 50 other ex-Coota girls turned up as well. One former Cootamundra girl, now a woman in her 50s, asked me not to be too hard on Hiscocks. 'She was only trying to do her best,' she urged me to remember.[21]

During her time as matron of the Cootamundra home, Ella Hiscocks adopted an Aboriginal ward, who had been removed from her family and placed in the home at the age of five months.[22] A memory retained by the girl, now a grown woman, is from about the age of five. Each night before she went to bed the matron would sit with her and make her pull her nose: '...stroke my nose down the side saying it would make it straight'.[23] This intimate example is a clue to the ways in which the rationale that led to the establishment of homes such as Cootamundra infused the daily actions and interactions of the board's employees. Individuals working for the administration may have believed themselves to be 'humane' in their relationships with Aboriginal wards, yet in their day-to-day work, and in their attitudes towards Aboriginality, they contributed to a daily undermining of the self-esteem and identity of the children and young adults in their care.

More overtly, memories of Hiscocks' humanity are matched with accounts of emotional abuse and the unremitting repression and deprivation experienced under her strict rule.[24] Others remember physical punishments, restrictions and a harsh authoritarianism. One woman told how as an adult she had finally 'forgiven Matron' who had 'held her spirit captive all her adult life'. She visited Hiscocks, by then in a state of advanced senile dementia, in a nursing home in Cootamundra in 1998.

'She lies there now looking very undignified,' recalled the ex-ward of the state with relief.[25]

***

In an interview recorded in 1980 with historian Peter Read, Ella Hiscocks stressed her disagreements and frustrations with the Sydney-based Aborigines Welfare Board and the miserable economic conditions she had worked under in the 1940s through to the 1960s. Describing the exhausting and ceaseless nature of her work, Hiscocks presented herself as a victim of the board's limited budget and their insistence on time-consuming bureaucratic processes. The long hours she worked, her heavy workload, the isolated geographic location of the home and the slow bureaucratic procedures associated with the centralised board were her main recollections of her working life. She remembered herself alone in her special responsibilities, stressing that while all the other staff would only work their set hours she was on call 'night and day'.[26]

Hiscocks remembered in particular the way the bureaucratic processes of the board interacted with the mainstream, 'white', welfare administration to frustrate her efforts to improve life for the girls at the home. The supply of both food and clothing at Cootamundra came from the mainstream state welfare agencies.[27] Food was ordered each week from a central government store, and each week Hiscocks had to submit quotes for each individual item.[28] This over-complicated the process of buying food, which could, if Matron Hiscocks had been entrusted with her own account, have been bought more simply in the nearby town of Cootamundra. The Prisons Department supplied the girls with clothing, which was of poor quality and inappropriate. Shoes, for example, were frequently too big and Hiscocks recalls that on more than one occasion they 'didn't match up'.[29]

Even in organising sport and recreation for the girls Hiscocks remembers being hamstrung by a central bureaucracy: 'I'll tell you something else that made me mad...the children liked sport and I had to send down to the Board for permission to take them anywhere... They'd take a long time to get back...sometimes the children would miss out because of it.'[30]

But direct criticism of board members, or policy itself, was not part of the matron's discourse. A widow throughout the 22 years she worked at Cootamundra, Hiscocks remembered fondly some of the men working for the board. Inspector Donaldson, loathed and feared among Aboriginal people throughout New South Wales for his tactics of child abduction, was, in her estimation, 'a fine old gentleman...did very good work amongst them'. (Her husband had applied for the job of inspector held by Donaldson, but died before he could begin.)[31]

Ella Hiscocks with a 15-month-old 'inmate' of the Cootamundra Girls' Home. Cootamundra Herald, *22 March 1967. National Library of Australia.*

Her loyalty and evident fondness of the men working for the board sit in an ambivalent relationship to the anger and frustration evident in her memories of the ceaseless workload, the slowness of the central bureaucracy to support her basic needs, her lack of financial autonomy, and her persistent sense of isolation from the Sydney-based administration.

Working far from the board's headquarters, Hiscocks formed allegiances outside the central administration. In seeking to improve the clothing ration, for example, the matron turned to the local town doctor, prevailing upon him, unsuccessfully, to add his weight to her complaints to the board about the poor quality of clothing issued to the girls at the home.[32] Hiscocks did receive support from locally based women's groups during her employment at Cootamundra. On her retirement, she praised the Cootamundra section of the Business and Professional Women's Association, the Country Women's Association and the Church of England's Women's Guild. Of these organisations Hiscocks said: 'I only had to mention something I wanted, and one or more organisation would respond.'[33] This support from local women's groups indicates, significantly, both an awareness and an endorsement of the work of the Cootamundra Girls' Home among prominent women in the rural community surrounding

Cootamundra.[34] This endorsement is today largely un-remembered, and forms part of a deep seam of shame and denial that lies at the heart of contemporary Australian race relations.

The home itself, in the old town hospital, engendered well-remembered feelings of isolation. The schoolroom where Hiscocks taught each day had been the isolation ward of the hospital and she remembered with dismay how ill-equipped and under-resourced it was: 'It was terrible... It was a terrible job to try and work it on your own.'[35] Aboriginal women incarcerated in the institution as young girls also recall their associations of the isolation of the old hospital with sickness and death.[36] Some recalled that one of the most feared punishments was being locked alone in what was believed to have been the old hospital morgue.[37] Rumours about bodies being found underneath the old storeroom where they kept the food still circulate today.[38] Several women recall being traumatised as girls by long hours spent locked there as punishment by Hiscocks and other staff members.[39]

Clean and moral

> Keep your bodies and minds clean, for by doing so you will help to form a wholesome personality. Assume the dignity and carriage, which are your heritage and your right.
> — Mrs Irene 'Inspector' English,
> Aborigines Welfare Board, 1955[40]

Amid Matron Hiscocks' complaints about the poverty of the administration and her ceaseless workload, two key, interrelated themes emerge from her memories that highlight the interaction of racial and gendered discourse: 'cleanliness' and 'morality'. Allusions to these and to the possibility of Aboriginal girls 'going bad' or 'getting into trouble with the opposite sex' proliferate in her accounts of home life.[41]

From her first impressions — that she would have 'known it by the smell of it' — Hiscocks ordered her memories of her work at the home through a sensory prism of cleanliness. Cleanliness, in Hiscock's world, was next to whiteness. During her time at the home she conducted a concerted campaign to get the Aboriginal girls from the home accepted at the local 'white' state school. Like the majority of schools around the state at the time, Cootamundra's was segregated when Hiscocks became matron of the home, and Aboriginal girls in her care had to be schooled at the home, in their 'under-resourced school room'. Hiscocks lobbied the principal of the local high school, the local Parents and Citizens group and the Department of Education's school inspector until she was successful in convincing the school to take the fifth- and sixth-form girls, and eventually (in 1950) girls of all ages.[42] One of her most persistent and persuasive arguments for why the school should take the girls, said Hiscocks, was that 'her girls' were as 'clean as local white girls'. In her recollection, she finally got the girls accepted at the local school after she had asked the school inspector: 'why the students can't attend the local school. They're *cleaner* [my emphasis] than a lot of the white girls.'[43]

In framing her argument to the school inspector in these terms, Hiscocks was engaging in what anthropologist Mary Douglas calls a 'dialogue of claims and counter-claims to status' in which ideas about cleanliness, dirt and pollution are crucial.[44] Wherever ideas of dirt are prominent, argues Douglas, their analysis discloses a play upon 'profound themes'. Reflection on dirt involves, among other things, reflection on the relation of 'order to disorder…form to formlessness'.[45] In Douglas's well-known summation: dirt is 'matter out of place'.[46] 'Dirt then, is never a unique, isolated event. Where there is dirt there is a system. Dirt is the by-product of a systematic ordering and classification of matter, in so far as ordering involves rejecting inappropriate elements.'[47]

As an agent of the state, Matron Hiscocks' memories of and associations with cleanliness and dirt are revealing of the system of beliefs at the core of the assimilationist policies and practices enacted haphazardly, but ruthlessly, by the Aborigines Welfare Board. The matron's exhausting, and futile, efforts to keep the young Aboriginal girls at Cootamundra clean and free from dirt coincided with a bureaucratic system that identified black as dirty and in need of expunging and assimilating into a 'clean' white culture and identity. Her particular role in the production and demarcation of boundaries between white and black, clean and dirty, coincided both with the broader assimilationist project and with ideas about white femininity.

Cleaning was women's work and in the racialised discourse about the 'deprivation' and 'filth' of Aboriginality Matron Hiscocks' work was never done. Anything that increased the level of 'dirt' also increased the workload of the matron, whose job it was to 'clean' the Aboriginal girls to make them acceptable to white society. She remembered angrily that to get to school each morning the board supplied the home with an old covered truck, 'like they used in the war'.[48] Each morning on the way to school the dust thrown up on the children in the back of the open truck threatened Matron's tireless efforts to keep them clean.

When he interviewed her in the 1980s Peter Read suggested to Hiscocks that in winter the girls must have been cold on the back of the open truck. She seemed angry at this line of questioning and cut short his comment with: 'You know what the dust is like. By the time they got down to school their navy blue tunics would be grey.'[49] Her response shows something of the way that, in Douglas's words, 'uncleanness or dirt is that which must not be included if a pattern is to be maintained'.[50] Paradoxically, in this instance it is the dirt that works to maintain that pattern. The 'pattern' in this instance was Hiscocks' belief that the 'polluting' factor that interrupted her best efforts to uplift the girls was the random element of dust or dirt. Yet at the same time as Matron was working ceaselessly to 'civilise' and whiten the girls in her care, stroking their Aboriginal noses to turn them straight, constantly checking their cleanliness, these same girls were driven into town on the open back of the truck, like cattle, like 'blacks'. In this case questioning her about the girls' experience of the cold seemed to disturb Matron Hiscocks' reminiscences of her own victimisation at the hands of the inefficient Aborigines Welfare Board.

Her constant fight against dust and dirt thus represented for Hiscocks an ideological struggle that was inseparable from her real struggle against the deprivation and endless work she was required to do in the home. Matron strove hard to participate in the constant cleaning and reordering of the identities of the wards of the state entrusted to her surveillance and supervision. In chasing dirt, in constantly seeking to tidy, the matron was not simply governed by an anxiety to purify; she was attempting to positively reorder her environment, and the girls' identity, to make both conform to an ideal of white female domesticity, an ideal promoted by the government and its agencies as the key to the 'successful assimilation' of Aboriginal people.[51] Finally, her futile struggle against dirt symbolises the inevitable exclusion and isolation from mainstream society of both the Aboriginal girls in her care and the matron herself.

Throwing her to the dogs

As with her constant battle against 'dirt', the pressures of work within an inefficient bureaucracy frustrated the matron in her efforts to maintain strict supervision over the 'moral welfare' and the sexual experiences of her charges. One of Hiscocks' duties, as the only employee at the home who could drive, was to travel out to country stations to meet prospective employers of young domestic service 'apprentices' who had reached the age of 15. She remembered that due to work pressures at the home she had to abandon the practice of interviewing prospective employers before taking the young 'apprentice' to work for them: 'In the end I'd take the girl out with me and if everything was in order I'd leave her there.'[52] She remembered only one occasion where she decided against leaving the young woman. Asked if she ever got the feeling the young apprentices were overworked or abused in some way, she replied flatly, 'no'.

Ex-apprentices sent out to work as domestic servants recall that often the matron was the only contact outside the household whom they could tell of the physical and often sexual abuse they experienced in these positions.[53] While Hiscocks' workload mitigated against her enforcing the high 'moral standards' she was expected to oversee, she expressed a real interest in the role she sought to play in 'reforming the girls'. She recalled in detail the time she was instructed to accompany a young woman to a remote Aboriginal station, where she was to be left in punishment for repeatedly running away from domestic service positions. Hiscocks remembered her own distress, as well as the young woman's. The apprentice, Hiscocks remembered, 'cried all night' and Matron 'cried too'. By morning she had decided, in a rare moment of open disobedience to the board, to refuse to leave the young woman at the Aboriginal station. In explaining her actions years later she said: 'I couldn't have left her...I would have felt like I was throwing her to the dogs. She was just of that age and all the boys would have been after her.'[54]

Ex-apprentices have since told how being returned to an Aboriginal station, although disorienting and frightening after years away, provided a desperately missed sense of family and community after the isolation and exploitation of institutionalisation and domestic service.[55] But Hiscocks saw the removal of young Aboriginal girls from sexual threat as one of the main reasons they were taken from their Aboriginal communities.[56] In this case, instead of 'throwing her to the dogs' Hiscocks was motivated enough to send the young woman to work once again as a domestic servant for a friend of hers in an isolated country location.

Matron's perception of a predatory Aboriginal male sexuality on Aboriginal stations reflected a common racist perception of Aboriginal men. Her tears are perhaps revealing of her misguided and merged identity with the young Aboriginal children and women in her charge. Yet Hiscocks' fears about Aboriginal stations and reserves, expressed in sexual terms, are contradicted by her own experience of working on similar Aboriginal stations before she was married: 'Very seldom…you'd come across a girl who'd get in trouble on the settlement and have an infant or anything like that you know. The law amongst them was very strict on that count.'[57]

And while official statements of assimilation policy stressed the importance of training Aboriginal women to 'merge' with whites, Hiscocks contradicted her expressed fears about Aboriginal men by remarking: 'The pity is few of them marry the dark men. You know the full bloods are very upstanding. I know only one girl who married a dark man, he was a Kinchela boy.'[58] Hiscocks appeared to have had no broader understanding of the gendered nature of the government's assimilationist child removal policy, nor of the board's long-term cultural and social purpose in removing girls from their communities.[59]

To justify the separation of Aboriginal girls from their mothers, Hiscocks relied on nostalgic recollections of the 'progress' made by 'her' girls and on ambivalent, but largely negative, attitudes towards Aboriginal mothering; for example, in the following confused but grudging acknowledgment of the importance of their Aboriginal mothers to 'her' girls:

> One girl, she became a trained nurse…her mother came, she was a terrible woman, but she came to the Home and that girl saw her coming up the path and ran towards her and threw her arms around her and made such a fuss of her…she's still a mother you see…but that girl, afterwards she worked with the Flying Doctors as a nurse for a long while.[60]

In this recollection the powerful emotions expressed by the daughter for the 'terrible woman' were not as important as her success and individual progress as a nurse with the Flying Doctors. In another instance, reflecting on the role of the board in removing children from Aboriginal stations, Hiscocks remarked: 'The parents were never asked. The police would come and take the girls…it was a terrible thing to have done.'[61]

The confusion between her own experience working in Aboriginal communities and the pervasive ideology, which emphasised Aboriginal women's worthlessness as mothers, the dangers of 'moral degradation', and the predatory nature of Aboriginal male sexuality, formed a contradictory mix in the matron's memories. Describing her time as a teacher on Aboriginal reserves, she remarked:

> ...that's one thing with a settlement, you never saw any of
> them being thrashed. The only unkindness was there was no
> food and that wasn't their fault. There was no food...a lot of
> malnutrition. You were restricted; you couldn't give the people
> rations except the old people unless they were working on the
> settlement; there was no money around anywhere those days.[62]

Her lived experience of Aboriginal communities was continually contradicted by a belief system in which Aboriginality was an inferior identity, and whiteness the goal. Asked again about the causes of malnutrition among the Aboriginal people she worked with, she replied it was because 'they only thought of today'. And finally, despite her own experiences of life on Aboriginal reserves which she contrasted favourably with institutional life, she concluded ambivalently in the late 1960s:

> I do not think that any institution can equal the natural home
> life. But these children are not getting a natural home life.
> Because dark people naturally live unto the day they do not
> look after tomorrow even, and very often they would be
> hungry and they would not get a natural life in that respect. I
> think they are very much better off in an institution than they
> would be in some of their home lives.[63]

Ending up in bother

A year before she retired from the Cootamundra Girls' Home, Hiscocks came before the Joint Select Committee of the Legislative Council and Legislative Assembly upon Aborigines' Welfare, which toured New South Wales in 1966.[64] The theme of young Aboriginal women's sexuality is a persistent trope here in both the matron's recollections of her role and records stemming from the wider administrative and political world in which she worked. The questions and answers exchanged by Hiscocks and the parliamentary representatives provide evidence for the argument made in recent postcolonial scholarship that sexual control is fundamental to the way racial policies are secured and administrative projects carried out.[65] The committee sought an efficient, 'modern' and mechanistic way of dealing with what appeared to them to be a self-evident 'problem': the sexuality of single Aboriginal women. As one committee member explained it: 'These girls are going to Sydney, finding a job and ending up in bother... Where is this thing to be tackled? What machinery have we set up to give these girls guidance?'

At the inquiry they asked Hiscocks to comment on what happened to the girls after they left the Cootamundra home. Hiscocks answered that 'all the girls' ended up pregnant within a short time: 'The same thing happens to the whole lot of them, they go to Sydney and in no time they are in trouble, as I told you, and the baby arrives.' When asked if the fathers were 'white boys', Hiscocks replied, '...mostly the whites, a terrible lot of the sailors I think. They meet every boat that comes in pretty well.' In another question and answer, Hiscocks explained that it was the lecherousness of men that created the circumstances under which the young women got pregnant: '...you only have to get on a train, and a few men will get in the train and they will never let up on them if you are not with them...they are only prey for the men there.'[66]

In their attempt to find an explanation for what they referred to as the girls' 'moral degeneration' upon leaving the home, members of the parliamentary inquiry ignored Hiscocks' perhaps controversial suggestion that some white men seemed to show an overtly sexualised interest in young Aboriginal women.[67] In the ensuing questions and answers they concluded dismissively that the number of girls 'getting into bother' was tied up with intellectual capacity and the fact that 'most [A]borigines are amoral not immoral'.[68]Hiscocks then seemed to dismiss her earlier opinion that the attitudes and behaviour of white men were largely to blame for much of the 'bother' the girls got themselves in, and instead put forward a culturally essentialist explanation of the young women's high pregnancy rates, concluding confidently that 'amongst [A]borigines themselves there is no courtship... I do not think it worries them at all'.[69] Thus the matron constructed herself as someone fighting a battle that could not be won — not simply against the indifference of the authorities and the base lusts of exploitative men, but against Aboriginal nature itself. In doing so she successfully avoided confronting the central role she herself played as a board employee in perpetuating and administering the very situation in which Aboriginal women were most vulnerable.

Hiscocks' statements reflect a consciousness caught between rationalisation of the board's policies and the role she played in the separation of children from their families, and a different understanding of Aboriginal communities gained from her years in the field. Ambivalent and sometimes contradictory statements are frequent in Hiscocks' recorded testimony before the government committee in 1966, at the

Matron Ella Hiscocks with her adopted daughter Coral Edwards. Cootamundra Herald, *22 March 1967.* National Library of Australia.

end of her long career, perhaps underlining her own confusion and, crucially, the inherent ambiguities of her position within the administration. She was part of a system that believed Aboriginality itself was an aberrant condition to be replaced with an 'assimilated' identity suitable for white society, yet her own emotional connection to the 'girls' in her care, particularly her adopted Aboriginal daughter, and her previous experience as a single woman working on Aboriginal reserves conflicted with her official role. This testimony and her memories of her time at the home reflect and enact the particular shifting intersections between 'race', 'class' and 'gender' as they were lived and understood by a woman at the bureaucratic 'front line'.

Hiscocks embodied some of the most abiding contradictions in the 'colonial' administration's economy of white female labour. She was protected by racial privilege but not by economic security. She felt inferior in the gender and class hierarchy of the central administration, as shown by her memories of being constantly frustrated by them, and the fact she never had her own bank account for the home, but apparently felt superior in the racial hierarchy. She lodged among 'black girls', on their way to a life of unpaid domestic service, but she was not one with them. The isolation experienced by the matron, the neglect by central office, and the indignity of having to rely on outside state agencies made her, in her working life, in many ways an abject figure. Marginal but necessary to the colonial state, she represents some of the boundaries and limits of women's role in the 'domestication of colonisation'.[70]

Notes

A different version of this chapter appears in *Aboriginal History*, vol. 27, 2003, pp. 146–62.

1. Ella Hiscocks in a taped interview with PJ Read, 1980 (hereafter Read interview), lodged at Australian Institute of Aboriginal & Torres Strait Islander Studies (AIATSIS), Canberra.
2. Aborigines Welfare Board Minutes (hereafter AWB Minutes), 25 April 1945, 4/8544, Archives Office of New South Wales (AONSW), Sydney.
3. 'Final episode in outstanding woman's story', *Cootamundra Herald*, 22 March 1967, p. 1.
4. 'Aboriginal welfare: superintendent appointed', *Sydney Morning Herald*, 9 February 1939.
5. NSW Public Service Board, *Aborigines protection*, report and recommendations of the Public Service Board of New South Wales, 1938, Government Printer, Sydney, 1940, p. 14.
6. See Goodall 1995. For further discussion of related points see also Bartlett, pp. 10–37.
7. Goodall 1995; Cole 2000.
8. NSW Public Service Board, *Aborigines protection*.
9. AWB Minutes, Item 13, 11/1945, AONSW, Sydney, p. 332.
10. See Cole 2000.
11. Explored in the larger project from which this chapter was drawn, through weekly reports of station matrons, the recorded memories of Matron Hiscocks and the critical correspondence of two school teachers at the Kinchela Home for Aboriginal Boys.
12. See Human Rights and Equal Opportunities Commission 1997.
13. AWB Station Reports and Returns, 1942–48, Cootamundra Monthly Returns, 4/10747.4, AONSW, Sydney; Read interview.
14. Taped interview with Amy Cockburn, ex-matron of Brewarrina Aboriginal Station, Newcastle, 20 November 1997, in possession of the author.

15. In 1940, for example, the manager at Cumeroogunga was paid £304 per annum. The matron's annual salary was £25. NSW Public Service Board, *Aborigines protection*, report and recommendations of the Public Service Board of New South Wales, 1938, Appendix A, 'Administrative staff', Government Printer, Sydney, 1940, pp. 37–38.
16. State School Records, SR 10/6626, 110/7912, 10/8262.2, 10/5528, AONSW, Sydney.
17. Read interview; AWB Minutes, 16 February 1945, 4/8544, AONSW, Sydney.
18. Link-up & Wilson, p. 12.
19. *Cootamundra Herald*, 22 March 1967, p. 1.
20. Anna Cole, interview with former Cootamundra Girls Home resident (name withheld), 12 November 1998, tape in possession of the author; Debra Jopson, 'Home ties', *Sydney Morning Herald*, 19 May 1998, p. 13; personal testimonies in Hankins 1982 and Link-up & Wilson.
21. Mary Perry, email conversation with the author, 19 March 2003.
22. *Cootamundra Herald*, 22 March 1967, p. 1.
23. Interview conducted by CE Hankins. See Hankins 1982, p. 4.5.5.
24. Hankins 1982, pp. 4.4.1–4.4.8.
25. Jopson, 'Home ties'.
26. Read interview.
27. AWB Station Reports & Returns, Cootamundra Monthly Returns, 1947–1948, 4/10745.2, AONSW, Sydney.
28. AWB Station Reports & Returns, Cootamundra, Monthly Returns, 1947–1948, 4/10745.2, AONSW, Sydney.
29. Read interview.
30. Read interview.
31. Horner 1994, pp. 7, 18; Hankins 1982, p. 2.1.13.
32. Read interview; see AWB Minutes, 1949, item 4, 'Matron's request', 4/8545, AONSW, Sydney.
33. *Cootamundra Herald*, 22 March 1967, p. 1.
34. Evangelical groups operating in the 1930s, such as the Oxford Group, were also known to take an interest in and visit the Cootamundra home. See Haskins 1998b, pp. 224–25. One Cootamundra inmate later told a researcher: 'Most of the time we wished that someone would come like [an] official or something, because we had a real Sunday dinner.' Cited in Hankins 1982, p. 4.3.10.
35. Read interview.
36. Anna Cole, interviews with former Cootamundra home residents (names withheld), 12 & 22 November 1998, tape in possession of the author; Jopson, 'Home ties'; personal testimonies in Hankins 1982 and Link-up & Wilson.
37. A small building some distance from the main building was generally believed by the girls at the institution to be the hospital's old morgue. See Hankins 1982, p. 4.4.3.

38. Betty Ellis, telephone interview with author, 12 March 2003.
39. Hankins 1982, p. 2.1.13.
40. 'Message to our people', *Dawn: A Magazine for the Aboriginal People of NSW*, March 1955, p. 2.
41. Read interview; Matron Hiscocks at NSW Joint Select Committee upon Aborigines Welfare, 1965–67, 4th session of 41st parliament, NSW Joint Volumes of Papers, vol. 5, NQ 3228.94401 8, State Library of NSW, Sydney.
42. Read interview, 1980; AWB Minutes, 13 April 1948, 4/8545, and 25 April 1949, 4/8545, AONSW, Sydney.
43. Read interview.
44. Douglas 1984, p. 3.
45. Douglas 1984, p. 44.
46. Douglas 1984, p. 3.
47. Douglas 1984, p. 35.
48. Read interview.
49. Read interview.
50. Douglas 1984, p. 40.
51. Goodall 1995; Bartlett.
52. Read interview.
53. Interview VG (name withheld), 7 October 1994; personal testimonies in Hankins 1982 and Link-up & Wilson; Tucker.
54. Read interview.
55. Haskins 1998b.
56. Read interview.
57. Read interview.
58. Read interview.
59. For work on the gendered nature of the removal and assimilation policies, see Goodall 1995, pp. 75–191; Goodall 1990; Walden 1995, pp. 196–207; Haskins 1998c; Austin 1990; Huggins 1988; Ruddick, Mills & Austin 1989; Patricia Jacobs 1986; Hankins 1982.
60. Read interview.
61. Read interview.
62. Read interview.
63. Read interview.
64. NSW Joint Select Committee upon Aborigines Welfare, 1965–67, 4th session of 41st parliament, NSW Joint Volumes of Papers, vol. 5, NQ 3228.94401 8, State Library of NSW, Sydney
65. McClintock 1997; Stoler 1997; Stoler 1989; Summers 1991.
66. Hiscocks at NSW Joint Select Committee, 1966, p. 9165.
67. Hiscocks at NSW Joint Select Committee, 1966, pp. 9094–9276.
68. Hiscocks at NSW Joint Select Committee, 1966, p. 9019.
69. Hiscocks at NSW Joint Select Committee, 1966, pp. 599–605.
70. On similarities with role of white governesses in South African colonies, see McClintock 1997, pp. 258–300.

8. 'For a brighter day'
Constance Ternent Cooke

Fiona Paisley

In 1926, Constance Ternent Cooke travelled on the recently extended north–south railway to see Aboriginal conditions for herself. Describing her Central Australian fact-finding mission two years later at an international women's conference in London, she reported her deep shock at seeing Aboriginal women, men and children starving in camps along the line. 'I was appalled by the misery, want and degradation that I saw,' she said. 'I felt ashamed of our treatment of these original owners of the land.'[1] For Cooke, unregulated white contact with Aboriginal people, their communities and families constituted a shameful aspect of Aboriginal affairs, a reality that few urban-living white Australians witnessed first-hand, and one most preferred to ignore. In Cooke's case, shame would turn to action. The desire to awaken the conscience of the nation to the conditions faced by many Aboriginal people inspired Cooke to several decades of activism in Australia and around the world.

By the time Cooke made her Central Australian trip, her interest in Aboriginal people already had begun to dominate her life. Five years earlier she had become a women's rights activist in the Women's Non-Party Association of South Australia, an organisation affiliated with the newly formed national Australian Federation of Women Voters. From the early 1920s, both these bodies included Aboriginal women's rights in their agenda — to no small degree through Cooke's influence. The year of her visit to Alice Springs, 1926, marked her increasing focus on Aboriginal rights as she joined the newly formed Aborigines

Protection League, a white humanitarian organisation calling for large tracts of land to be provided for Aboriginal use. One year later she brought her specialised knowledge of Aboriginal issues to international women's and humanitarian networks based in London when she spoke on the Aboriginal question, particularly the status and conditions of Aboriginal women, at the London-based dominion women's British Commonwealth League conference, and then at a meeting of the Anti-Slavery and Aborigines' Protection Society. These were incredibly busy and important years for Cooke as she circulated information about Australian Aboriginal conditions to a growing international as well as local and national audience.

What motivated a woman like Cooke? Rejecting the idea that white women were naturally concerned for Indigenous rights during the inter-war years (or before and since), the exact source for her life of activism remains hard to identify. Cooke did not write about her own activist career, so we can only guess at how she might have reflected on her achievements. Without the luxury of her own interpretation, Cooke's story can best be appreciated as one of activity and determination. Unapologetically, therefore, this chapter focuses on the 'what and how' than on the 'why' of her activism. It does not speak for the inner voice of its protagonists, white or black. In this sense it is at odds with many recent studies of white women in the colonies, that set out to investigate their opposition to and/or complicity with the brutalising effects of colonialism,[2] an approach problematic for its bifurcation of white women's agency as either good or bad, as well as for its preclusion of the agency of non-white women and men.[3] This chapter, then, aims to show the contingent and practical elements in alternative politics, as well as to make it clear that Aboriginal people are crucial in understanding the radical quality of Cooke's politics.

While Cooke was one of a cohort of white Australian women who became outspoken campaigners for the reform of Aboriginal policy during the inter-war years, in several ways she was unique among their number.[4] Firstly, she conceived of the immediate inclusion of Aboriginal people within the nation. This conception of diversity within unity was not widely accepted until after 1967, when a referendum led to a change in the Constitution so that Aboriginal people, previously excluded, were counted in the national census.[5] Secondly, despite her frequently harsh criticisms of racial policy and racialist attitudes in Australia, she was to become a widely respected expert who maintained her women's activism while accepting a government appointment. Considered one of Australia's leading experts in Aboriginal affairs, Cooke was invited by the federal government in 1929 to participate in a conference on the Aboriginal question. The same year, she was appointed to a select group of predominantly white male experts on the South Australian government's Advisory Council of Aborigines. Strikingly, Cooke remained critical of Aboriginal policy even as she worked within its parameters as a government adviser.

Because of her dual status as reform activist and government employee, Cooke is an important crossover figure in the history of Aboriginal rights. Determined to help make 'a brighter day' for the original owners of the land, Cooke worked assiduously locally, nationally and internationally over several decades in both government and non-government organisations.[6] She brought to inter-war humanitarian and feminist politics her awareness of Aboriginal claims for land and self-determination: claims reinforced by her work for the South Australian Government as an inspector of local missions from the late 1920s. In turn, she applied her already formed focus on Aboriginal women's rights to her government work. Her dual agenda was grounded in the exchanges she had with Aboriginal people, whether indirectly through a train window in the outback, or directly as a visitor to their communities. While she was ready to work for incremental change in government policy, however small, Cooke continued to seek out reform groups sharing her hopes for a dramatic change in Aboriginal affairs in Australia. But this complex, even pragmatic, existence had its fair share of disappointments. Her vision of a just future for Aboriginal people outgrew the peak women's organisation of her day, the Australian Federation of Women Voters. By the mid-1930s, she had pushed well beyond the limits of white women's politics on 'race' in Australia.

Wherever and however Cooke pursued Aboriginal rights, she applied her formidable energies, and she could be tireless in her determination. JB Cleland, her future colleague on the South Australian Advisory Council and a leading Australian anthropologist (he later became Professor of Anthropology at Adelaide University), quipped that Cooke's middle name ought to have been 'Tenacious'. (It was a remark delivered with affectionate humour, but no doubt also a degree of exasperation.)[7] The seeds of this tenacity were sown early. When Cooke was a young woman (she later reported), an unnamed anthropologist had warned her of the imminent demise of the Aboriginal race, adding that reserves would provide the only chance of preserving its remnant populations.[8] Although her own approach and that of other humanitarians among her peers rejected the idea of this doomed race theory by the inter-war years, the dire prediction may indeed have provided the initial spark for her interest in Aboriginal affairs as a young woman.[9] A Christian maternalism seems to have formed the emotional wellspring for her later vision of independence and social equality founded on large, self-determined reserves for Aboriginal people. What makes her so different to most of the women activists of her day was her direct interaction with numbers of Aboriginal people. In her mature years, Cooke gained considerable first-hand knowledge not only of the survival of Aboriginal people, but of their vibrant and vocal communities working for their own rights agenda.

***

Constance Mary Hoare was born to a large, middle-class Anglican family in Adelaide in 1882. They were part of Adelaide's educated elite with a cosmopolitan view of the world. Her father was an accountant; her mother was of French extraction. Constance was educated at home, as was the norm for girls from wealthy families in the late 19th century. As a young woman she became a teaching assistant in a school run by her second cousin, thereby entering one of the few professions open to women of her class and generation. In 1907, aged 25, she married Dr William Ternent Cooke of the Department of Chemistry at Adelaide University. They had two children, and, until William's death in 1957, lived comfortably in the Adelaide suburbs.[10]

But Cooke would not conform to the requirements of respectability where the Aboriginal question was concerned. The social liberalism of her childhood was redirected in her adult life into controversial views on 'race' as she engaged in campaigns for Aboriginal women's and community rights. Increasingly, her participation in the reform movement brought her into contact with some of the very worst aspects of Australian Aboriginal policy and its management, and she became ever more determined to change the political culture in Australia.

In Adelaide, Cooke was well positioned to pursue an interest in Aboriginal rights. Before 1911 (and the formation of the Northern Territory) the borders of South Australian government extended into northern Australia, and South Australians were responsible for a considerable Aboriginal population. While the large numbers of 'tribal blacks of the outback' were remote to urban South Australians, local Aboriginal people represented a valuable potential workforce.

Constance Cook in regal pose c. 1930. League of Women Voters Collection, Mortlock Library, State Library of South Australia.

From the 1830s, schools were established for Aboriginal children so that they would become trained for work in white households. The government quickly abandoned the scheme, however, declaring Aboriginal parents an obstacle to uplift for regularly keeping their children from school. Instead, it funded two missions, one Lutheran and the other Moravian, at Point McLeay and Point Pearce respectively, both on the Yorke Peninsula. These were established under the auspices of the Aborigines Friends' Association, the white humanitarian organisation with strong mission links formed in 1858 and led by Reverend John Sexton. Sexton would later dominate the first decades of the Advisory Council in Adelaide and became a central figure in Cooke's life as a government expert.

Point McLeay was a mission Cooke would visit often. According to historian CD Rowley, in the early days of the mission Reverend

George Taplin set out to relentlessly 'smash a culture…[he] could not understand'.[11] At the same time, however, Aboriginal people from the mission were also actively involved in negotiating settler culture, and they are notable for their success. Aboriginal convert James Unaipon (Ngunaitpori) was elected first deacon of the mission church, and co-authored a book on his people, the Ngarrindjeri, with Taplin.[12] Unaipon's son David became one of the most celebrated Aboriginal people of his generation, an author, minister and scientific inventor who worked for a number of years studying his own and other cultures at the South Australian Museum during the first decades of last century. David Unaipon's collection of Ngarrindjeri legends has been recently reissued under his authorship, having been appropriated by a non-Aboriginal author in the mid-1920s.[13]

Point McLeay is also noteworthy for its place in Aboriginal voting rights history. Prior to Federation, when all states except Queensland and Western Australia provided Aboriginal people with the franchise, only Point McLeay had its own polling station, established in 1896. With 100 names on the rolls, inmates voted in the elections that year, and in the following years on Federation matters. While the Federation Council was concerned with the question of who would be citizens in the new nation, Aboriginal people were expected to die out within the next generation. So it was the state voting rights of white women in South Australia, who were already enfranchised by Federation, rather than those of Aboriginal people in the state, that were to be protected by section 41 of the Constitution. By taking this provision at its most literal, and declaring that only those on the rolls in 1902 were entitled to the federal vote, subsequent governments sought to diminish Aboriginal citizenship rights. In 1921, joint state and federal enrolment cards issued in South Australia implied that Aboriginal people were barred from voting in federal elections. Between 1922 and 1946, the 17 long-term voters still living at Point McLeay lost their Commonwealth vote. This blatant misrepresentation of the Commonwealth *Electoral Act* attracted little or no attention from South Australians interested in Aboriginal rights, including from Cooke.[14]

South Australian Aboriginal people had a history of participating in government inquiries into their own conditions. In 1913, a Royal Commission had considered the management of Aboriginal people on reserves in South Australia. Its findings that government administration had to be mediated by mission advisers led to the formation of the Advisory Council. In this sense, those living on Point Pearce and Point McLeay may well have viewed the council as their own achievement, through their evidence to the 1913 inquiry. Matthew Kropinyeri of Point McLeay had advised that while parents were interested in opportunities for their children, they opposed removal and institutionalisation: '...to be subjected to complete alienation from our children is to say the least an unequalled act of injustice.'[15] Undoubtedly Aboriginal people's impressive history of political engagement in South Australia provided inspiration for the next generation in their exchanges with Cooke.

As they saw their voting rights evaporate, Aboriginal residents on reserves also witnessed the increasingly draconian impact of 'protective' legislation on their communities. For governments, but also for humanitarians and certainly for women activists, miscegenation was the feared outcome of unregulated contact between white and black. From early in the 20th century, the protection of Aboriginal women had been widely understood as central to the modern management of Aboriginal populations. The *Aborigines Act 1911* (SA) had set out various provisions for the care and protection of natives, including reserves managed by local administrators to protect the Aboriginal race from 'injustice, imposition and fraud'.[16] As became apparent in following decades, however, the problems associated with contact had worsened as increasing numbers of whites settled in Central and Northern Australia (Cooke had seen this first-hand during her 1926 trip). The Women's Non-Party Association of South Australia, to which Cooke belonged, identified the scandalous conditions of Aboriginal women and girls in outback areas such as Alice Springs as their most pressing issue.

When Cooke joined the association, the Aboriginal woman question was already part of its reform agenda. In previous years, the renowned Daisy Bates had published disturbing accounts of the behaviour of itinerant white men working along the east–west railway line, and of her work to save Aboriginal girls from disease and immorality, aiming to reduce the birth of mixed descent children (see Chapter 10). Where Bates drew upon late 19th-century assumptions that Aboriginal people were doomed to extinction (see Chapters 9 and 10), the association identified the treatment of Aboriginal people living in contact with white society as a matter of social justice and welfare extending into the future. In 1920, the Women's Non-Party Association wrote to the Women's Service Guilds of Western Australia expressing concern about plans to extend the trans-Australia and north–south railways across Central Australia into the west. The South Australian association wanted to know the likely impact upon

Aboriginal people living in previously remote areas, and in particular questioned what was being done to protect '[A]boriginal women against the vices of white men' along the West Australian section of the line.[17] The West Australian organisation resolved to support the association by lobbying the South Australian government, especially in relation to white men living and working along the railway line.[18]

As president of the association from 1924 to 1927, Cooke emphasised the need for proactive, as well as reactive, forms of protection for Aboriginal women. Previously, the South Australian association's protective work had entailed inspecting the conditions of Aboriginal women sent from Alice Springs to work in white homes in Adelaide.[19] The organisation soon began to develop a more interventionist line based upon individual and collective rights to wages and land. Over the following years, it began to help Aboriginal women previously in domestic service to access their wages. These moneys, held in a trust fund by government authorities supposedly until the women reached 21 years of age, were still to be paid.[20]

Protective reserves were not only to provide safe zones for Aboriginal women; they were to acknowledge the falsehood of *terra nullius*. In 1924, Cooke proposed a resolution for protective reserves at the first conference of the Australian Federation of Women Voters, the national body affiliating the Women's Non-Party Association with the British Commonwealth League in London. According to Cooke, the setting aside of sufficient, inviolable land was to recognise the 'right of the original inhabitants' to hold a portion of 'their own country'.[21] This vision of an Aboriginal state within the nation-state proved too controversial for her peers. After heated discussion, they resolved to support the provision of areas of land only, thus doing little more than confirming the existing reserve system. No doubt spurred on by this negative response, Cooke instigated and then became the convenor of an Aboriginal welfare committee within the South Australian Women's Non-Party Association from 1928, thereby effectively forming her own women's focus group on the Aboriginal question.

In 1926, Cooke consolidated her commitment to the Aboriginal cause by joining the Aborigines Protection League as one of its founding members, and (as her 1924 resolution to the Australian Federation of Women Voters indicated) she brought with her an existing reform agenda. Led by Colonel JC Genders, and counting Mary Montgomery Bennett, a staunch colleague and friend of Cooke (see Chapter 6), among its members, the Aborigines Protection League was a lobby group aiming to win greater provision of Aboriginal land from state governments. Cooke was its vice president for the next 20 years. A large reserve had been established in Central Australia when state and federal governments endorsed the Aborigines Friends' Association campaign, and another would be established in Arnhem Land in far northern Australia from 1929. The Central Reserve soon felt the impact of mining interests, however, and quickly proved to be less than the inviolable space first proposed. What became known as the Model State Movement confronted the state government's interest in allowing mining and other forms of economic development on reserve land, as well as its strong resistance to Aboriginal independence. The movement argued that Aboriginal people should negotiate their own form of advancement rather than submit to a white version forced upon them. The 'native states' they proposed were to provide Aboriginal people with 'self-determination' of their own path.[22]

Although success in changing state government attitudes towards reserves would prove elusive, Genders and Cooke did not join other humanitarians, including the women of the Australian Federation of Women Voters, in promoting responsibility for Aboriginal affairs at the national level. Cooke was not inclined to support a national policy for Aboriginal people, having seen the federal government's failures through lack of funding or concern for Aboriginal people in Northern Australia. The formation of the Northern Territory in 1911 had stirred hopes for a new level of interest and funding from federal authorities, but these were short-lived. Where the federal government inherited decades of neglect of Aboriginal people in northern Australia and Central Australia from the South Australian Government, in following years it made little improvement, establishing the children's home in Alice Springs but without sufficient funds. The home and its successor, the Bungalow, were a source of scandal throughout the inter-war years, as described in chilling terms during these decades by various official and unofficial visitors.[23] As Cooke advised the London Anti-Slavery and Aborigines Protection Society in 1934, the superintendent of the children's home in Alice Springs had been found guilty of abusing one of his young charges.[24] As we saw at the start of this chapter, already sceptical of a national approach to what was considered to be the Aboriginal question, Cooke spoke passionately about these dreadful conditions while she was in London in 1927.

The British Commonwealth League was a London-based dominion women's organisation formed in 1921 under the auspices of the International Alliance of Women. In 1926 the executive, including the sometime president of the Australian Federation of Women Voters, West Australian Bessie Rischbieth, stressed the responsibility of the 'Commonwealth citizen woman' to take an active role in improving the conditions of native peoples, particularly women.[25] In 1927, when Cooke presented a paper to the annual conference in London on behalf of Australian women on the status and conditions of Aboriginal women, she seemed just such a responsible settler woman. Yet her views already conflicted with those of Rischbieth and the Australian Federation of Women Voters, and her relationship with that organisation would only worsen over the next decade. In her paper Cooke described 'vicious' frontier men encouraging the prostitution of Aboriginal women. Once the 'burden bearers' of the tribe, Aboriginal women, she asserted, had been reduced to the white man's 'prey', bartered by Aboriginal men. While there was a significant amount of miscegenation between Aboriginal women and European men, it was white men's access to Aboriginal girls that was most disturbing. Particularly disgraceful, Cooke reported, were the conditions under which the government kept young Aboriginal women and girls at the 'half-caste home' in Alice Springs. In fact conditions were so bad they had inspired a Women's Non-Party Association campaign to publicise them. Cooke explained that:

> ...the Federal Home for half-castes, in which there are over 50 children...is situated next to a hotel and consists of iron sheds with no windows other than sheets of iron propped open. There is no fence around it and it seemed to be common knowledge that some of the older girls left the home at night, and it was this and other rumours that stirred the women a thousand miles away [in Adelaide] to take action.[26]

Land would provide Aboriginal people with their own future, safe from the debilitating influences of 'our environment...[which is] not suitable for their stage of culture'. While laws to protect Aboriginal people were on the books, they had not been enforced. As a result, she advised: 'I know that in the Centre the natives possess nothing; there are no settlements of a happy contented people, only poor outcast wanderers.'[27] This important paper established Cooke as a formidable critic of the federal government. It was admired in the West Australian women's newspaper, the *Dawn*, for drawing attention to the destructive effects of 'advancing civilisation' on Aboriginal people.[28]

While in London, Cooke presented the same paper at a meeting of the Anti-Slavery and Aborigines' Protection Association, a highly respected organisation engaged in campaigns on native rights around the world. She joined one of its deputations to the Australian High Commission, calling for the improvement of Aboriginal rights in Australia.[29] In following years, she would be one among a small coterie of correspondents supplying information to the society on the Aboriginal cause.

At the same time, a broader acknowledgment of the need to reform Aboriginal policy began to slowly infiltrate Australian public debate. In 1929, an Australian federal government report endorsed the descriptions of dangers faced by Aboriginal girls and young women (as had been circulated by Cooke and others within humanitarian and women's networks). Reporting for the federal government on conditions in Northern and Central Australia, the Queensland Chief Protector, JW Bleakley, gave a damning indictment of neglect and white men's aggression. Cooke would draw on his report to support her own analysis, particularly in his account of the endemic abuse of Aboriginal women, and of the lack of white women in the outback.[30]

Wishing to appear responsive to the Bleakley Report, in 1929 the federal government called a Melbourne conference of representatives from missions, societies and associations. Cooke was invited, along with Genders and others, and spoke for the appointment of women experts as protectors.[31] This was part of a long-term campaign promoted by women's groups in these years, but governments continued to reject the idea of replacing honorary policeman protectors in a reformed outback administration that would include women.[32] A change of government only a few months later resulted in the shelving of Bleakley's recommendations and those of the conference. Cooke would later report that the Minister for Home Affairs, CLA Abbott, whose portfolio included Aborigines Affairs and who had seemed amenable to the reform of policy during the conference, was not the 'strongman' she had hoped for, and had soon backed down from his conference commitments.[33]

Elsewhere more lasting progress was being made. In 1918, the Commissioner of Public Works in South Australia, the Hon. J Bice, had formed the Advisory Council of Aborigines in order to improve the administration of Aboriginal policy. Comprising of white men, predominantly from the Aborigines Friends' Association, its members were charged with reporting on the 'protection, control, training or education' of Aboriginal people. Accordingly, one of the first recommendations the council made was for the vocational training of young Aboriginal people otherwise 'allowed to drift into idleness'. Education was to provide Aboriginal young people with the means to protect themselves against exploitation by whites, and to become 'useful members of society'.[34] From as early as 1922, these male councillors resisted the persistent lobbying of the Women's Non-Party Association for a lady member, asserting that they preferred to remain a group of 'gentlemen'. In the 'unlikely' event that the appointment of women should eventuate, they advised, at least two women would be required to undertake inspections of settlements.[35] Clearly they believed that a white woman should not travel alone in the company of white men colleagues, nor be alone among Aboriginal men. The vulnerability of white women involved in Aboriginal issues had been made all too clear in 1928, when Annie Locke, who provided crucial evidence of the Forrest River massacre to a local missionary in Western Australia, was castigated for living among Aboriginal men.[36] Locke wrote to Cooke from Alice Springs several times; perhaps they had met during Cooke's visit in 1926. She saw them both as engaged in changing deeply ingrained white racism. They were waging a 'great battle with the whites [in the outback]'. Of the authorities, she observed: '...they do not like them [Aboriginal people] to be enlightened, but [keep] them in ignorance so they can...drive them as they please.'[37]

Given the widespread opposition to white women's involvement in Aboriginal affairs, the women's campaign was remarkable for its success in finally securing the appointment of two white women to the council in the late 1920s. Ida McKay, a fellow member of Cooke's Aboriginal Welfare Committee who had lived in Central Australia for a number of years, was appointed in 1927. Cooke joined her in 1929. Ten years later, Alice Harvey Johnston replaced McKay, and she and Cooke continued to work on the reformed council until the late 1950s. But their reform aims were largely thwarted by government intractability and public inertia. Even the more conservative Sexton recorded the frustration felt by the council. While the needs of 'full blooded blacks' living in outback regions had once been answered by the ration system, he asserted, continuing to treat Aboriginal people as if they were children could no longer be defended.[38] Breaking the ration system mentality was hugely difficult, as the council discovered, and recommendation after recommendation was sidetracked by the government.

Nonetheless, these new appointments helped to revitalise the advisory council, ushering in a new era in its influence and significance. Women councillors brought greater attention to the protection of

Aboriginal women. Informed by their inspections of local settlements, Cooke and McKay were eager to improve the conditions of women and their families. In May 1931, for example, when Miss Green of the City Mission voiced concerns about 'native girls visiting the city', a meeting ensued between 'the lady members' of the council, a representative of the Women Police of South Australia, and the Chief Protector of the Aborigines.[39] One of Cooke's first actions was to propose that she and McKay make a visit to Point Pearce, and over the years, they made regular inspections of Point Pearce, Point McLeay and Ernabella mission stations. Along with other members of the council, Cooke submitted reports on the provision of housing, education, medicine and food. She was also involved in the Girl Guides company established at Point Pearce in the mid-1930s, sending a picture of herself in Guide uniform to her friend Mary Bennett.[40] In the same years, the South Australian branch of the Girl Guides promised to send second-hand uniforms to company leader Mrs Archie Bray.[41] Cooke also attended meetings of residents, who were encouraged to air complaints, presumably reassured by the presence of the council members. However, the intermediary role played by the council, though meant to facilitate greater understanding between government and Aboriginal communities, was largely cosmetic, as Aboriginal grievances expressed at these meetings were never formally recorded.

Cooke's interests in a Model State for Aboriginal people found their echo in the concerns of Aboriginal people who approached the council during these years calling for land and self-determination: two demands also interconnected in Cooke's work. In June 1929, several residents at Point Pearce, including Joe Edwards, wrote to the council and the government asking to be 'placed on blocks of land with the assistance of the Government'. They described starvation from the insufficient provision of rations, and the despair of their younger generation facing a future without meaningful employment.[42] Lack of response to their plight over the next two years led them to more formal organisation. In September 1931, eight Aboriginal men calling themselves the Point Pearce Mission Committee advised the council that they were petitioning their local member of parliament, Mr Pattinson (Yorke Peninsula, Liberal Party). Enclosing a copy of their petition, they advised that despair and ill health was continuing to take a terrible toll on their community: 'Conditions must become worse and further lower the moral standard of the people, more especially the younger generation.' If land for farming was not available, they suggested that residents could 'become self-supporting' through the provision of boats to establish a small, self-managed fishing business.[43]

Given the difficulty of gaining government response to their conditions, the interest of sympathetic whites like Cooke must have been a last hope to many Aboriginal people living on reserves. Numbers of Aboriginal women and men from Point Pearce and Point McLeay wrote to Cooke as their supporter, and some addressed her even as their friend. In October 1930, for example, Mrs Joe Edwards sent a letter to her 'dear Mrs Cook[e]', apologising for not having written earlier. She reported that conditions were serious: her boys were at starvation point, and her husband was still waiting for an answer to his request for land. If Cooke had 'a spare suit that was of no further use', could she send it for her son? And, as she had shown an interest in her daughter Doris, would she like to see a photo of her recent wedding? Above all, could she find out if there was any news on their request for land to farm?[44] The conditions faced by residents on government-funded missions during these years, though noted in general terms by Cooke and others in their reports, emerge graphically in these letters. While they were sent and received within the deeply hierarchical context of colonial race policy and its administration, their flesh and blood details disrupt the liberal principles of disinterest perpetrated by government 'protection'. They were transgressive because they made personal claims on this white woman, a government appointee but also an advocate of humanitarianism. Although Cooke and other council members were limited in their capacity to change policy in any larger sense, throughout the late 1920s and 1930s Cooke did her best to respond with interest and sympathy to local Aboriginal communities and to send them all-important parcels of food and clothing.

For Cooke, personal obstacles existed *within* the South Australian council as well. In 1929, Sexton had blocked her attempt to join the General Committee of the Aborigines Friends' Association because he was unhappy with her criticisms of the government and her membership of the Aborigines Protection League. And he resented the fact that she had spoken on the scandalous conditions of Aboriginal people while she was in London the previous year.[45] He considered criticisms overseas gave the wrong impression that Australians were uncaring about Aboriginal people.[46] Moreover, he feared that the Model State Movement would force all Aboriginal people onto one central reserve.[47] In turn, Cooke and McKay opposed Sexton's position that mining could be allowed on reserves.[48]

Resilient as ever, Cooke responded by forming a subcommittee of her own, this time within the council, and she began to write new policy for the Aboriginal people in South Australia. Overall, she reported optimistically, change was increasingly likely as 'people are becoming conscious of what is going on in the outback'.[49] True to her prediction, Sexton's and his generation's domination of the council gradually diminished. In 1939, as the council was reformed under new departmental conditions, he was compelled to admit — somewhat patronisingly — that the women members had been 'zealous' in taking on their full share of discussions and responsibilities, while bringing a 'spirit of enthusiasm into the work' and 'a great graciousness of spirit into the proceedings...'[50]

Over the following decades, women councillors were encouraged by new appointments to the reformed council from within the anthropological community in Adelaide. One of them was Professor John Burton Cleland, a central figure on the Board of Anthropological Studies at Adelaide University. Cleland considered that 'pure bloods' could be preserved and 'half-castes' merged, but that even those Aboriginal people merely in contact with whites were doomed to cultural and social absorption.[51] While his views were more biologically deterministic than Cooke's, the attention he gave to 'traditional' culture on the one hand, and rapid assimilation for those of mixed descent on the other, mirrored her own. She promoted the provision of reserves where cultural practices might continue, yet could encourage full citizenship for all Aboriginal people.

Taking her message overseas once again, in 1930 Cooke was invited by the Pan-Pacific Women's Conference committee to speak at its next meeting on the subject of the status and conditions of Aboriginal women in Australia. These conferences, the first of which was held in Honolulu under the auspices of the Pan-Pacific Union in 1928, were designed to facilitate the exchange of information and the development of friendship between leading women activists and social reformers of the Pacific Rim. Among their interests were education and health reform, including that of native women.[52] Widely recognised as an important moment in white women's activism for Aboriginal rights in the inter-war years, Cooke's Pan-Pacific paper to the 1930 conference, 'The status of Aboriginal women', extended its campaigns from the

British Commonwealth into the Pacific region.[53] A comprehensive account of the difficulties faced by Aboriginal women, her paper condemned the inaction of governments and their failure to protect or provide a viable future for Aboriginal people.

Once again, Cooke confronted the limitations of feminist politics concerning 'race'. Several months before the conference took place, she realised that the organisers hoped she would dilute her position, and she began to doubt the value of attending at all. When the Commonwealth government approached the Pan-Pacific Women's Conference organising committee shortly before the event, concerned that a critical paper was to be presented by one of its Australian delegates, president Dr Georgina Sweet agreed. She advised that she had already taken 'a great deal of trouble and pains, and had many private conferences and communications with the various experts in Australia...[so that] the paper...[had been] modified to some slight extent by the writer [Cooke]...'[54]

Worse was to come. As the papers were being finalised for distribution to delegates (during which her own had apparently been 'modified'), a member of the Liberal Women's Branch Committee in South Australia warned federal minister C Hawker (Wakefield, Liberal Party) of an impending public relations disaster. Mrs CR Morris had learned from an undisclosed source that a paper to be presented at the forthcoming conference would make:

> ...some very serious allegations on the treatment of the Aborigines by successive governments in Australia...in the hope of stirring up the public opinion of the world against the management of the original inhabitants of our country so that action may be taken to bring public pressure to bear on the Government that it may mend its ways.

While Morris was at pains to assert that her sympathies lay with the campaign and that she held 'no brief for our treatment of the Aborigines', would it not be '...in the best interests of our country [if] this public washing of our dirty linen could be prevented?' Arguing that native affairs was an internal matter, she concluded: 'I believe the treatment of the Aborigines needs serious amendment, but it is peculiarly our own business which we ought to amend ourselves and not ask other countries to interfere with it.' Perhaps a confidential word to the prime minister might bring 'influence to bear' on the conference.[55]

Morris's letter was relayed to Australia's Minister for Internal Affairs, A Blakeley.[56] A copy was sent to the Prime Minister's Department, along with a request for further information concerning the 'status of the conference, the names of the Australian delegates, the date of meeting, and any other particulars available' from the Department of External Affairs.[57] As their patriotic informant could provide useful information essential to the 'refutation of defamatory charges against Australia which may be made at the Conference', her wish for anonymity was to be respected.[58] Thanks to a press clipping supplied by Morris, government officials learned that at the triennial AFWV conference that year, Cooke had asserted she had 'heard from reliable sources that in North Australia even the children of [A]borigines were not safe from white men. Conditions were a disgrace to a civilised country.'[59] No wonder the Minister for Home Affairs feared international condemnation!

With some haste, the Secretary of the Department of the Interior, JA Carrodus, wrote a response to Cooke's paper. Carrodus would become acting administrator of the Northern Territory in 1934 and was to be a significant figure in the formation of Aboriginal policies from the late 1930s.[60] His response to Cooke's paper comprised 'Comments' and an overview of government policy. Several copies of Carrodus's rebuttal were circulated among members of the 'British and American Press'.[61] Simultaneously, Blakeley advised parliament that a rebuttal to overseas criticism of Aboriginal affairs had been prepared for a Pan-Pacific conference soon to be held in Honolulu.[62] In a letter he sent to the conference committee, Blakeley requested that both papers be read there in 'conjunction'.[63] One of the surprising aspects of this intervention is his apparent ignorance concerning Cooke's involvement in the South Australian Advisory Council and of her key role in the Model State Movement.

How much Cooke knew of this confidential exchange is unclear. Certainly she began to look for a replacement. On the recommendation of her friend Baldwin Spencer, she approached Daisy Bates. The idea was ill-conceived: Bates was enamoured of the 'dying race' theory, putting her out of step not only with the Pan-Pacific women's conferences, but also with Cooke. Their accounts of Aboriginal affairs in Australia would surely have been different in tenor and approach. Luckily, Bates turned down the opportunity, using the moment to assert anyway that her knowledge of 'wild and semi-civilised and fully civilised' Aboriginal people was 'unequalled in Australia'.[64]

Without a replacement, Cooke resigned herself to attending. No doubt her dismay over the government's attempt to censor her paper increased during her voyage out and while in Honolulu. In a letter written on her return to Australia, the Chair of the Australian delegation, Elizabeth Clapham, advised the minister that every care had been taken not to criticise Australia during the conference. She had undertaken the 'task of watching the question on behalf of the Commonwealth Government', as requested, carefully noting 'all references to the subject'. There is no evidence that Clapham did make such notations.[65] However, Cooke was either advised not to go ahead with her paper, or she decided to protect the organisation from further compromise. Her paper was published nonetheless in the conference proceedings (with international circulation) and Carrodus's reply appeared in a poor second place, effectively reducing his statement to a defensive addendum.

The published conference proceedings show that Cooke's 1930 paper was almost the same as the one she had presented to the British Commonwealth League three years earlier. Despite government pressure, the two versions exhibit fewer differences than one might expect (Cooke had obviously resisted Sweet's attempts at modification). The only clear excision is her damning description of federal government homes in Alice Springs and Darwin. Yet even in this case Cooke managed to make her point, stating that she would not 'touch upon' their dreadful conditions. Instead, she made full use of the Bleakley Report's criticisms of government policy, and she added Mary Bennett, who asserted the morality of 'native women', to her collection of leading expert opinions on Aboriginal people. Her paper still asserted that the contradictory status of Aboriginal people as British subjects governed by restrictive legislation resulted in their status as 'outcasts in white society', a situation only land and citizenship rights could remedy.[66]

In his reply, Carrodus countered that medical treatment, wages and Arnhem Land for the 'nomadic tribes' was evidence of the government's humane approach. He acknowledged Bleakley's recommendations that Aboriginal women were insufficiently protected from white men, and contended that new homes for 'half-castes' in Darwin and Alice Springs were being considered. In his defence of the humanity of government policy, Carrodus subscribed to the institutionalisation of Aboriginal girls 'as soon as possible after reaching an age when they can be removed from their native mothers'. While his version of removal was carefully angled to the government's benefit, in surprising contrast Cooke's paper contains no account of removal at all. Apart from her disgust at conditions in government homes — for removed children — she never referred to the subject directly. Her silence is in marked contrast to the voluble critique of her friend and colleague Mary Bennett who widely denounced the brutality of removals.[67] This failure stands as the one significant blemish on Cooke's admirable activist record.

Despite this difference, Bennett lauded Cooke's work at the 1930 Pan-Pacific Women's Conference, not so much for her international work but for her influence on her fellow Australian delegates. In a letter to the Anti-Slavery Society of London she advised that Cooke 'did splendid work winning Australians to an understanding of the [A]boriginals on the voyage to Honolulu. She was precluded from reading the paper she had been asked to prepare...although] [s]he [had] made the paper very mild, hoping to get it through.' Furthermore, Cooke would be able to use the government's lengthy reply 'as a lever to enforce laws'. Throughout the conference, Bennett reported, Cooke had pleaded for the rights of the 'backward peoples with the result that they are on the map for the next conference'.[68] Indeed Cooke's resolution, 'That the study of family life and interracial relationship shall be included in the study of indigenous people governed by a dominant race, especially in regard to their fundamental right to land ownership', was passed that year.

Ultimately, the Pan-Pacific women's organisation would not prove an effective forum for Aboriginal rights activists.[69] In retrospect, Cooke described her participation in the Honolulu conference as a useful experience, given that she had been able to 'discuss the question of the treatment of Aboriginal people with delegates from other countries'.[70] Perhaps this positive spin reflected her meeting with the leader of the New Zealand delegation, Elsie Andrews. In her conference diary, Andrews recorded her exchange with Cooke en route to Honolulu. Their conversation on Indigenous rights was a significant moment in the development of her own ideas on Maori rights: Andrews would include Maori women in the delegation she led to the next Pan-Pacific Women's Conference held in 1934.[71] Perhaps Cooke's attendance had been worthwhile after all.

In following years, Cooke continued to promote her dual interests in land and citizenship. In 1933, through the Women's Non-Party Association of South Australia, she presented a resolution on large reserves to the fourth triennial conference of the Australian Federation of Women Voters.[72] As almost ten years earlier, she was unsuccessful, but Bennett for one encouraged her to continue with her agenda to 'creat[e] a desire for justice' for Aboriginal people.[73] One of her Aboriginal correspondents also expressed appreciation of her efforts. William Taylor, 'Native' of Point Pearce, wrote to Cooke of his support for her efforts concerning the 'control and welfare of the Aborigines generally'. He had read about her work in the local press:

> With a feeling of deep interest I have watched the *Advertiser* for the results of the conferences held by the Women's Non-Party Association together with other bodies...also the other bodies and also the last conference now ended by the Women Voters and the compromise reached.
>
> It seems just splendid to think that we as a down trodden people have such noble Ladies and Gentlemen taking up the cause for the welfare of the Aborigines because I think we would be long waiting on the Government alone for justice.
>
> The question of land has been a long felt want with some of us to work out our own destiny personally.

Taylor looked forward to the inclusion of:

> ...educated Aboriginals and Halfcastes in a national commission appointed of men and women.
>
> This suggestion came to my mind about six years ago but how to accomplish it I was at a loss knowing that we are such poor people financially though we might have brains enough for the purpose.[74]

Both the Australian Federation of Women Voters and the British Commonwealth League had passed resolutions for the inclusion of Aboriginal people on advisory committees. Taylor endorsed Cooke's political stance because it corresponded most closely to his own. He wrote to her of Aboriginal people's desire to govern their own destiny, to find justice as a downtrodden people, and to participate directly in national political life.

Over the next decade, Cooke continued to extend the scope and aims of her humanitarian reform agenda. Internationally, her Aboriginal Welfare Committee became part of a network of research groups endorsed by the Anti-Slavery and Aborigines' Protection Society as a way of better circulating information and ideas. The society hoped that her 'study circle' in Adelaide would be copied in other states.[75] It also attracted the interest of Professor AP Elkin,

Head of Anthropology at the University of Sydney and president of the recently revitalised Association for the Protection of the Native Races. Elkin sent her several of his publications on Aboriginal people.[76] Hoping to further encourage national interest in Aboriginal rights — and to carry out the Anti-Slavery Society's advice to encourage similar circles in other states — Cooke toured Australia in 1932, accompanied by a letter of introduction from the Aborigines Friends' Association written by Sexton himself.[77]

One of Cooke's most extraordinary attempts to change the whole approach of Australian women's organisations to the Aboriginal question came in 1936. To commemorate the centenary of settlement in South Australia, a special committee (including Cooke as an Aborigines Protection League delegate) commissioned a collection of women's writings celebrating white women's role as pioneers. Echoing Bleakley's assertion in his 1929 report that Aboriginal women were the unacknowledged pioneer women of Australia, Cooke suggested that an Aboriginal woman should write one of the contributions. A radical departure from the supposed incapacity of Aboriginal women to speak, let alone write, of their own lives, her idea was considered unfeasible, and a disappointed Cooke left the committee.[78]

In another path-breaking move, Cooke called for the 1936 conference of the Australian Federation of Women Voters to mark the centenary of the abolition of slavery in the British Empire by supporting equal citizenship rights for Aboriginal people. Her radical resolution was thrown out on the grounds that a women's organisation should be concerned with equality with men rather than equality between the races, the latter detracting from their cause. Mary Bennett summed up the significance of this lost opportunity to the Anti-Slavery Society in London: 'To my thinking the truly important thing is that an Australian lady has brought forward a Resolution asking for equality of status for Aborigines. This is something to dream of and work for...Mrs Ternent Cooke...has made history.'[79]

**

Throughout her life, Constance Cooke was a force to be reckoned with. She was a dynamic individual whose energies were directed towards overturning many of the conventions of her day. She envisaged a world in which Aboriginal people were part of the national community, with full rights but also recognised as the original Australians with a unique land-connected social and cultural heritage. Her personal relationship with some of the most politically experienced Aboriginal people in Australia, the people of Point McLeay and Point Pearce, shaped her perspective and marked her apart from most of her peers. Cooke remained determined throughout, valiantly promoting a sea change in Australian race relations. She was awarded an MBE for her work for Aboriginal rights in 1964, and died in 1967, the year of the referendum that began a process finally leading to the inclusion of Aboriginal people as citizens. To this day the dual aims of land and self-determination occupy a central place in Aboriginal politics.

Notes

1. British Commonwealth League, *British Commonwealth League Conference Report*, London (henceforth BCLCR), 1927, p. 29, National Library of Australia.
2. Perhaps best illustrated by Chaudhuri & Strobel 1992.
3. As noted by Stuart Hall in his overview of theories of identity and their implication for contemporary politics. Hall 1996, pp. 345–46. On this effect in histories of white women imperialists and colonists, see Haggis 1990.
4. Paisley 2000.
5. Attwood & Markus in collaboration with Dale Edwards & Kath Schilling.
6. Cooke to Buxton, Secretary of the Anti-Slavery Society, 9 May 1934, Anti-Slavery and Aborigines' Protection Society Papers (henceforth ASAPSP), s 19, D2/21, Rhodes House, Oxford.
7. Anderson 2002, pp. 200 ff; personal correspondence with Bridget Jolly, Adelaide, 2 May 2003. Jolly is the granddaughter of Alice (Maude) Johnston, a member, with Cooke, of the South Australian Advisory Council.
8. BCLCR, 1927, p. 29.
9. Historian Russell McGregor has noted that theories about race can be mapped across the end of the 19th century and into the 20th century as shifting from doomed theory (dying out) to mergence (biological and then social). Individuals, however, often adhered to elements of both in their accounts of racial policy. Thus AP Elkin, one the most well known proponents of assimilation, would at times mobilise older, contradicting accounts of racial demise. McGregor 1993a.
10. Macilwain.
11. Rowley 1980, pp. 103–05, 204–05. See also Richardson 1992 and Ball 1992, pp. 36–45. For a broader account of missions, see Brock 1993.
12. National Library of Australia, Federation Gateway, 'James Unaipon', viewed 3 February 2005, <www.nla.gov.au/guides/federation/ people/ unaipon.html>.
13. Muecke & Shoemaker.
14. Stretton & Finnimore.
15. Mattingley, p. 119.

16. 'An Act to make provision for the better Protection and Control of the Aboriginal and Half-caste Inhabitants of the State of South Australia', no. 1048, 1911, Sec. 7, *Statutes of South Australia*, Adelaide Government Printer, 1911.

17. State Executive Minutes, September 1920, Women's Service Guilds Papers, 1949A/3f, State Archives of Western Australia, Perth.

18. State Executive Minutes, September 1920, Women's Service Guilds Papers, 1949A/3f; Perth Guild Minutes, October 1920, Women's Service Guilds Papers, 1949A/12, State Archives of WA.

19. McGregor 1997, p. 154.

20. Cooke to Buxton, 3 October 1934, ASAPSP, s. 19, D2/28, Rhodes House, Oxford.

21. Australian Equal Citizenship Association, later the Australian Federation of Women Voters, first interstate conference, 1924, Women's Service Guilds Papers, 1949A/30, State Archives of WA.

22. McGregor 1997, pp. 118–19; Markus 1990, pp. 168–72. See also Blackburn 1999.

23. Markus 1990, pp. 23–29 ff.

24. Cooke to Buxton, 9 May 1934 and 3 October 1934, ASAPSP, s. 19, D2/19, Rhodes House, Oxford.

25. *BCLCR*, 1926, p. 3.

26. *BCLCR*, 1929, pp. 30–32.

27. *BCLCR*, 1929, pp. 30–32.

28. *Dawn* (Journal of the Women's Service Guilds of Western Australia), 15 February 1928, p. 12.

29. National Archives of Australia: 'Anti-Slavery and Aborigines Protection Society', A431, 48/273.

30. Cooke 1930, p. 136.

31. 'Conference of representatives of missions, societies and associations interested in the welfare of Aboriginals to consider the report and recommendations submitted to the Commonwealth by JW Bleakley Esq., Melbourne, 1929', Papers of Bessie Rischbieth, MS 2004/12/506, National Library of Australia.

32. This campaign has been well described elsewhere. Paisley 1997 and Holland 2001a.

33. Cooke to Buxton, 19 August 1929, ASAPSP, s. 19, G374, Rhodes House, Oxford.

34. Advisory Council of Aborigines, Minutes Book, Department of Aboriginal Affairs, GRG 52/12/1, pp. 36 ff, State Archives of South Australia, Adelaide.

35. Advisory Council of Aborigines, Minutes Book, p. 92.

36. Markus 1990, p. 163.

37. Annie Locke to Constance Cooke, DAA, GRG 52/32/32, pp. 35, 49, State Archives of SA.

38. John H Sexton, 'The Advisory Council of Aborigines: the origins of the board', DAA, GRG 52/10/5A, 1939, p. 1, State Archives of SA.

39. 'Native women in the city', DAA, GRG 52/32/10, State Archives of SA.

40. Mary Bennett to Constance Ternent Cooke, 2 November 1931, DAA, GRG 52/32/52, State Archives of SA. See also Andrew Wilson, 'Indigenous culture: exploring the past to inform the present — Aboriginal family history and state records', paper presented to the History Trust of South Australia, Renmark Conference, 24–25 May 2003, pp. 1–4.

41. Rose Jarvis, state secretary, Girl Guides Association of South Australia, to Mrs Bray, Guides Australia, 21 July 1930, Archives of the Girl Guides Association of South Australia.

42. WH Harvey, Walter Hutley & Constance M Cooke, 'Report of visit to Point Pearce Mission Station, June 15th to 17th, 1929', DAA, GRG 52/10/19, State Archives of SA.

43. Edward Chester, acting secretary, Point Pearce Committee, to Rev. JH Sexton, Secretary, Advisory Council, September 1931, DAA, GRG 52/37/10, State Archives of SA.

44. Mrs Edwards to Constance Ternent Cooke, 29 October 1930, DAA, GRG 52/32/40, State Archives of SA.

45. Sir John Harris (Secretary) to Cooke, 19 January 1928, ASAPSP, s. 22, G374, Rhodes House, Oxford.

46. Sexton, 'The Advisory Council', p. 1.

47. Cooke to Buxton, 4 March 1928, ASAPSP, Rhodes House, Oxford.

48. Bennett to Buxton, 18 March 1929, ASAPSP, s. 22, G374, Rhodes House, Oxford.

49. Cooke to Buxton, 19 August 1929, ASAPSP, s. 19, G374, Rhodes House, Oxford.

50. Sexton, 'The Advisory Council', pp. 5–6.

51. McGregor 1997, pp. 124–25, 227–28. See also Anderson 2002, pp. 195 ff; Thomas 2002, pp. 57–79; Cheater 2000.

52. Paisley 2002.

53. Woollacott 1998; Lake 2000.

54. NAA: Mrs W Thorn and Miss EM Griffin to Minister for Home Affairs, 2 July 1930, A1/15, 30/8749.

55. NAA: ES Morris to CAS Hawker, 11 June 1930, A1/15, 30/8749. Thanks to Julia Pitman for informing me that Morris was a South Australian active in the women's guilds of the Congregational churches. Julia is completing a postdoctoral thesis at Adelaide University, entitled 'Prophets and priests: women in the Congregationalist churches of Australia, 1920–1977'.

56. Under Blakeley, the scandalous history of the Alice Springs home for 'half-caste children' continued unabated. Markus, pp. 30–31.

57. NAA: Arthur Blakeley to CAS Hawker, 19 June 1930, A1/15, 30/8749.

58. NAA: CAS Hawker to A Blakeley, 1 July 1930, A1/15, 30/8749.

59. NAA: newspaper clippings and letter, ES Morris to CAS Hawker, 25 June 1930, A1/15, 30/8749.

60. McGregor 1997, pp. 167, 172, 182; Markus 1992, Chapter 8.

61. NAA: handwritten memo, signature illegible, addressed to Mr Carrodus, 3 July 1930, A1/15, 30/8749.

62. NAA: Clipping, Hansard, 11 July 1930, n.p.n, A1/15, 30/8749.

63. PE Deane (Sec, Minister for Home Affairs) to Miss EM Griffin, 8 July 1930, A1/15, 30/8749.

64. Daisy Bates to Cooke, 20 October 1929, DAA, GRG 52/32/34, State Archives of SA, Adelaide. Thanks to Tom Gara for this reference.

65. NAA: Clapham to Blakeley, 15 January 1931.

66. Cooke 1930, pp. 127–37.

67. Paisley 1999.

68. Bennett to Buxton, 6 December 1930, ASAPSP, G441/A, s. 22, Rhodes House, Oxford.

69. Bennett to Buxton.

70. League of Women Voters Papers (formally the Women's Non-Party Association of South Australia), 'Minutes', 1 November 1930, SRG 116/1/2, Mitchell Library, Sydney.

71. Elsie Andrews, 1930 diary, p. 38, Elsie Andrews Papers, Taranaki Museum, New Plymouth, New Zealand.

72. Australian Federation of Women Voters, fourth triennial conference, Women's Service Guilds Papers, 1949/5, State Archives of WA.

73. Bennett to Cooke, DAA, GRG 52/32/52, State Archives of SA.

74. Mr William Taylor, Point Pearce, to Constance Ternent Cooke, 29 May 1933, DAA, GRG 52/32/61, State Archives of SA.

75. Buxton to Cooke, 2 November 1932, DAA, GRG 52/32/60, State Archives of SA, Adelaide.

76. Elkin to Cooke, 8 August 1932, DAA, GRG 52/32/57, State Archives of SA, Adelaide.

77. Sexton to 'Whomever it May Concern', 5 August 1932, DAA, GRG 52/32/56, State Archives of SA.

78. Lake 2000, pp. 169–70.

79. Bennett to Edith Jones, enclosed in Jones to Harris, 30 December 1936, ASAPSP, s. 22, G378, Rhodes House, Oxford, quoted in Lake 2000, p. 173.

Part 4
'Knowing' the Aborigines

9. 'Bye and bye when all the natives have gone'
Daisy Bates and Billingee

Cynthia Coyne

The relationship between an Anglo-Celtic colonial woman, Daisy May Bates, and an Ngumbarl Jukun Aboriginal man, Billingee, at the beginning of the 20th century in Western Australia was one of exceptional and historic rapport. Their artistic and ethnographic collaboration produced a 20-page artists' drawing book, with sketches made by Billingee and notes by Bates, presented in 1907 to the Governor of Western Australia, Admiral Sir Frederick George Denham Bedford. While it remains unclear whether or not Billingee was producing the images in the drawing book only for Bates or for both Bates and Bedford, the collaboration between them was an extraordinary event that traversed the racial divide in colonial Australia. They both had markedly different socio-cultural, political and gender perspectives on life, with dissimilar experiences and visions. Yet they worked together to produce an enduring Australian antiquity, contributing to our understanding of the dynamics of Aboriginal art tradition. This record might well be the earliest account of an Aboriginal man from the Kimberley region using European art media to depict his cultural heritage. An analysis of the drawing book in the context of contact history in the Kimberley during the late 19th and early 20th centuries offers us insight into the cross-cultural historical experiences between an Aboriginal man and a European woman in colonial Australia.

As a descendant of the Jukun-Yawuru clan, the collaboration between Daisy Bates and Billingee has both personal and political significance. It has provided a rare opportunity to view and investigate the original art, cultural heritage and stories represented by a clansman almost 100 years ago. This priceless experience has strengthened my political view that the culture and art traditions of Indigenous clans in the West Kimberley operate in a dynamic and continuous way.

Introducing Daisy May Bates and Billingee

'[B]ye and bye when the natives have all gone, the work done by Billingee will be exceedingly valuable from an anthropological point of view,' Bates wrote to Sir Frederick Bedford in 1907, in a letter accompanying the presentation of the drawing book.[1] Bedford was governor from 1903 to 1909. During his tenure Daisy Bates had been working for the West Australian Government, documenting information about the language and culture of Aboriginal people, including the man she called Billingee. Bates referred to Billingee as 'an untaught artist...an intelligent native, and his knowledge of the customs of his people is entirely native'.[2]

Bates' observations about Billingee and Aboriginal culture epitomise the social evolutionist perspective of her day, which considered it natural and inevitable that the 'native' people of Australia would eventually disappear with the spread of Anglo-Celtic settlement and the introduction of Western technology. Supporters of this notion, like Bates, believed that the anthropological task was to 'save' examples of this 'vanishing' culture. Bates encouraged Billingee to make drawings of material cultural objects, which she then annotated. Ironically, the project has had quite a different outcome: the drawing book offers us first-hand information about Indigenous aesthetics, subsequently becomes an affirmation of Indigenous cultural identity during colonial times in Broome, and supports the contemporaneous nature of art tradition.

After seeing the drawing book I became enthused to learn more about the collaboration between Bates and Billingee. I was curious about Bates' connection to and knowledge of the Indigenous people in the region, and the relationship of the non-secret subject matter in the drawing book both to art and cultural items held in Australian museum collections and to contemporary life. A number of the sketches in the drawing book relate to a secret sphere in Aboriginal life, and I am therefore unable to examine or discuss them. The means by which Bates accessed such secret information and the impetus behind it are matters for further discussion and debate elsewhere. Throughout academia there has been extensive debate about the credibility of Daisy Bates as an anthropologist, and 'her motivations and methods have become a matter for heated discussion in her time and thereafter'.[3] For example, in relation to the integrity of Bates' research work, Ronald and Catherine Berndt wrote:

> ...much of her work did not graduate to what can be considered as being seriously anthropological, although since she worked in areas that were rapidly changing under stress, her notes are the only ones available for some groups of Aboriginals. In spite of the legendary aura that has grown up around her, her writings leave much to be desired.[4]

The non-scholarly style of Bates' writing in her 1938 book *The passing of the Aborigines* has contributed to this opinion. However, despite her unethical data collection methods and lack of academic training, Bates was the first person to gather and record linguistic, socio-cultural and kinship information about Aboriginal groups in Western Australia in a systematic way. Bates' compilation of Aboriginal language vocabularies in Western Australia has significantly contributed to the depth of information we have about Aboriginal people in colonial times. The Jukun and Ngumbarl dialects that Billingee spoke and recorded with Bates are no longer spoken in Australia.[5] A large number of Aboriginal words and phrases that Bates wrote in the drawing book also appear in the Jukun and Ngumbarl vocabularies that she produced with Billingee as her informant.[6] We can speculate that Billingee's sketches and these vocabularies were produced at the same time, near the beginning of the 20th century, and form a level of connectedness — a unique collaboration between the artist and the ethnographer.

There is a lack of published or other documentary information about Billingee, the only example I have found being in Isobel White's compilation *Daisy Bates: the native tribes of Western Australia*. Bates herself, however, provided information about Billingee in her ethnographic notebooks and manuscripts.[7] In these papers she referred to him as a crippled 'native' living in Broome during the early 20th century, and acknowledged him as her linguistic informant in the compilation of Ngumbarl and Jukun vocabularies. Bates also wrote that 'Billingee's country and the country of his relations stretched from above Beagle Bay to Roebourne', and identified him as a Gularabulu or sea coast man from Weeraginmarree (Willie Creek).[8] From Bates' account, it would seem that Billingee had kinship connections that spanned vast territorial distances, knowledge to produce cultural objects and designs, and the ability to inform her about his language, people and heritage.

It appears Bates had a great regard for Billingee and his artistic abilities. Some time between the years 1904 and 1912 she wrote:

> I watched him making his native weapons and chipping designs of animals, etc., on rock faces and I sat beside him while he made and finished a glass spearhead with the femur bone of a kangaroo. His fineness of touch in this most delicate task and the absolute precision, which directed each stroke so that the evenness of the Serature should not be impaired, was exquisite in its way and showed him to be the possessor of the genuine artistic faculty.[9]

After seeing Billingee work, Bates commented that he was the best material culture maker in his group. She then acquired a box of crayons and a drawing book and asked Billingee to reproduce his work. Bates did not record Billingee's age nor make any estimate. I have not been able to identify any photographs of him in her photographic collections at the National Library of Australia. However, given his role as a linguistic informant and the type of images he drew — which only men of age or status would have had the authority to produce in his society — Billingee would have been either middle-aged or older.

Preserving and documenting written accounts of Aboriginal people was not a priority of historians during colonial times; thus, biographical knowledge of Aboriginal men such as Billingee was either not gathered or not maintained. In contrast, the story of Daisy Bates is relatively well known in academia and in popular culture. She has been the focus of a number of books, films and academic studies, and her life history has been comprehensively published in three separate biographies between 1970 and 1985.[10] Major libraries in most capital cities of Australia have copies of her ethnographic writings within their special collections.[11] Her life and life-myth are analysed by Jim Anderson in Chapter 10.

In May 1904 Bates commenced employment with the government of Western Australia, in the Department of the Registrar-General. Her job was to assemble a record of the Aboriginal languages of the state.

She spent the first year in a government office in Perth gathering, reading and compiling existing literature on the languages and cultures in Aboriginal Australia. In the second year of her employment she erected a tent 10 kilometres from the centre of Perth and, for the next two years, used this workstation to gather linguistic and socio-cultural information about Aboriginal groups living in the south-west of the state.

During 1907 and 1908 Bates travelled from Esperance to the goldfields, collecting information about Aboriginal groups in these regions. Over the following couple of years she worked in an office in Perth arranging and writing up the results of this research. In the interim she had written a number of newspaper articles and papers for scholarly journals, during which time she had also become a popular speaker for a number of organisations in Perth.

In 1910 an opportunity arose for Bates to travel with an anthropological expedition from Cambridge University to the north-west of Western Australia. This expedition was organised and managed by AR Radcliffe-Brown, the now famous British anthropologist. The personalities of Radcliffe-Brown and Daisy Bates clashed, and this had a lasting effect on her work and life. Bates was also unable to get her manuscript published through the West Australian Government, which undermined her authority as an expert who had gathered original information over the previous decade.

In 1912 the government returned her manuscript and ended her employment. After this Bates went to live on Rottnest Island, then spent a year near Eucla, moved eastwards to Fowlers Bay, and finally settled in Ooldea, South Australia. During this time she continued to gather data and write about Aboriginal people, making only short trips to Western Australia. On 18 April 1951 she died in Adelaide. Amazingly, it was another 30 years before her manuscript on the Aboriginal tribes of Western Australia was published.

Contextual matters associated with the drawing book

The drawing book is located in the private archives at the JS Battye Library of West Australian History, catalogued as 'Drawing Book' and authored in the name of Billingee with footnotes by Daisy Bates.[12] Two letters from Bates to Sir Frederick Bedford are located on the inside front cover of the book.[13] All the 20 pages in the blue cloth-bound book have pencil and wax crayon drawings done by Billingee, interleaved with tissue. Billingee drew images of material cultural objects, such as weapons (including boomerangs, shields and spears); pearl shell and other ritual decorative objects (including headdresses, plumes and the like) used in performance, dance and ceremonies; as well as representational images of native flora and fauna. Bates pencilled handwritten annotations near these drawings. Her footnotes on the pages included Ngumbarl and Jukun language words and phrases with, in most cases, English translations.

An examination of the sketches and their annotations reveals historical, cultural and social information about Aboriginal societies of the early 20th century. The drawing book also sheds light on contemporary relationships between people, and between people and their environment.

Although Bates referred to Billingee as an 'untaught artist', she did not consider the aesthetics of his work, nor place them as a product of fine art, nor think much about Billingee's intended messages through his art production. Marcia Langton, however, suggests that 'Aboriginal artists have intended since earliest colonial times to reveal their vision and to assert its power'.[14] I believe this is the case for Billingee. The drawings he produced are an assertion of his culture in Broome during the early 20th century.

Art historian Andrew Sayers has written extensively about the work on paper produced by Aboriginal artists during colonial times in Australia.[15] Throughout the 19th century artists from the southern regions of Australia, notably Black Johnny, William Barak, Tommy McRae and Mickey of Ulladulla, first started to work on paper in collaboration with colonial settlers. Billingee drew the sketches in this drawing book a couple of decades after five Aboriginal artists, who were prisoners at Fanny Bay Jail in Darwin, were commissioned by John George Knight, the then deputy sheriff, to produce drawings on paper. Then, from the 1930s onwards, Norman Tindale and Charles Mountford collected crayon drawings produced by Aboriginal artists for the South Australian Museum. Billingee's work on paper can be located in relation to these early Aboriginal artists. For the most part they were the first to work on paper, thus using a new and nontraditional art medium to engage in a kind of collaboration across the racial divide, producing work that had similar themes: hunting, food gathering and ceremonies.

These works on paper are similar in that they provide us with an Aboriginal perspective about life during this period of Australian history, an alternative to what the colonial records document or what colonial ethnographers like Bates believed about 'vanishing' cultures. Yet the collaborative influences that Aboriginal artists experienced when working on paper had some dissimilarity, as reflected in the reception of their work by the wider Australian community. John George Knight, for example, had an art and architecture career background and his interest in the works on paper produced by the Aboriginal prisoners was primarily artistic. He displayed their work at the Dawn of Art Exhibition held in Melbourne in 1888–89 under the category of art rather than ethnography — the more common practice of this era when interpreting Aboriginal art and material cultural works.

Similarly to Tindale and Mountford, Bates focused on the ethnographic and material cultural aspects rather than the artistic or aesthetic. When reviewing Billingee's work on paper, Bates did so primarily through the contemporary 19th-century social evolutionist ideology practised in museums and by other anthropologists, and in keeping with her assigned task of documenting Aboriginal languages from 'a dying culture'. For some 70 to 80 years after Australian Federation (1901), material cultural objects and art made by Aboriginal people were deemed by a whole array of anthropologists and others involved in the art market to be either ethnographic artefacts or tourist objects, not fine art. Australian museums collected an array of works produced by Aboriginal people, using local wood, fibre and natural pigments, and presented them for their material cultural rather than aesthetic value. In terms of the aesthetics of Aboriginal art, Howard Morphy has argued:

> The colonial process has been a battle not only between different economies but between different ways of relating people to land, and since aesthetics has been close to the heart of Aboriginal relationships with land, colonialism has also been a struggle over the aesthetics of the Australian landscape.[16]

The collaboration between Billingee and Bates should really be accorded the same kind of 'unique status' that Andrew Sayers attributes to Von Guerard and Black Johnny.[17] The drawing book is a visual record not only of Billingee's experiences and aesthetic world but of the intellectual encounter between him and Bates as individuals with different cultural and gendered viewpoints. Billingee has provided cultural and intellectual knowledge, and Bates has annotated this knowledge, resulting in a combined visual and ethnological account of his people. But it is important to mention from the outset that the understandings we are able to gain from Billingee's sketches and Bates' notes are limited by the gaps in knowledge between what the artist depicts and the ethnographer documents.

Wider historical context

Anglo-Celtic people first started to explore Billingee's country in the north-west and central Kimberley regions during the late 1830s. Lieutenant George Grey, a senior military officer in the British Army, commanded a party of explorers on expeditions to the north-west of Western Australia during 1837–38 and 1839. Grey reported that:

> The main objects of the expedition were then specified to be: – To gain information as to the real state of North-Western Australia, its resources…and the course and direction of its rivers and mountain ranges; to familiarise the natives with the British name and character; to search for and record all information regarding the natural productions of the country, and all details that might bear upon its capabilities for colonisation or the reverse; and to collect specimens of its natural history.[18]

Some 20 to 30 years after Grey's expeditions, Europeans began to establish their own pearling industry in the north-west Kimberley, and an array of social, economic and cultural interactions between European, Asian and Aboriginal people followed. Anglo-Celtic cultural interpretations of landscapes during this time involved the ongoing settlement of whites and the continued employment of this and other colonisation strategies. This meant Anglo-Celtic people were taking possession of land, water, mineral and other natural resources, and changing the existing Aboriginal economy, supplanting it with one based primarily on Western forms of pearling and pastoralism. The pearling and pastoral industries, in combination with the 1886 gold rush in Halls Creek, made for hostile race relations in the Kimberley.[19] This in turn affected the Aboriginal construction and representation of cultural landscapes.

The dislocation of Aboriginal people from the Kimberley landscape through massacres, slavery and other forms of containment, such as the setting up of ration depots and mission stations, was commonplace. Jane Jacobs argues that the 'desire to establish settler colonies depended upon the will of erasure or, when this failed, systematic containment of indigenous peoples'.[20]

The effects of this colonising society on clan structure differed across specific clans. Those located nearest the places where settlers arrived bore the brunt of hostilities and subsequently experienced a more significant decrease in their populations, which in turn restricted their members' ability to engage in clan and cultural activities. This was probably the case for Billingee's clan group, the Ngumbarl, in the Dampier Peninsula.

Christianity, introduced through white settlement and mission stations in the Kimberley, affected Aboriginal beliefs and practices, as well as the production of material culture and art. Missionaries in the Kimberley during Billingee's time encouraged Aboriginal people to produce material cultural objects, and to paint on bark and board for sale. In fact, the people from the Ngarinyin, Wunumbal and Worora clans, and territorial landowners of the northern and central Kimberley region, were one of the major groups that missionaries targeted to produce this type of mobile art.[21] Billingee would have experienced first-hand the effects the settlers had on his landscape and culture, and Bates was in a unique position to document these changes.

The encounter between Daisy Bates and Billingee during the early 20th century was extraordinary not least because it was rare for a 'white' woman to have any relationship with an Aboriginal man during the time when the colonialists were in power. Without doubt Bates' relationship with the Beagle Bay Mission and with Bishop Gibney influenced her motivations and attitudes. During this time Bates recorded that Billingee extensively produced material cultural objects. It is plausible to think that Billingee's work was among that collected by the missionaries, or other collectors and connoisseurs.

During Billingee's time and thereafter it was common practice for anthropologists, missionaries and people who worked for the Native Affairs Department to collect Aboriginal art and material cultural objects and give them to museums in Australia to be stored or exhibited. However, because the general policy of the day did not record the names of Aboriginal artists, it would be extremely difficult, if not impossible, to identify the work that Billingee produced. It is the aesthetic and ethnographic collaboration with Bates, therefore, that has given him a name and produced new historical information about Australian colonial life.

The subject matter in the drawing book

The images of material cultural objects in the drawing book can be loosely divided into weaponry and ornamentation. In conjunction with Bates' other ethnographic writings, images and text in the drawing book inform the viewer about the relationship these objects have to the local environment; to social and cultural issues (such as identity, gender and age); and to performance activities, 'love magic' and dispute processes.

Even though Bates acknowledges that Billingee's work shares some of the features of Aboriginal rock art, the placement of sketches on a page has overtones of Western displays — in fact it is reminiscent of museum displays, where objects are lined up in glass-covered boxes for public exhibition.[22] Hence, several questions arise: Where did Billingee get the notion to draw objects using a museum layout? Are there some connections between his artistic style and his knowledge of the European artistic style? What art styles had he viewed to produce these kinds of sketches? Billingee has drawn many of the objects in a systematic, Western style. Was Bates perhaps present, directing the style of the artwork?

In some parts of the book, sketches drawn on one page appear to be connected to those on another, together forming a part of one story. Elsewhere, the sketches on the one page seem rationally connected, such as drawings that depict weaponry, yet those on another appear to be an arbitrary collection of images; for example, the decorative ornaments of necklaces drawn near images of a bird and fish. We might also ask the question, is the drawing book an artefact of the colonial encounter? And what lies beyond this encounter? Marcia Langton writes: 'There remains the difficulty of mapping the detailed world of Aboriginal religious life and culture proper...and [what] Aboriginal people bring to this encounter.'[23] For Billingee, then, the images in the drawing book provide us with an insight into aspects of 'Aboriginal religious life and culture proper', even as it illuminates the colonial encounter.

Billingee sketched five boomerangs that were coloured with either a zigzag or straight line design. Bates pencilled the word *lanjee*, which is translated as meaning boomerang, next to each. The other words that are written near the word *lanjee* look like *koolmee* and *jarrnigur*, which, in translation, are the names of local trees used to make boomerangs.[24] In her ethnographic notebook on dances, songs and ceremonies Bates remarked that *lanjee* music 'is called *jerrum-jeerum* or *jerim-jerim*'.[25] While her notes in the drawing book did not comment on the decorative patterns that Billingee drew on the boomerangs, the designs he made on three of them are identifiable with people from the Dampier Peninsula.[26] Billingee shows, through his collaboration with Bates, the objects used by his people and how the landscape is used to make these objects — the relationship of the land and people in his society.

Billingee sketched the images of a number of spears, a spear thrower and two shields on one of the pages in the drawing book. Bates noted that these objects were from the Broome and Roebourne areas in Western Australia. She also wrote the word 'mangrove' underneath four of the spears. Presumably, then, some spears were made from the wood of the mangrove tree, a common plant in Billingee's landscape. Bates further wrote the word *jimbala* near two of the spears. This is a Ngumbarl language word meaning a structured or heavy war spear.[27]

Alongside the spear thrower Billingee drew on this page, Bates pencilled in the words 'spear thrower' *yungara*. This is interesting because, as Akerman reports, 'people from the Dampier Land Peninsula [Billingee's territory] did not…use the spear-throwers or stone-tipped spears found in other parts of the Kimberley'.[28] This being the case, Billingee has drawn fighting and hunting tools from different places in Western Australia, not just his own locale, and the notes written by Bates on the page support this notion.[29] Billingee, then, seems to be informing us about objects used in Aboriginal societies throughout the Kimberley, not just his own.

The two shields Billingee drew on this page appear large and flat. Roman Black records that five different types of shields have been produced and associated with specific regions in Western Australia.[30] Kim Akerman identifies one kind, the 'large flat shield', as being used to defend people from the onslaught of boomerangs and spears.[31] Although Billingee drew bold zigzag designs on the two shields, the notes by Bates, on the page, do not offer any insight into their meaning. Akerman records that oblong, rounded shapes and zigzag designs are visible on the *wunda* shields, and are identifiable with groups living in the Murchinson and Gascoyne regions of Western Australia. Murchinson/Gascoyne shields were used in trade exchanges that spanned great distances northward into the Kimberley.[32]

Regardless of the specific origin of the shields and their designs, the drawings tell us about the designs and diversity of material cultural objects produced by Billingee and his people in the early 20th century. Bates' footnotes and Billingee's sketches also reveal the selection of wood used to produce objects that were part of the cultural heritage. This would have been at the forefront of Billingee's vision because the

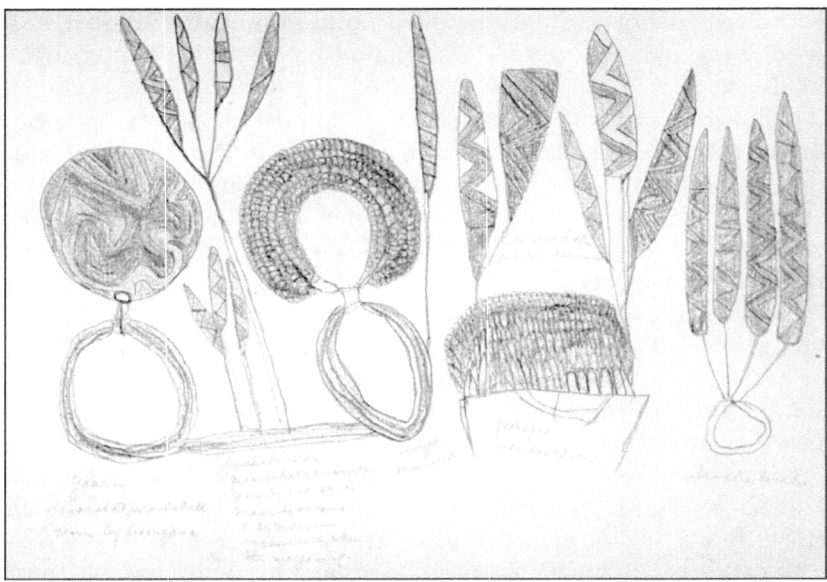

Drawing by Billingee (footnotes by Daisy Bates) of male and female ceremonial dress and ornamentation: tassels (aprons), hair belts and decorated pearl shell. Courtesy Battye Library Private Archives Collection.

Drawing by Billingee (footnotes by Daisy Bates) of nose pins made from wood (represented by the tree) and bone (represented by the kangaroo and emus). Courtesy Battye Library Private Archives Collection.

natural resources he and his compatriots relied on in their territory for maintaining their way of life were under threat. Billingee had witnessed the destructive processes involved in colonial settlement: the felling of timber and land clearing for the introduction of European pastoral industry.

On another page in the drawing book, Billingee sketched images of decorated men who were holding weapons and appeared to be engaged in a dispute. The accompanying notes made by Bates on this page are also limited. Although she provides information about these objects using Jukun, Ngumbarl and English language words, she does not elaborate about the meaning or story that Billingee intended through this drawing. However, if an association is made between the images of the spears, boomerangs and shields and those of the men involved in the dispute, it becomes possible to identify the men with Broome and Roebourne.

Furthermore, both text and images on these two pages in the drawing book appear to be linked with Daisy Bates' records of 'corroborees', songs and dances from Broome and the north-west of Western Australia.[33] This gives us a brief insight into some of the Aboriginal rules of social behaviour of the time, and a glimpse of the cultural and social relations of Aboriginal people in these places during colonial times. Additionally, the visual record of the dispute process provides another ethno-historical reference for researchers interested in the traditional law and weapons used by Billingee and his compatriots during the early 20th century.

As already mentioned, Billingee's images included human ornaments and naturalistic representations of fauna. Under one of these images Bates has written in the words *lingmeree* 'kangaroo sheath'. She elaborated on the contextual use of the kangaroo sheath by Aboriginal people in ethnographic notes she made about dances, songs and ceremonies. The kangaroo sheath appears to have been an object of central importance to the outcome of an elopement dispute story; however, as the story Bates has documented may be located in a secret domain of Aboriginal life, I will not elaborate on it.

Nevertheless, it is important to mention that Billingee and Bates, through their collaboration, have provided us with a snapshot of the ritual and decorative objects used by Aboriginal people to maintain their cultural heritage in colonial times. On the same page as the 'kangaroo sheath' illustration, Billingee has drawn images of a bird and fish, which might seem irrelevant to the other sketches. Underneath one of the small fish Bates has written the words *noongan barredee*. Bates explains that this fish is 'not eaten by' certain people 'for some time', which suggests that Billingee and his people considered the *noongan barredee* fish as taboo for specific people during particular times. Here Billingee and Bates' collaboration provides us with a fleeting glimpse of the cultural rules associated with food taboos in the area.

Billingee has devoted one page in the drawing book to Aboriginal dress and ornamentation. On this page he has drawn male and female tassels (aprons), hair belts and decorated pearl shell ornaments. Bates has pencilled in Aboriginal words and phrases near these objects with some English translations. She identifies one of the decorated pearl shell objects as a *goarn*, another one as *bindha bindha*, and writes that men and women wear different looking tassels (aprons). In the Kimberley and Western Desert regions of Western Australia, Kim Akerman notes: '...men and women wore small blades, discs and crescents of pearl shell for personal adornment...[and the] wearing of smaller pieces of shell is considered to be informal, and the larger, more cumbersome shells are usually associated with formal events.'[34] Through representing Aboriginal dress and ornamentation on this page Billingee was engaging in the aesthetics of artistic heritage, giving evidence of the connection between material cultural and the landscape, and therefore expressing his cultural identity in the face of the colonising society.

In one of the most intriguing images of the book, Billingee has drawn what seems to resemble a royal crest of the British Empire. In the centre of the page is a large fruiting tree (or flowering shrub) with elongated branches that envelope images of two emus and a kangaroo. On the far left, five bright-red, vertically elongated objects stand separately, and Bates has pencilled in each the words *warangaji*, 'nose bones'. Bates has not written anything much about the fruiting tree, nor whether these images are connected to the other objects on the page. However, a common form of beautification or embellishment for ritual practice in Aboriginal societies is the wearing of nose bones. These objects, about 40 centimetres long, are made either from the bone of a kangaroo or emu, or from lengths of wood, and placed in the septum of the nose.[35] The composition of this drawing shows us the range of raw materials used to make nose pins, as well as one of the relationships between material culture, people and the environment. It would also appear Billingee was attempting to use a form

Anglo-Celtic people were familiar with to communicate information about the native flora, fauna and associated decorative ornamentation significant to his people, territory and law.

The use of headdresses in Aboriginal societies — which Billingee reveals in images of two men decorated and wearing headdresses for performance — is of great antiquity. Paintings on rock art galleries in the north of Australia, according to Ian Howie-Willis, show 'people wearing a range of headdresses...the designs are related to particular Dreamings so that performers in a ceremony would all wear the headdress of one design'.[36] Bates also pencilled in words and phrases near the men and near the ornaments they were wearing and holding. She wrote the words *pander womba*, 'decorated man' underneath the sketch of one man, and *joordajoorda*, 'made from wood' alongside the headdresses. In other ethnographic notes Bates recorded that when men wore *joordajoorda* they sang a specific song.[37] Headdresses are currently associated with song and dance sequences in Billingee's territory and throughout the Kimberley, as currently shown by the Pelican Dreaming story and dance, produced by the late Nyigina Lawman and artist Butcher Joe Nangan.

Akerman notes that 'the distinctive *niwalki* thread-cross Pelican headdress has become a local icon of Aboriginal culture'.[38] Indeed, the construction of the headdresses and the diamond-shaped objects that Billingee drew are visually similar to the *Ilma*, or woven wool head-dresses, that have been recently produced in the Dampier Peninsula. Roy Wiggan, a senior Bardi man from the Dampier Peninsula, is renowned in the Australian art world for his production of hand-held sculptural *Ilma* dance emblems. According to Akerman: '*Ilma* emblems are derived from thread-cross artefacts, once originally made from hair or animal-fur string and constructed on frameworks of sticks...or in some areas they are primarily used in public or open dances.'[39]

Decorated men feature on yet another page in the drawing book, this time enacting a performance. Again the bodies of the two men are painted; they are also holding emblems and wearing headdresses. Bates wrote *pander womba*, 'decorated man' underneath both figures. Billingee has drawn a circular object that encompasses the head of one of the men, and Bates has pencilled in what appears to be the word *booga*, without an English translation. She uses the same word to describe the diamond-shaped objects on the previous page. Both the diamond- and circular-shaped objects on these two pages appear to be woven or thread-crossed, an artistic production technique used by Aboriginal people in this region when they make objects for performance.

***

The drawing book, then, is a valuable source of historical information. This collaboration between an Anglo-Celtic woman and Jukun Ngumbarl man in colonial Australia reveals much about Aboriginal society and relationships between humans and the landscape. It also shows the continuity of Aboriginal traditional culture in the face of colonisation and the corrosive effects of missions, government policy and capitalism. Ironically, it mocks Bates' original aim of documenting a 'dying culture' by contributing to our contemporary knowledge of how much is still alive.

When Sir Frederick Bedford received the drawing book in 1907, he gave Bates a piece of gold for Billingee's labour. But upon receiving the gold, Bates claims, Billingee replied: 'Please tell Governor that I nothing want him money. He look at things and think of Billingee.'[40] The prevailing social evolutionary values of the period are very likely to have influenced both Bates' relationship with Billingee and the reception of Billingee's work by Governor Sir Frederick Bedford, but we can only hypothesise about how Billingee wanted his work to be seen by the governor. The question is particularly interesting in regard to the correspondence between Bates and Bedford, the outcomes of contact history in the Kimberley, and the ensuing inequitable relationships between cultural groups in the 19th and early 20th centuries.

Billingee might have wanted to inform Bedford about the significance of pearl shell to his people, culture and law. During 1906 the government passed legislation that banned the trading of pearl shell, and this had a devastating effect on the ability of clans in the Kimberley to engage in their own cultural, spiritual and economic activities. I propose that Billingee and Bates both wanted to inform Bedford about the material culture of the local Aboriginal people, and how it connected to ceremony and the environment; however, they went about it by very different means. Bates applied ethnographic methods to Billingee's art on paper in her interpretation of his worldview, whereas Billingee identified with his worldview, and informed others about it by aesthetic means — using the materials of his 'oppressor'. As Howard Morphy observed, the 'history of the European colonization of Australia has also been a history of Aboriginal attempts to assert the equality of value of their culture and way of life against the economic and political objectives of the invaders'.[41]

Billingee's art informs us about a world that 'lies behind the colonial encounter', revealing Indigenous socio-cultural rules and connections to the environment. It is plausible that Billingee collaborated with Bates in an endeavour to affirm the excellence of his 'culture and way of life' to Bedford, through aesthetics, and that the money offered by Bedford was of secondary or little importance.

Half a century later, the State Library of Western Australia purchased the drawing book for its archives from a second-hand bookstore in London. The state librarian corroborated Bates' earlier prediction, that the historical value of Billingee's drawing book would be 'priceless'.[42]

Notes

1. 'Daisy Bates' letters to Sir Frederick Bedford', Daisy Bates Papers, MN 1315, accession record 4123A/2, 1907: 2, JS Battye Library of West Australian History, Perth.
2. 'Daisy Bates' letters', 4123A/2:2.
3. King.
4. Berndt and Berndt 1988.
5. This is my own observation, based on my recent field research in the area and life experience as a descendant of the Jukun-Yawuru clan.
6. See 'Native vocabulary compiled by Billingee, 1904–1912' and 'Vocabulary Broome District: Jukan Ngangga, Informant = Billing-gi, 1904–1912', in Daisy Bates Papers, MS 365, Box 26, folio 52, pp. 1–51 and 105–31, National Library of Australia (NLA), Canberra.
7. For a comprehensive record, see *Daisy M Bates: a guide to her papers*, NLA, Canberra, 1966, revised 1988.
8. 'Native vocabulary compiled by Billingee, 1904–1912', in Daisy Bates Papers, MS 365, Box 26, folio 52, p. 49, NLA, Canberra.
9. White 1985.
10. White 1985; Salter 1971; Hill 1973.
11. For a comprehensive guide to the literature about Daisy Bates held in Australian libraries see King 1985.
12. See 'Billingee' in Daisy Bates Papers, MN 1315, accession record 4123A, JS Battye Library.
13. See 20-page artist drawing book with annotations by Daisy Bates, 1907; 'Daisy Bates' letters to Sir Frederick Bedford', in Daisy Bates Papers, MN1315, accession record 4123A/2, JS Battye Library of Western Australian History, Perth.
14. Marcia Langton, 'Religion and art from colonial conquest to post-colonial resistance', in Kleinert & Neale, p. 24.

15. See Sayers 1994.

16. Morphy 1998, p. 266.

17. Sayers 1994, p. 3.

18. Grey 1841.

19. Caruana, 1993.

20. Jacobs 1996, p. 105.

21. Ryan & Akerman 1993.

22. For where Daisy Bates likens Billingee's work to rock art painting see White 1985, p. 269.

23. Marcia Langton, 'Religion and art from colonial conquest to post-colonial resistance', in Kleinert & Neale, p. 16.

24. I was not able to authenticate the spelling of the last two words in any of the vocabularies in Bates' papers.

25. See 'Dances and songs, 1904–1912', in Daisy Bates Papers, MS 365, Box 17, folio 34, NLA, pp. 102–05.

26. See the Kimberley collections held by the National Museum of Australia and the West Australian Museum.

27. See 'Vocabulary Broome district...', Daisy Bates Papers, MS 365, Box 26, folio 52, NLA, p. 110. I was not able to authenticate the spelling of the last two words in any of the vocabularies in Bates Papers.

28. Kim Akerman, 'The traditional Aboriginal art of the Kimberley region (WA)', in Kleinert & Neale, p. 226–30.

29. See 'Native vocabulary compiled...'Daisy Bates Papers, MS 365, Box 26, folio 52, NLA, pp. 1–51.

30. Black 1964, p. 83.

31. Kim Akerman, Richard Fullagar & Annelou van Gijn, 'Weapons and *wunan*: production, function and exchange of Kimberley points', *Australian Aboriginal Studies*, no. 1, 2002, pp. 13–24.

32. Akerman et al., Weapons and *wunan*', pp. 17–19.

33. See 'Dances and songs, 1904–1912', pp. 1–136; also, 'Corroborees, songs, etc. Broome and N.W. West Australia, 1904–1912', in Daisy Bates Papers, MS 365, Box 18, folio 35, pp. 125–144, NLA.

34. Akerman & Stanton, p. 22

35. E Ride, 'Body adornment', in Kleinert & Neale, p. 544.

36. Howie-Willis, Ian 1994, 'Headdresses', in *The encyclopaedia of Aboriginal Australia: Aboriginal and Torres Strait Islander history, society and culture*, ed. D Horton, Aboriginal Studies Press, Canberra, pp. 453–54.

37. See 'Corroborees, songs, etc.', p. 132.

38. Kim Akerman, 'Nangan', in Kleinert & Neale, p. 658.

39. Kim Akerman, 'From boab nut to Ilma: Kimberley art and material culture', in Ryan & Akerman, pp. 106–17.

40. See 'Daisy Bates' letters to Sir Frederick Bedford'.

41. Morphy 1998, 266.

42. 'Daisy Bates was right', *Australian*, 16 April 1958.

10. 'A glorious thing is to live in a tent in the infinite'
Daisy Bates

Jim Anderson

It was common for British colonies to become the locus for personal reinvention, and that is precisely what Irish-born Daisy Bates (1859–1951) did, spending much of her life living with, and writing about, Aboriginal tribal groups in Western and South Australia. She was, however, so eccentric, her later writing so palpably racist, and her life story now so much contested, that she is no longer much believed or respected, although she still remains something of a populist, iconic figure. While she found both limited fame and notoriety in her own lifetime, she never seemed to find much happiness until she created her own small realm in the Australian bush.

Despite the persistent social-Darwinian notion that proclaimed their imminent racial demise, Aboriginal people survived the colonial enterprise and, in 1967, were finally admitted into society as full human beings, deemed worthy to be counted in the national census. Some 16 years before, Daisy May Bates, for whom the 'doomed race' theory was axiomatic — '[t]ruly a dying people whom no effort can save' — passed away in an Adelaide nursing home.[1] Of humble Irish origins, her life had been one of constant reinvention and crossing of borders, both geographical and social, as she recast herself as a lady, a journalist, an ethnographer, philanthropic agent of the British Empire and Aboriginal spirit woman.

Bates was in her 40s before Aboriginal people became of any interest to her, initially as the subject of her journalism. This interest developed into an extensive ethnographic inquiry, and she 'made the decision to dedicate the rest of [her] life to this fascinating study', spending almost 50 years travelling across the outback, living frugally, pitching her tent near Aboriginal encampments, and recording their lore and language.[2] She considered that they were fast disappearing as a result of contact with civilisation, and it became her life's mission 'to make their passing easier'.[3] In these endeavours she became something of a legendary figure and created a place for herself in Australian history. Although this legend has become somewhat contested, built as it was on her deception and self-delusion, her narrative does reveal a true delight in the Australian landscape and the freedom and solitude it afforded her. Her life was one of constant movement and frequent disappointment, yet she found meaning in the role she created for herself and she found her place in the outback.

The wonderful, horrible life of Daisy Bates[4]

Daisy Dwyer was born in 1859 to poor Catholic parents in post-famine Ireland. She was, however, obviously possessed with intelligence and drive, and sought to improve her place in the world. By 1883, when she arrived in Australia as part of the Irish diaspora, it appears she'd had some training as a governess for she found such employment with a Queensland pastoral family. She was briefly married to the man who would gain notoriety in the Boer War as 'Breaker' Morant, and later worked in Victoria where she bigamously married another horseman, Jack Bates, a drover for her employer. Her marriage to Bates was also a failure but she bore him a son, Arnold — an unwanted child whose very existence seemed to cramp Daisy's independence, and who she later abandoned to foster and institutional care.

During these early years in Australia, Bates seems never to have found her own place, but 'travelled with her child to various parts of Australia, staying with friends'.[5] Jack Bates had promised to buy a property where the family could settle, but he continued his droving life. This eventually caused her to become depressed, which her doctor, somewhat improbably, diagnosed as 'nostalgia'; he suggested a voyage to England and Jack Bates offered to pay her fare.[6] Arnold was placed in a boarding school and in 1894 Daisy left son, husband and adopted colony and returned to London. There, having found work with WT Stead, editor of the *Review of Reviews* and the spiritualist magazine *Borderlands*, she 'learned much of the craft of journalism' while living in genteel poverty.[7] When reports appeared in the London *Times* that pastoralists in Western Australia were mistreating Aboriginal people, Bates took the opportunity to investigate these claims and in 1899 sailed to Perth. There she met up with her family but, having transformed herself into a lady journalist, she quickly fostered out her son and took delight in genteel Perth society before sailing north to join her husband, who was in the process of buying a property near Carnarvon.

It was on this trip that she began writing and contributing articles for publication, demonstrating an imaginative skill in her description of place and a delight in landscape, as shown in this example from one of her biographers:

> ...the grotesque brown mounds of the white ant, that crouch ghoul like over the vast bare flat'...The sight of a myriad cockatoos rising with 'a sudden and simultaneous frou frou of wings' she compared with 'a women's meeting, when all are asked to rise'...She saw a 'mock sun, shining and sending forth rays irrespective of the real sun, which was in another part of the horizon' and heard a singing 'glade of birds, their song beginning at 2 a.m. and kept up until sunrise', when daylight revealed only a clump of scrub 'with neither sight nor sound of a single bird' to explain the phenomenon.[8]

It was also at this time that Bates began to write about Aboriginal people. Significantly, in light of her later spiritual relationship with them, one of her first observations was that 'they have no Deity, but many devils' who could be frightened away by the bullroarer whose 'booming and most depressing noise [was] sufficient to send any devil flying from it'. She was also intrigued by Aboriginal basket-weaving and delighted in their rock art 'limned in the days when the world was young'.[9]

Negotiations for the property completed, Daisy returned to Perth and took the opportunity to visit a remote Trappist mission at Beagle Bay on the far north-west coast in order that '[t]he world would be given the truth about the Aborigines'.[10] Here, Bates had her first extended contact with them, catching 'but a few stray glimpses... of the strange hidden life of this last remnant of the palaeolithic man'.[11] She was obviously smitten for, relying solely on her income from journalism, she went on to live for eight months with the Koolarrabulloo tribes near Broome, where she began to develop a

The Duke of Gloucester and Daisy Bates conversing at Ooldea during the Duke's tour by train in 1934. Photograph courtesy State Library of South Australia.

deeper interest in Aboriginal culture. In 1904, she finally left her droving husband and, having made something of a reputation from her articles, found employment with the West Australian Government. She was commissioned to collect ethnographic data, and set up her tent near Aboriginal camps on the outskirts of Perth and all around the south of Western Australia. She submitted papers on Aboriginal people to learned journals, such as the *Transactions of the Royal Geographical Society of Australia*, and in 1910 was invited to join an expedition led by the Cambridge anthropologist Arthur Radcliffe-Brown.[12]

In 1912 Bates applied for the job of Protector of Aborigines but, despite glowing references from several West Australian worthies, was turned down on the grounds that as a white woman she would be the one in need of protection. She had to console herself with the

— unpaid — title of *Honorary* Protector of Aborigines. Undeterred, she continued her work. Now 'a confirmed wanderer, a nomad even as the [A]borigines', she roamed the south-western part of Western Australia and in 1914 crossed into South Australia and set up camp at Wirilya near Yalata on the Nullarbor Plain.[13] Here she gloried in the solitude and particularly delighted in the company of birds, of which she wrote that every species 'has its own personality, so to speak'.[14] Yet she continued to relate to Aboriginal people from the perspective of the doomed race theory and Bates locates herself within the ancient landscape where:

> ...sunsets blaze and fade, and blaze again in these great empty wilds, and dawn sets her diadem over them. The light loitering winds carry delicate perfumes hither and thither, but all these places that once echoed with song or war-cry are now left to the birds and animals whose forebears witnessed the arrival of humans, and who themselves are now witnessing their passing.[15]

By 1918, at nearly age 60, the deprivations of her nomadic existence began to take their toll on her health; she travelled to Adelaide to recuperate, but the following year she was back on the Nullarbor Plain. Ooldea Soak had long been a permanent watering hole and an ancient locus for Aboriginal ceremony, but with the coming of the transcontinental railway the water had been tapped and piped to a nearby siding to replenish the six locomotives that crossed the Nullarbor each week. Denied their ancient watering rights, 'some hundreds of derelict natives' had camped beside the railway tracks, and for 17 years Bates remained at Ooldea offering them a meagre nursing and hospice service and collecting her data.[16] Her nursing skills she 'derived from experience only, without regard to medical theory', and all she could really offer the sick was the plain diet which she alleged was the source of her own good health and 'made them healthy too'. She would bandage their burns, and for coughs offer them what she claimed as an Irish folk remedy: 'honey, brandy, lemon, olive oil, powdered candy and vinegar (a tablespoonful of each)'. Nevertheless, it was as anthropological specimens that Aboriginal people really held her interest since, '...first and last, their old ways were studied, and so these times of sickness were spent in tranquility, and they passed over in peace among their own kind.'[17]

In 1920 Bates was asked 'to arrange a display of [A]borigines...in honour of His Royal Highness, the Prince of Wales' who was on a tour of Australia.[18] The display seems to have gone off well, with Bates sharing the dais with the prince as she explained to him the significance of the Aboriginal dances. Twelve years later Bates was visited by the journalist Ernestine Hill, with whose help she began a series of articles, 'My natives and I'. Syndicated across the Australian newspapers, this series was eventually to find publication as the bestselling *The passing of the Aborigines* (1938). In 1934, Bates finally gained recognition for her long years of sacrifice to the 'dying race' and was awarded the Order of Commander of the British Empire. On this triumphant note, Daisy Bates, CBE left Ooldea later that year for Adelaide and civilisation.

The contested narrative

Bates' purported autobiographical account *The passing of the Aborigines*, which begins in 1899 with her return to Australia, is couched in the paternalistic and racist terminology of colonial discourse. The doomed race theory is substantiated in her expressed notions of eugenics and racial purity, since for Bates 'half-castes' were anathema. Full of self-glorification and false humility, her narrative reads much like a 'Boy's Own' adventure story of the period; indeed, Arthur Mee, promoter and publisher of such stories, wrote a glowing introduction. Her aggregation of all Australian Aboriginal people to the small, marginal and marginalised desert groups with whom she had most contact is both divorced from and obscures the broader discourse of white settlement and Aboriginal dispossession.

Most strikingly, in this work Bates sustained and extemporised upon the myth of Aboriginal cannibalism. 'Baby cannibalism was rife among these people,' she wrote — a point she returns to time and again, for her index contains 14 references covering some 25 pages.[19] In 1930 she sent the bones of what she claimed were the remains of a cannibalistic feast to Adelaide University for investigation. They turned out to be 'undoubtedly those of a domestic cat'.[20] Yet Bates is still quoted, some 70 years later, by politicians of the right who would use these claims of cannibalism in seeking to deny Aboriginal people justice.

Thirty years after Bates' death, Elizabeth Salter published a rather uncritical and romantic biography, *Daisy Bates: the great white queen of the Never Never* (1971). Drawn largely from Bates' own notes, it depicts her early life as one of Anglo-Irish gentility somewhat fallen on hard times — a depiction later revealed by historical research to be a complete fabrication on Bates' part.[21] An even more sycophantic paean,

Kabbarli: a personal memoir of Daisy Bates by Ernestine Hill (the journalist who had helped Bates with her own book), appeared two years later. Hill also accepted the story of Bates' genteel origins at face value and, like Salter, she was somewhat in awe of the 'White Grandmother of Ooldea', casting Bates as a lady and heroine of empire.

Bates' voluminous ethnographic work filling 94 folios never appeared in print; however, in 1985 an edition of some of her early papers was published as *The native tribes of Western Australia*. Bates' articles on Aboriginal folklore, collected from the Perth area and which had appeared over a period of 30 years in various Australian newspapers, were published (together with some previously unpublished pieces) in a 1992 collection, *Aboriginal Perth and Bibbulman biographies and legends*.[22] Some of the Aboriginal Dreaming stories that she collected have reappeared in an illustrated, narrative format.[23] To the non-specialist, these stories read as objective accounts, rich in cultural and linguistic detail, and containing none of the pompous self-promotion nor the paternalistic racism of the biographical works. Indeed, the biographical narratives have become so contested by writers such as Isobel White that it becomes difficult to place Daisy Bates in the ever-shifting ground of her own reinvention and her lionisation by others. Ernestine Hill, her amanuensis in the writing of *The passing of the Aborigines*, claims that Bates never made 'any corrections or contradictions' to Hill's manuscript.[24] Yet as the book was being prepared for publication, Hill received a letter from Bates that said: 'As I read through the chapters, I come upon so many evidences of your own words and sentences...that I shall always look upon the completed work as much as as [sic] yours as mine.'[25]

So how much was Bates and how much was Hill? The self-aggrandisement expressed in *The passing of the Aborigines* is corroborated in Salter's biography, but then she and Hill were both promoters of the Bates legend. It must be assumed that although the poetic licence probably belongs to her sycophants, there is at least a kernel of Daisy Bates in these texts. Knowing just how much, however, is problematic; as the Bates legend shifts, so Bates reality becomes more difficult to pin down.

Border crossings

As a girl born into a poor, Irish Catholic family, Daisy Bates suffered from four-fold marginality in a world dominated by a masculine, Anglo-Protestant empire mapped out in boundaries of class, religion, race and gender. Yet, in one way or another she was to cross all of those borders. As a woman who 'all through her life never lacked courage', she had managed early to transcend the restrictions a post-famine Ireland would have placed upon such a girl of humble origins and had become at least sufficiently skilled to find work as a rural governess in the British Empire's farthest flung colony.[26]

Daisy Bates was never wealthy, although Jack Bates later signed over the Carnarvon property to her and, from the proceeds of its sale in 1912, she was able to sustain her austere, nomadic lifestyle for a while. Although her needs were small, she nonetheless had to supplement this income with her journalism and the beneficence of friends. In later life she subsisted on a small government pension.

While she was not so successful at crossing the poverty line, on her return to Australia in 1899 she did manage to cross the line of class. In Perth, Bates met up again with her family but, having recently arrived from five years at the hub of the Empire, she described her husband as having become 'loose and flabby and common – above all common!'[27] With the status of 'English Lady Journalist' bestowed upon her by the Perth press, she fully lived up to the role, and the degree to which she was successful is demonstrated by her acceptance into the exclusive Karrakatta Club and her formal presentation to the Duke and Duchess of York, the future King George V and Queen Mary.[28]

Central to her makeover into a lady was Bates' strong identification as an Anglican. That she should have crossed the denominational divide to aid her own upward mobility and identify with the dominant imperial orthodoxy is perhaps not surprising, given that the King Emperor to whom she owed devoted allegiance was also the head of the Anglican Church. Yet Bates became more than just Anglican, for at a time when Australia was struggling with its own religious and national identities, she became vehemently anti-Catholic. She had been very happy to avail herself of the friendship of the Catholic bishop Matthew Gibney and his priests during her visit to the Beagle Bay monastery: 'I had then, and have now in retrospect, the greatest admiration for the Trappist missionaries,' she later wrote.[29] But in 1926 she was writing to the *Australasian* newspaper with dire warnings of a Catholic conspiracy to take over Australia, by breeding-up the 'half-caste' population. The archbishops, 'Mannix, Kelly of Sydney, Clune of W.A. ...all have their armies constantly at work,' she wrote. '...the Broome Caste Missions are R.C.

and hence the menace is quadrupled — the offspring of these offscourings of the world are evil to look at, evil in thought, word and deed. No found-ation for good citizenship in any of them.'[30] She also became equally 'obsessed with suspicion' about the loyalty of Lutheran missionaries, and in 'making these views known' she lost a great deal of respect in South Australia.[31] Among her recommendations for the appointment of a high commissioner for native affairs was her insistence that, in representing the Crown, he be 'an anglican and a gentleman'.[32]

Whether she could no longer maintain the pretence, had run out of money, or simply developed wanderlust, Bates did not remain for long in polite metropolitan society, although she was forever to retain its mores. Throughout all those years in the bush she maintained an upper-class posture and 'always preserved a scrupulous neatness, and all the little trappings and accoutrements of my own very particular mode of dress'. This consisted of 'a neat white blouse, stiff collar and ribbon tie, a dark skirt and coat, stout and serviceable, trim shoes and neat black stockings, a sailor hat and fly-veil'.[33] She always carried her umbrella which, having been touched by the royal personage at her presentation in Perth, had taken on something of the aura of a sacred object. The maintenance of this persona was, as Ann Standish has remarked, 'partly an "othering" tactic', serving to maintain racial superiority rather than cross the racial divide.[34] Unlike the male heroes of empire, such as Sir Richard Burton and TE Lawrence, Bates couldn't simply pretend to 'go native'.

Bates never denied her Irish heritage and indeed because of it considered herself to have a cultural affinity with Aboriginal people. In Aboriginal dot-painting she saw the whorls of ancient Irish art, and the clue to her purported success in being able to think with a 'black man's mind' lay in her claim that: 'If you are Celt you can sense what the [Aboriginal person] is unable to express.'[35] Despite this claim, and in order to gain their confidence in her gathering of ethnographic data, Bates stooped to deception and created yet another persona for herself: 'I pretended that my name was Kallower, and that I was a *nirruroo-jandu* or magic woman.'[36]

In 1910 she visited the isolation hospitals on the Dorré and Bernier Islands, off the West Australian coast, and became 'a constant traveller between the two islands and the mainland' carrying *bamburu* or letter sticks.[37] She claimed that in order to fulfil this task she had first to be adopted into the Aboriginal kinship structure, and used this and her other 'little errands of mercy' to transform herself from *kallauer*, or grandmother, into a spirit being called '*kabbarli*, the Grandmother… [which] I was to remain in all my wanderings, for the name is a generic one, and extends far among the western-central and central tribes'.[38] This was perhaps her greatest self reinvention, as 'the revered grandmother of ancient tribes, the great white queen of the desert, a goddess'.[39] Just how much of this mythological persona was bestowed upon her by Aboriginal people and how much was her own invention is now difficult to determine, for Kabbarli became the legendary central character of her self-promoting narrative.

Clearly, married domesticity did not suit her, and although even in the bush she maintained the posture of a genteel lady, her free, nomadic lifestyle challenged the gender stereotypes of her age. Yet, ironically, it was in her contact with Aboriginal people as the feminine, yet mythical, persona of Kabbarli that Bates actually crossed the boundary of gender. As Isobel White points out, having 'been admitted to the men's secrets, the [Aboriginal] women would not have admitted her to theirs, as they would not have regarded her as a real woman'.[40] It was the story of Daisy Bates' life: having crossed one border, she had created another.

Apart from her own reinventions, perhaps the border that Bates crossed more than any other was the truth about Aboriginal people. In sustaining the doomed race theory, her account creates the impression that the only 'true' Aboriginal people were the marginal desert groups with whom she became acquainted. In attributing their extinction to simply being 'unable to withstand civilization', Bates disguises the complex and violent reality of Aboriginal dispossession.[41] She refuted those claims of settler cruelty that she had early set out to investigate, and throughout her narratives settlers are always portrayed in a kindly light. Her account also disguises the fact that the majority of Aboriginal people were, from the turn of the century, subjected first to policies of settled apartheid and then to assimilationist attempts at 'biological absorption'.[42] Daisy Bates' own fabrications of cannibalism were perhaps a journalistic device with which to pepper her narrative, to add piquancy to this genre of 'my life among the savages' colonial discourse. Yet, despite evidence to the contrary, she persisted in the lie and may not be forgiven for such perniciousness. One border that she reinforced was that of racial purity, for she maintained a loathing for miscegenation; for her, 'the only good half-caste [was] a dead one'.[43]

Although she believed she was a philanthropic agent of the Empire, Bates in fact achieved little for 'her natives' that was of long-lasting significance. All she could provide was an impoverished, one-woman hospice service. While in the 1930s women activists such as Mary Bennett and Ada Bromham were advocating for Aboriginal rights, Bates was simply living out her own fantasy in the desert.[44]

The place of Daisy Bates

Where then was the place of Daisy Bates, the eternal expatriate who had crossed so many borders? If we are to rely upon her accounts, we should take care. 'They accepted me as a kindred spirit,' she declared, yet throughout all her years of contact Bates never actually lived *with* Aboriginal people but camped some distance from them.[45] At the Beagle Bay Mission she had been happy to show off her grooming to the delight of the Aboriginal girls, but later behind her brush fence at Ooldea she established an exclusive domain, a goddess realm into which no person could intrude: 'I daren't invite a gentleman to set a foot inside that breakwind, or even be seen talking to him alone, or my reputation's gone as Kabbarli… I had to refuse admission one day to a bishop who came a-visiting.' She also had to chase away a visiting anthropologist who had refused to leave and wrote that she '…fled him from tree to tree. I'm quite sure he went back and reported my insanity.'[46]

Only in her 70s did Bates finally open up to Ernestine Hill, who alone gained entry into Bates' sanctum sanctorum. This consisted of a humble tent (measuring 8 feet by 10) which contained only the minimum of furniture and the trunks that 'held the Quality Street suits, coats, toques, shoes…[o]f architecture rather than tailoring' that Bates daily wore.[47] She might be impoverished, but here she was totally free, accountable to no one, and could solitarily indulge in her Kabbarli fantasies.

More than the passing of a native race, Bates' narratives are about her own struggle to find her place, and if there is any gladness, any ring of truth in any of her attributed writing, it is to be found in her delight in the bush. At Wirilya, she describes the idyllic setting:

> At all times it was beautiful, whether in the quivering heat of summer which sent waves of soft colours dancing over still trees and brown surface, or in the cool and misty winter mornings, when just to look upon its beauty was an ecstasy; the tall golden grasses nid-nodding with every breeze, the growing

greens of tree and bush mingling in utmost harmony with the greyer or browner older leaves, the tree-tops of the edging slopes beyond the vale silhouetted against a brilliant sky, or rising out of a white lake of morning mist; and all round and about, winter and summer, the wild life of the bush adding its voice and movement to the general harmony.[48]

Later still, at Yuria Water, she describes a landscape that, she implies, was exclusively hers to adore: 'Always the blue hills are visible, and always the colours change on hill and valley; yet in the native dialect, there is not one expression that would tend to show the native's admiration of his beautiful surroundings.'[49]

While people might not be welcome in Bates' little world, bush creatures certainly were: 'That's one of the chiefest joys of living in a tent, with the birds, the lizards and small furry friends that come to call on me.'[50] The first part of the chapter 'My friends the birds' is given over to a wonderful description of Australian bush life, that sings with Aboriginal names:

I might be solitary, but I was never lonely. The breakwind that enclosed my garden of sand was a veritable sanctuary of wildlife… I invariably rose at sunrise, when the days are at their most glorious, and the whole world is full of beauty and music and dreaming, waking from its slumbers under the mists. I made my toilet to a chorus of impatient twittering… My first greeting was for the birds… With a flash of bright wings and an excited chattering they were all about me. Melga…the little spotted and chestnut-backed groundthrushes became tame chickens…Miril-yiril-yiri…the wren, and Minning-minning his wife were other cherished friends… Jindirr-jindirr, the wagtail, and I sang duets together.[51]

She was fascinated by reptiles and developed a particular liking for the horny, or mountain, devil with whose aid Bates kept her tent free from 'the pestiferous little ant', and she was enthralled to witness combat of 'Jaggal, the bicycle lizard'.[52]

Beautiful as her landscape might have been, the cost of creating her remote and humble tent-realm was poverty and physical hardship. It remains one of the mysteries about Daisy Bates: why, having emerged from post-famine Ireland, did she choose to return to and remain in marginal penury for so long? To simply dismiss this as madness is, as Ann Standish says, 'probably accurate, but insufficient'.[53] For Ernestine Hill it was simply that Bates 'was Irish [and] that explained everything…the idealism, endurance, self-sacrifice, the prejudice and pride, her fearlessness…her delight in folk lore, her perpetual adoration of royalty'.[54] Whatever satisfaction Bates derived from her self-created role, the most persistent evidence of what captured her is that of the remote landscape and her solitary place in it.

In 1941, at the age of 82, Bates returned once more to the Nullarbor, to Wynbring siding east of Ooldea, but by this time not only were her eyesight and general health failing, she was also losing her mind. The old Kabbarli magic had gone, too. In 1944, she sent a telegram to Prime Minister John Curtin claiming that she had been attacked by a mob of hostile Aboriginal people and had to defend herself with a revolver. She requested him to finance her move to the safety of Adelaide. But when the matter was investigated by the railway authorities, they found there had been no mob; she had imagined it all. Finally, in 1945, suffering from malnutrition, she had to be rescued by ambulance and returned to Adelaide. In 1951 Kabbarli, she 'who had yearned for the red roads of Yuria, which gleamed from the white rock like the points of a star, died alone under the prosaic roof of a suburban rest-home'.[55]

***

All the hardships that Daisy Bates endured, all the border crossings, geographical and social, that she attempted, and all the personas she created throughout her life reveal an essentially lonely woman, searching for her place in the world. Having gained entry into Perth's exclusive set, she headed off again as an inveterate adventurer in an age when adventure was a colonial lifestyle. To find her place Daisy Bates had crossed many borders and in doing so had created many others. Although we can never be sure about her early years, she certainly moved up and out. After two failed marriages and an unwanted child, she traversed the world to reinvent herself time and again. The absent mother of a living child, she became the legendary 'Grandmother' of a dying race. It was in her tent-realm in the solitude of the bush that she took greatest delight and it was here, perhaps, that Daisy Bates found her true place:

> Apart from the joy of the work for its own sake…the freshness, the freedom, the far-ness meant much more to me now than the life of the cities. A glorious thing it is to live in a tent in the infinite — to waken in the grey of dawn, a good hour before the sun outlines the low ridges of the horizon, and to come out into the bright cool air, and scent the wind blowing across the *mulga* plains.[56]

Notes

1. Daisy Bates to the editor of the *Australasian*, 1926, cited in McGregor 1997, p. 125.
2. Bates 1972 (1938), p. 115.
3. Bates 1972 (1938), p. 243.
4. Note the heading for this section was taken from the documentary film *The wonderful, horrible life of Leni Riefenstahl* (1993). Without drawing too long a bow, she and Daisy Bates were each in their own way fantasists for an imperial project.
5. Isobel White, introduction to Bates 1985, p. 5.
6. Salter 1971, p. 36.
7. Isobel White, introduction to Bates 1985, p. 5.
8. Salter 1971, p. 75. Salter gives no annotation, but presumably is citing Daisy Bates 1901, 'From Port Hedland to Carnarvon by buggy', *Journal of the Western Australia Department of Agriculture*, vol. 4, pp. 183–382 (see bibliography in Salter 1971, p. 252).
9. Salter 1971, p. 76.
10. Salter 1971, p. 78.
11. Bates 1972 (1938), p. 22.
12. Isobel White gives a bibliography of Bates' articles published at this time in Bates 1985, p. 373.
13. Bates 1972 (1938), p. 115.
14. Bates 1972 (1938), p. 141.
15. Bates 1972 (1938), p. 143.
16. Bates 1972 (1938), p. 168.
17. Bates 1972 (1938), p. 232–33.
18. Bates 1972 (1938), p. 181.
19. Bates 1972 (1938), p. 107.
20. Cited in Hall 1998, p. 159.
21. See White 1993, pp. 47–65; Standish 1999.
22. Bates 1992.
23. Bates 1972.
24. Hill 1973, p. 105.
25. Hill 1973, p. 150.
26. White 1993, p. 49.
27. Cited in Salter 1971, p. 69.
28. Salter 1971, p. 70.
29. Bates 1972 (1938), p. 13.
30. Cited in McGregor 1997, p. 138.
31. White 1993, p. 56.
32. Salter 1971, p. 219.
33. Bates 1972 (1938), pp. 18, 198.
34. Standish 1999, pp. 56.

35. Bates 1972 (1938), pp. 25, 143.
36. Bates 1972 (1938), p. 24.
37. Bates 1972 (1938), p. 103.
38. Bates 1972 (1938), p. 104.
39. Standish 1999, p. 58.
40. White 1993, p. 62.
41. Bates 1972 (1938), p. 67.
42. Haebich 1988, p. 352.
43. Daisy Bates, *Sunday Times*, 2 October 1921, cited in Haebich 1988, p. 129.
44. Lake 1998.
45. Bates 1972 (1938), p. 24.
46. Hill 1973, p. 109.
47. Hill 1973, p. 110.
48. Bates 1972 (1938), pp. 139–40.
49. Bates 1972 (1938), p. 161.
50. Hill 1973, p. 109.
51. Bates 1972 (1938), pp. 198–99.
52. Bates 1972 (1938), p. 202.
53. Standish 1999, p. 58.
54. Hill 1973, p. 106.
55. Hill 1973, p. 246.
56. Bates 1972 (1938), pp. 115–16.

11. 'I drew very close to these men, sharing their dilemma…'
Elizabeth Durack

Franchesca Cubillo

In the late 1990s Elizabeth Durack (1915–2000), known throughout Australia as an established artist and a member of a very prominent Irish pastoral pioneering family, became the centre of attention within Aboriginal arts. Many discussions, interviews, television programs and angry debates emerged following her confession in 1997 that she had created a fictitious Aboriginal artist by the name of Eddie Burrup and submitted artwork under his name. Issues of appropriation of Aboriginal culture and art forms, positions of power, authorship, authenticity, racism and intellectual property rights became major topics for discussion within this debate.[1]

In his interview with Elizabeth Durack in *Art Monthly* in 1997, Robert Smith revealed how the incarnation of Eddie Burrup took place. In 1975 Elizabeth began producing what she called her 'morphological paintings'. They were conceived as elementary works and at first she sought, unconvincingly, to place them conceptually in Mediterranean antiquity. Her daughter Perpetua saw that they made 'much more sense in the Aboriginal context'. This 'was in effect the genesis of "Eddie Burrup"'. This didn't become problematic for her until, Elizabeth stated: 'Eddie suddenly emerged as a fully developed artistic persona towards the end of 1994.'[2]

Elizabeth not only painted under the guise of Eddie Burrup; she had invented his identity, created his biography and produced manuscripts of interviews that had apparently taken place. Elizabeth Durack had in fact created an Aboriginal identity according to her own parameters, put forward in dialogue and illustrations her interpretations and notions of Aboriginality, and interpreted the Kimberley landscape according to her own perception.

The identity of Durack's alter ego is interesting in that it was male. Burrup was a 'traditional' Aboriginal man from a particular historical era, a composite of several Aboriginal men she had known. A manuscript bearing Burrup's words was produced for inclusion with artwork in the *Native Title Now* exhibition held at Tandanya National Aboriginal Cultural Institute, Adelaide in 1996. It is worth noting that the manuscripts produced by Elizabeth were written in Kriol, hence suggesting that English was her fictional character's second language. Presumably Durack also wanted to show that 'Eddie' had had minimal contact with the white man because he still, despite his old age, spoke Kriol; for example:

> Well now, I tell'm you — My old uncle 'e bin learn'm me for read'm country — we two-fella *gissa-gissa* — we follow'm up all t'em oldenday track place where Dreamin' time mob bin put'm first time.
>
> A'right — by'n bye he'n fella allabout knock up — 'e go underneat' for sleep. Place where 'e go down 'e leave'm mark longa rock — you see'm? 'E there alright! 'E t' one allday singin' out l'a me...
>
> Same now I put'm l'a picture...[3]

Another characteristic Elizabeth highlighted in her fictional character was his knowledge of cultural practice. She hinted at him being a law man. Again Elizabeth was conscious of her audience, and produced what she thought was an authentic and authoritative statement on Aboriginality and cultural relationship to 'country', pointing out that he had a special relationship with the landscape. And not only was Burrup amicable and cooperative, as all 'good' Aboriginal people should be, he was at a loss to stop the encroachment and domination of Western civilisation over his culture.

Elizabeth Durack strongly believed that 'an unknown factor was at work on the Eddie Burrup story', and that he was 'a character in his own right with a life and career of his own'. She told Smith: 'At times over the last two — going on three — years since working in direct union with Eddie I have experienced a feeling of tremendous happiness and a sense of deep fulfilment.'[4]

Non-Aboriginal people believe that there are many benefits to be gained if you identify as an Aboriginal. These benefits are not only financial, but also social, spiritual and political. A white male author, Leon Carmen, specifically set out to prove a point regarding the level of support marginal groups (like women and Indigenous people) now get. He posed as an Aboriginal female author and submitted a novel under the name Wanda Koolmatrie (a well-known South Australian Aboriginal family). This novel was published and she/he received an award in recognition of the quality of the material. It was Leon's belief that if it had been submitted under his own name he would not have won any award. A Sydney sculptor, Lawrence Gundabuka, revealed that he had changed his name and begun to identify as an Aboriginal person because his grandmother looked Aboriginal and he 'felt' Aboriginal.

In the case of Elizabeth Durack and Eddie Burrup, I'm not sure why, as Julie Marcus put it, a 'wealthy and distinguished Irish-Australian painter should find such personal fulfilment in working under the name and identity of an Aboriginal man'. I too find it questionable that 'the identity of Eddie Burrup should emerge at this late stage of Durack's career'.[5] Durack was in fact quite successful and well known as an established Australian artist; therefore, she had no need, either financial or for artistic recognition, to create and promote this identity. What it did provide, however, was a mechanism for her to speak as a voice of authority on issues of Aboriginality and race relations within Australia. Marrianna Annas refers to Elizabeth's activities as not only 'bad method acting' but also 'the ultimate in paternalistic colonialism'.[6]

In this chapter I will not discuss, however, whether Elizabeth Durack was right or wrong in inventing Eddie Burrup, or whether she had the right to allow him to emerge and coexist within her public persona; rather, I will attempt to explore what motivated her to develop a male Aboriginal alter ego, and highlight how she managed to establish herself through the creation of this identity as an authentic and sensitive commentator on Aboriginality.

***

'If I think things through, I would say that Eddie Burrup is a synthesis of several Aboriginal men that I have known,' Elizabeth told Robert Smith:

> ...there is a great deal of Argyle Boxer...although I only knew this man when he was in retirement, travelling around with a plant of horses of his own on vague prospecting expeditions in

liaison with my father, and generally seeing that things were to rights on the properties and reporting any irregularities… Then there is also a lot of my classificatory son: Jeff Chunuma Rainyerri Djanaiwan of Ivanhoe Station… Both these men were *gissa-gissa*; i.e. arm in arm…their philosophy being one of going in harmony — black and white together — and as equals… Then old Jubul and old Roger of the Ivanhoe Bush camp lived in what Boxer and Jeff would have regarded as the past — they lived apart from change and felt change to be a challenge to the way of life they were responsible for — for the continuance of the old way of life but against overwhelming odds… I drew very close to these men, sharing their dilemma… They are part of Eddie Burrup too, as also were the old Goanna men who let me walk with them on what must have been one of the last of such journeys — this was out from Moola Bulla down toward the desert in 1947… And similarly the old men at Cundarlee Mission outside Zanthus… Then too there is an unknown factor that was at work on the Eddie Burrup story and that knows him to be a character in his own right with a life and career of his own…[7]

It is evident that Aboriginal people, stories and culture had a major impact on Elizabeth Durack's life. These themes appeared frequently throughout her work and set her apart from other artists of the day. It was her unique way of depicting Aboriginal people and their culture that contributed to her success, her artwork appearing in publications and exhibitions throughout Australia and overseas.

Elizabeth, or Betty as her family referred to her, was born in Claremont, Perth, on 6 July 1915 and had four brothers and one sister. Her parents were Michael Patrick (1865–1950) and Bess Ida Muriel Durack. Elizabeth was educated at Loreto Convent in Perth from the age of six but spent her holidays in her teenage years on her father's cattle stations in the Kimberley. Michael Patrick, MP was the eldest son and heir apparent to Patrick (Patsy) Durack (1834–1898), a wealthy Irishman who had made his fortune in the pastoral industry in northern Australia. The Durack family was well known throughout the Kimberley region of Western Australia, as they were responsible for owning and managing several cattle properties, including Argyle and Ivanhoe stations. The Duracks were also one of a small handful of non-Indigenous families pioneering this remote part of the country. One of the legacies of this family is that its name has been commemorated into the Kimberley landscape: the Durack River and the Durack mountain range (Burrup Peninsula).

The far north-western Kimberley landscape and the Aboriginal people of this region had a major influence on Elizabeth Durack and her older sister Mary (1913–1994). Their unique relationship to this landscape is portrayed vividly through their work. In the early part of her career, Elizabeth's illustrations accompanied Mary's stories. These stories were in the format of children's books, and in the period 1935–1943 the sisters produced seven publications. Many of their short stories appeared in the *Bulletin*.

In the 1950s and 1960s, Elizabeth 'sympathetically illustrated the plight of Aborigines in remote and fringe bush camps. Her sensitive line drawings reveal the pathos of the situation but, as she noted, she was fascinated by the aesthetic qualities of the desert background and the shapes of the people and their dwellings.'[8]

In an interview recorded in 1965 Elizabeth stated that she was often asked 'what on earth do you want to draw an old native for? Nobody would want to look at an old native.'[9] An exploration of the Durack sisters' work clearly shows that their relationship with Aboriginal people was intimate and contrary to the general Australian population's understanding of Aboriginal cultural practice. To appreciate the extent to which Elizabeth had been exposed to Aboriginal cultural knowledge, one just needs to look at her painting series 'The cord to Alcheringa', 1953, in particular *The elders of the tribe*. These ten paintings depict what appears to be restricted men's ceremony; the men are covered in elaborate body paint, wearing ceremonial headpieces and sitting on extensive ground paintings. If you look carefully you will see Western Desert–style concentric circles that identify significant ceremonial sites, including obvious Dreaming tracks that connect these sites. This was the first time Aboriginal Western Desert–style paintings/ceremonies had been produced as artwork by a non-Aboriginal person. So even before the Papunya Western Desert art movement took place, the iconography of the desert region had already entered the public arena via this woman's art.

It is worth noting that these two sisters were depicting Aboriginal culture at a time when Aboriginal people were being marginalised from Australia society. The governmental order of the day was to segregate Aboriginal people from the rest of the Australian community by placing them on reservations and missions throughout the regions. Often these facilities were on the outskirts of populated towns, some distance from the main business area. However, the Durack family did not live in these settled areas, but on remote cattle properties. In this environment they had to rely on Aboriginal people to assist them in working their land, and on Aboriginal knowledge of the landscape to move their cattle safely through the arid terrain.

Mary Durack described how the Durack men were viewed by the local Aboriginal community:

> My father was generally known as MP and as 'Miguel' to his family and other close associates. The Aborigines rendered his initials as 'Umpy', though after his father's death he inherited the various terms of respect by which they had referred to Grandfather — Yamagee ('old man'), Ngirragull or Goorung ('big-boss-belong-me and all-about').[10]

The Aboriginal people of the Kimberley region were in a position of power in the early days of pastoralist activities, as they had an extensive knowledge of the landscape, unlike non-Indigenous people working and living in the region. Non-Indigenous people were reliant on Aboriginal people for their survival in this new and harsh environment.

The relationship established by white pastoralists with the Aboriginal community was in the first instance practical; that is, Aboriginal men were used for navigating stock and white people through the landscape. White pastoralists were also dependent on them for mustering, maintaining fences, branding, and the other essential tasks of this large-scale farming. Aboriginal women were also utilised as domestic staff: cooking, cleaning, gardening and taking care of the pastoralists' children. These children often formed different relationships with Aboriginal people because of their familiarity with the Aboriginal women who cared for them and the Aboriginal children they grew up with.

As young teenage girls, Mary and Elizabeth were given access to Aboriginal lore and culture that was not available to the majority of white Australia. Elizabeth spoke of being taken by her father and Argyle Boxer, an Aboriginal guide, to rock art sites in the Keep River Gorge area. She noted that this was one of the many localities in which she began to appreciate Aboriginal art styles and practices.[11] This not only highlights the privileged access the Durack family had to Aboriginal culture, but indicates the level of intimacy and respect that Argyle Boxer had for Michael Durack and his family. In taking them to sites that were culturally significant to the local Aboriginal community, Boxer demonstrated this trust.

Boxer — Warramunga to his countrymen — spoke several languages, including the local Miriwung, into which tribe he was formally initiated. He was acknowledged in later years as a 'dreamer' of song cycles and corroborees connected with Miriwung mythology, including the long cycle of Moolarli, a spirit hero to whose magic the formation of the Ord River Gorge was attributed.[12]

The Durack men, Patsy and Michael, had developed special relationships with certain Aboriginal men. Patsy Durack's relationship with a man known as Pumpkin was firmly established before Elizabeth's father, Michael, was born. On his deathbed Patsy bequeathed a watch and chain to Pumpkin, and had apparently referred to him as his 'brother'. Mary reflected on how her father 'had brought the watch and chain that Grandfather had left to him, and with it a message from his sister Mary that the old man had spoken of his Aboriginal "brother almost with his last breath"'.[13]

Patsy had been totally dependent on Pumpkin because of the man's extensive knowledge of the country. For Patsy, who was fresh from Ireland, Australia was harsh, uncontrollable, unknown, desolate and remote. Pumpkin, Patsy's Aboriginal 'brother', had in fact come from Cooper Creek, western Queensland, and travelled across to the Kimberley with Patsy in 1887. Mary recalled:

> Pumpkin had been part of MP's life for as long as he could remember. Always at his father's right hand, this remarkable Aboriginal had regarded Patsy Durack as a brother and his sons as nephew, their welfare always foremost in his mind. It was, as my father often reminded us, Pumpkin himself who had insisted on joining JW (Michael's younger brother) and himself at Argyle more than 20 years earlier, and had Grandfather not arranged for them to travel to Wyndham by ship together, he would probably somehow have made his own way overland. It could not have been an easy thing for an Aboriginal to leave his country and tribal associations, but he had finally won the respect of the local Aborigines and had become as much a part of Argyle as he had been on Thylungra... Pumpkin had been associated with the interlopers ever since he offered Patsy Durack a fish from his own tribal waterhole in 1868... Pumpkin's story was that he had recognised Patsy Durack as a brother he had lost years before, who had simply rejoined him as a 'jumped-up white-fellow'.[14]

Then, in the late 1880s, Pumpkin had taken the eight-year-old Boxer under his charge. Boxer was originally from Mt Isa and had travelled to the Kimberley with his mother and a man called Wesley Lyttleton. Mary stated that Pumpkin, 'so the story goes', 'took a fancy to the boy and acquired him in exchange for a good packhorse and a tin of jam. What became of Boxer's mother is not recorded, but Wesley Lyttleton soon returned from the goldfields and worked thereafter on Argyle.'[15]

Another Aboriginal boy, Ulysses, joined this small family unit in 1890, then later another, Theology. Pumpkin taught each of them how to be good stockmen. Pumpkin obviously also felt responsible for the two Durack boys, Michael and John (JW), who he had watched grow up in the Kimberley landscape.

The impact of Pumpkin and Boxer on Durack can't be under-played; to do so would be to do the men themselves a disservice. It is obvious that they were significant cultural leaders and held positions of authority within their local Indigenous community. They were also valuable facilitators and participants in the develoment of the pastoral industry in the Kimberley, Pilbara and northern regions of Australia. Elizabeth strongly believed she had a responsibility to acknowledge the colonial history between white and black men in the Kimberley region during the early 1900s. This history was romanticised, as she sought to legitimate her father and his role in the development of the pastoral industry, but also to place him as a respectful/considerate coloniser on the frontier. 'Eddie Burrup' provided Elizabeth with a legitimate voice. With her romanticised notion of Aboriginality she saw the work as some form of homage to Aboriginal Australia, as well as a concrete example of reconciliation between two communities and two cultures, between which relations were, in Elizabeth's view, 'floundering so badly at the present time'.

The identity of Eddie Burrup provided for Elizabeth, most import-antly, a reminder of the intimate ties that her father and grandfather had had with the older Aboriginal men of the Kimberley region, and the intimate relationship her family had with the Kimberley landscape. Elizabeth Durack's identity developed within this environ-ment as well as her notion of Aboriginality. I believe that Elizabeth Durack's invention of Eddie Burrup was her attempt to recapture the mythology of her childhood, of a region, cultural landscape and particular time in history. It may have been her attempt to lay a legitimate and authentic conceptual claim to this cultural landscape that she has strong affiliations to. It was an attempt to reassociate with the landscape of her youth, past ideology, and previous race relations between black and white people. In essence, she did this by drawing upon a publicly recognisable icon — that is, Aboriginal art/ Aboriginality — and using it for her own advantage.

Notes

1. The author published an article at the time, from which this article has been further developed: see Cubillo 1998.
2. Robert Smith, 'The incarnations of Eddie Burrup', *Art Monthly Australia*, no. 97, March 1997, p. 5.
3. 'Eddie Burrup transcripts', excerpts quoted in Smith 1997, p. 4.
4. Smith, p. 5.
5. Julie Marcus, '"...like an Aborigine": empathy, Elizabeth Durack, & the colonial imagination', *Olive Pink Society Bulletin*, vol. 9, 1997, p. 46.
6. Annas.
7. Smith, p. 5.
8. Gooding.
9. Hazel de Berg, interview with Elizabeth Durack, 31 May 1965, Oral History Collection, National Library of Australia, Canberra.
10. Durack 1983, p. 23.
11. Smith, p. 5.
12. Durack 1983, pp. 513–14.
13. Durack 1983, pp. 68–69.
14. Durack 1983, pp. 274–75.
15. Durack 1983, pp. 513–14.

12. 'To put on record, as faithfully as possible'
Catherine Martin

Margaret Allen

The South Australian writer Catherine Martin wrote about Indigenous people in some of the work she produced in her long career, which spanned the years 1865–1923. Although her output in relation to Indigenous issues was quite small, she often wrote in a more sensitive and progressive way than most of her contemporaries. In particular her book *The incredible journey*, published in 1923, presented a positive view of Indigenous motherhood and raised the issue of stolen children at a time when white public opinion had little interest in or sympathy for these issues. Only in recent years, with the publication of Indigenous life stories like Margaret Tucker's *If everyone cared* and Sally Morgan's bestselling *My place*, and with the release of *Bringing them home*, the report on the stolen generations, have the issues explored in *The incredible journey* been discussed widely in Australia. *The incredible journey* was written and published in an environment that was unreceptive, even hostile, to the views it advanced. This chapter explores the novel and the at times contra-dictory discourses that informed it. It also seeks to explain why a settler woman should choose to write such a text in early 20th-century Australia, and to place that decision within the context of her personal and family history.[1]

***

Catherine Martin was born Catherine Mackay on the Isle of Skye in 1847. In 1855, her family was able to emigrate to Australia with the assistance of the Highland and Island Emigration Society, a philanthropic body that sought to ameliorate the social and economic distress of destitute Highlanders. Her family, described in the society's records as a 'poor family but very eligible', were thus effectively cleared from their homeland.[2] They settled in the south-east of the South Australian colony, where they worked on the run of another Scot, Robert Lawson. Catherine's father, Samuel Mackay, died within a year or so of their arrival in the young colony. Her older siblings supported the family. The older brothers worked as labourers, drovers, stockmen and overseers in the pastoral industry in the Naracoorte district, and across the colonial border on stations in western Victoria.[3] Able to set their lives on a more secure footing than they could have expected in their Scottish homeland, some of them used the capital they amassed in the south-east to establish themselves as wealthy and influential pastoralists in the north-west of Western Australia.

As the fortunes of the Mackay family rose, so the Indigenous peoples of the area were decimated and dispossessed. When Catherine, her sisters and their mother, Janet (Jennette) Mackay, were running a ladies school in the town of Mount Gambier from 1866 to 1876, the local Indigenous people, the Buandig, had been reduced to existing on the fringes of settler society. One estimate was that in the first 30 years of European settlement, from about 1840, the local Indigenous population fell from 900 to 17.[4] Some of those who survived worked for the new owners of their lands, while others were taken in by the missionary, Mrs Christina Smith (a friend of Catherine's sister Mary), who had set up a home for Aboriginal people in Mount Gambier in 1865.[5]

Catherine Mackay began writing verse, short stories and serials during the years she lived in Mount Gambier. She moved to the colony's capital, Adelaide, in 1877, where she worked as a correspondence clerk in the fledgling Education Department, while continuing her writing. She published her work in the press, both in South Australia and Victoria. After her marriage in 1882 to Frederick Martin, an accountant and would-be littérateur, she continued her work as a clerk, but left at the end of 1885 and from then on devoted herself to literature. Her best-known work, *An Australian girl*, was published in London in 1890 and was followed by *The silent sea* in 1892. She and her husband travelled extensively in Europe between 1891 and 1894 and again from 1904 to 1907. They had no children, and after Catherine was widowed in 1909 she travelled in Europe for long periods of time. She died in Adelaide in 1937, aged 90.

While Catherine Martin's work was well known in the 1890s, by the time of her death it had slipped from public notice. She seems to have been a reticent writer, publishing her work under a number of different pseudonyms; indeed, *The incredible journey* was the only book that appeared under her real name. It was also the only one of her works that focused on Aboriginal people. Here, when she was 76 years old, she finally found a broader canvas on which to expound her views on Aboriginal people and their history.

The incredible journey tells the story of a young Aboriginal woman, Iliapa, whose son is taken from her as a result of collusion between two men: a 'bad' white man and a 'traditional' Aboriginal man bent on punishing her family. It is set among the 'Arunta' people of Central Australia in the early 20th century, who are represented as living a mixed life of 'traditional' practices and beliefs as workers on the pastoral stations run by white bosses.[6] Although Iliapa has been promised in marriage to an older man, Yukuta, her aunt Labea connives to ensure the marriage does not take place, flouting the wishes and the honour of Iliapa's father, Erungara. Instead, Iliapa marries Nabulka, a young man on the run from the police for a murder he did not commit; in fact, he is in danger of being 'framed' by a corrupt white policeman for this crime.

Nabulka and Iliapa live happily for some years as valued workers on Balkara Station, where the white 'Master' and 'Mistress' are kind and understanding towards them. The birth of their son, Alibaka, completes the happy family. Erungara lives with them and Alibaka is the centre of their lives. They are represented as a nuclear family, bound by love: 'It would be hard to say which of the three was the proudest of him — his father, his mother, or his grandfather. But no one else in the world could love him quite as much as his mother did.'[7]

But the family is broken up when Nabulka has to go into hiding for some years to avoid being captured by the policeman. Then Yukuta punishes the family for breaking their promise by enticing Alibaka away. He 'sells' him to a white man, Simon, who wants Alibaka to be a jockey for him. Caught between his respect for the old ways and his love of his family, Erungara dies, leaving Iliapa alone to cope with the crisis.

Iliapa is determined to recover her son. With the assistance of her employers, she sets out for a long trek across the desert to Labalama.

She is accompanied by her friend, Polde, another Aboriginal woman. On this trek they tell stories to each other and endure hardships together. They are assisted by kindly white folk and face the dangers presented both by 'traditional' men and by evil white men like Simon and his cronies. Their great courage and endurance is rewarded; Iliapa is joyously reunited with her son and then, a little later, with Nabulka.

The text is remarkable for its contestation of contemporary white views of Aboriginal women and Aboriginal motherhood. In her introduction, Martin says she set out 'to put on record, as faithfully as possible, the heroic love and devotion of a black woman when robbed of her child'.[8] She wrote at a time when all Australian states had an official policy of removing Indigenous children from their families and placing them in state or religious institutions, where they were to be trained as servants or manual workers in the general community. Aboriginal women were seen as inadequate mothers, and the policy of removal assumed they would forget their children soon after they were taken away.[9] *The incredible journey* directly refutes this view.

Martin offers a positive view of Aboriginal motherhood. In representing Iliapa's 'heroic love', she challenges, as Anna Haebich notes, 'negative stereotypes of Aboriginal women as mothers, endowing them instead with the idealised and essentialist attributes of motherhood generally reserved for white women'.[10] Motherhood bestows upon Iliapa an agency usually denied Indigenous women. Susan Sheridan has commented: '*The Incredible Journey* is the only colonial women's text of this period that I can find in which the Aboriginal woman is central to the narrative and is constructed as a subject in her own right.'[11]

Martin suggests commensurability and reciprocity between black and white motherhood. The white 'Mistress' of Balkara once lost her two young children in the bush. For two days and nights she was overcome by 'fear and misery' while everyone on the station searched for them. It was Erungara, Iliapa's father, who found them and 'fed and cared for them and brought them back in safety!'[12] Now she understands Iliapa's anxiety and helps her regain her son.

But while there is a notion of equality and reciprocity here, in the text white women are represented as being capable agents. There is no mention of white women as victims of male power, unlike in Martin's other works; for instance, her story 'Breaking the law' which explores the situation of a white woman whose husband has taken her children away from her.[13] However, the idealised notion of motherhood serves to bring black and white women together in common emotion; thus, when Iliapa shares her story with a white woman she encounters on her trek, 'the white woman on seeing Iliapa cry for her lost boy, could not keep back her own tears'.[14] The tale of Iliapa's quest to regain her son is constructed so as to draw the reader's sympathy with Iliapa's plight and with her struggles. The triumphant reunion of the young man and his devoted and determined mother serves as the climax:

> It was the voice of Alibaka, and on hearing it, Iliapa gave a low, stifled cry. The next moment he was in her arms — Alibaka, her own boy. At last, at last she held him close. It was as if she could never let him go. How many nights had she lain awake, and wept, fearing that she might never again set eyes on him. But here he was at last — alive and well.[15]

The question of why Martin wrote this book is interesting. She published it just as campaigners, particularly in her home state of South Australia, took up the issue of child removal.[16] I have not been able to establish that she had links with the people and organisations active in these campaigns; indeed, the fact that the story was written in the main by 1906, well before the campaigns of the 1920s, suggests Martin may have worked quite independently.

In her introduction to *The incredible journey*, Martin confesses that she found Iliapa's story difficult to write. She had heard the story from someone 'who knew the details at first hand', but while a 'touching story vividly told bites into the hearer's mind', she found that putting it down in 'cold type' destroyed both the emotion and the message and she rejected 'one version after the other'. But Martin was driven to complete the task: 'Iliapa's story clung obstinately to my mind as one that must be told.'[17]

Given *The incredible journey*'s equation of Indigenous and non-Indigenous motherhood, it is notable that Martin says her driving reason for telling the story was 'the influence of a mother who, so far from looking on the Blacks as outcasts or untouchables, treated them with the unfailing kindness of a gentlewoman in contact with lowly and very destitute kinfolk'. She recognises that her mother's attitude was not widely held, and was to many 'almost an offence, or at best an eccentric fad'. But, she adds: 'To shirk the trouble of recording the story — though it might quite probably evoke but scant enthusiasm — felt like a sort of treachery.'[18]

Martin's acknowledgment of her mother's influence raises a number of questions when we look at the record of some of her older brothers in their relations with Indigenous people in the Pilbara region of Western Australia. Roderick, Donald and Donald McDonald (referred to as 'Dody') Mackay took large tracts of land in the Pilbara in the mid-1860s, where they established a number of sheep stations. Mundabullangana, Roy Hill and their other stations were built on Aboriginal land and with Aboriginal labour. In 1893 there were reported to be 125 Aboriginal people on Mundabullangana:

> All shearing is done by the native labour. Also all teamstering both with horses & bullock teams. Through a great part of the year a large number of these natives are constantly employed in water-drawing, Several young fellows are occupied on the schooner 'Myra'. Others are often on the road droving from this to an inland Station. The greater part of the fencing has been put up by native labour indeed the bulk of the improvements have been made by their aid. The women assist their men at whatever work they are engaged upon.[19]

Aboriginal people were stationed out on the run, drawing water for the sheep from the 27 wells out in the paddocks. Aboriginal women with children carted water from the river for the garden and troughs. They worked in the homestead and also with the stock. A photograph taken at shearing in 1898 shows four women and a huge mob of sheep in front of the substantial shearing shed. The women standing up on the railings are directing sheep into the races leading into the shed.[20] These people received food rations and clothes.[21]

The Mackay men were also involved in kidnapping Aboriginal men from the interior and bringing them to the coast to work on their stations and luggers. Sam Mackay had an Aboriginal polo team on Mundabullangana and Aboriginal jockeys for his racehorses.[22] Indeed, between 1907 and 1914 he brought seven young Aboriginal men and boys from the Pilbara to work as grooms on his station near Melbourne.[23]

There was an understanding in the area that the Mackays, along with the MacRaes, dominated the Pilbara. These big station owners were largely above the law. Historian Kay Forrest has described the Mackays in the Pilbara region as 'a strong, violent family'.[24] In 1896, Catherine's brother Dody was elected a member of the West Australian Legislative Council, to defend the interests of the northern pastoralists. In one of his earliest speeches, he attacked claims that the Aboriginal people of the north were being treated in 'a cruel and inhuman manner', as 'a despicable perversion of the truth'.[25]

The Mackay brothers and Donald's sons, Jack and Sam, were known for their cruelty towards their Aboriginal workers on the stations and on the pearling luggers that they ran off the coast.[26]

In light of this history we must ask: was Martin's *Incredible journey* intended, in part, as a rebuke to her brothers and nephews, who, like the character Simon, took Aboriginal boys away from their mothers? Could it be seen as a critique of some of the behaviour and values of her brothers and nephews in the Pilbara? Was she trying to honour her mother's memory and the respect and kindness she modelled, and somehow atone for the sins of her brothers and nephews?

Catherine Martin was determined to tell this story and to get it published. It seems that she first offered a version of it for publication in 1906 under the telling title *His mother's boy*. The publisher, Macmillan, rejected it. The reader of the manuscript found it hard to appreciate the different style of the work, commenting: 'There is none of the humour, the pathos, the picturesque and glowing atmosphere of Mrs. Martin's former stories.'[27]

Significantly, the reader saw *His mother's boy* as intended 'for quite young readers'.

Martin put the work aside, perhaps distracted by her husband's illness and then his death in 1909. Years later, after the First World War when she was again in Europe, she once more sought to get it published. In June 1922 she sent the manuscript, or part of it, now entitled *Back of beyond*, to Grant Richards, a London publisher. He quickly rejected it: 'The fact that the story deals with Australian life and conditions would make it difficult to sell in England, and I am afraid we could not count on a sufficient sale to make the venture profitable.'[28]

Martin then began negotiations to have the book published at her own expense. She settled upon a cost of £140 for a thousand copies with Grant Richards, the book being due out early in 1923. However, in November 1922 she wrote to Richards asking for the 'arrest of action'.[29] Her book, now titled *The incredible journey*, appeared in 1923 under the Jonathan Cape imprint.[30] Although the Cape correspondence is not extant, Martin may have paid for the publication with Cape. Perhaps she was able to negotiate a lower publication price with Cape.

Martin was correct when she predicted that a work depicting Aboriginal people positively would muster only 'scant enthusiasm'.

The book was not widely distributed. The Cape ledger reveals that '1000 were printed, 634 sold or given as free copies, 356 in quires wasted'.[31] It is not clear how many were bought within Australia and how many elsewhere. The work did receive a short and favourable review in the *Times Literary Supplement*. After summarising the story, the reviewer wrote: 'It is an inspiriting story and clearly and tensely described. The characters of the two women are admirably distinct... The author tells us that she was in some doubt as to the best way of telling this story. The one she has chosen is exactly suited to express the strong and simple nature of the women whose courage she records.'[32]

The only Australian review I could uncover also commended the book to readers. The reviewer had clearly absorbed its message about the common humanity of Indigenous and non-Indigenous peoples: 'Australian [A]borigines are not often made the heroes of romance. Yet they are human, and have the powerful instinctive love of offspring from which our codes of citizenship and ethics of family life are derived.' The reviewer declared that Iliapa and Polde's long journey was 'one of the best narratives of hardship and suffering endured under the hot blank Australian skies that has been told in Australian literature', finally recommending that other writers follow the example of 'Mr Martin' in including Aboriginal stories, 'before the material is lost. It is the best way of preserving the only folk-lore that Australia can boast of'.[33] There was no discussion, however, of the major contemporary issues the book had broached.

It appears that the book was not reviewed in any South Australian newspaper. Perhaps with Martin's friend Catherine Helen Spence long dead, there was no one to insist upon a review in the Adelaide papers. As Martin had predicted, there was little enthusiasm among settler readers. When I asked Martin's great-niece, the late Jean Cook, about the book's reception in Adelaide, she remembered that people dismissed it for presenting a far too favourable picture of Aboriginal people.[34]

Martin, as the author of this text, might be seen as the first Australian writer to critique the removal of Indigenous children in a literary work. But it is important to note that she represents the kidnapping of Alibaka as the outcome of Indigenous practices and treachery as well as a result of the greed of the white man, Simon. The work relates in different ways to a notion of Aboriginal history, and an exploration of these further complicates our understanding of the text.

Martin sketched out a history of Aboriginal people in Australia in this work, pointing out elements of their past situation and contemporary experience as well as pointing to a future scenario. In her introduction, which she appears to have completed just as the proofs were being checked early in 1923, Martin put forward some radical observations on the founding of settler society in Australia. She described the taking of Indigenous land as trickery, if not theft, and ridiculed the contract purporting to record Batman's 'purchase' of the site of Melbourne:

> In the Public Library of that city there is a document in which [A]boriginal chiefs — so-called — make over to John Batman in return for blankets, food, beads, etc., about half a million of acres of land. Nothing in *opera bouffe* can be richer in comedy than this treaty, the weird hieroglyphics standing for the signature of Jagajaga, Coloolock and Bugbarie, neither side to the bargain understanding a word the other spoke.[35]

In relation to South Australia, in which the story is set, she comments: 'Not even the customary string of beads seems to have changed hands on this occasion.' She imagines one of the old men of the tribe watching the formal proclamation of the South Australian colony, 'under the shade of a gum-tree', saying: 'My inside is turned to water. They look as if they had come to stay. This country belongs to us. Here we have the right to walk about, to fish and to hunt; to say when the grass should be burned, and when the animals and birds of the air should be killed. What will they give us if they take all this?'[36]

Martin goes on to compare the colonists to a brazen Highlander who takes a cow and then stoutly maintains that 'he did not steal the animal but took her in the sight of all men as his own'.[37] She does not explore this further, and the notion that the Australian lands were stolen sits uneasily at the beginning of the book. Indeed, much of the rest of introduction is framed within a discourse of progress. She comments favourably upon the spread of white Australians into the bush and the modern technology that can facilitate this. Thus she commends the Mundaring reservoir, a contemporary development project in Western Australia, as a marvellous feat of 'skill and labour' which will support a greater population in the arid regions.[38]

For Martin, 'traditional' Aboriginal people belong to the past; they are 'fast dying and…their passing will form but a minute entry in the record of extinct races'.[39] Her imagined historical trajectory contains a notion of Indigenous people falling from past greatness as a result of white invasion. In her introduction, Martin also refers to the 'invaluable work of Messrs Spencer and Gillen', and they may have influenced her in this view. Certainly, the story of Iliapa is overlain by quite a lot of anthropological information which Martin derived from her readings of Spencer and Gillen. Perhaps, in 1902, she also heard Frank Gillen's lectures on 'The Central Australian Aborigine' given in the Adelaide Town Hall, accompanied by 'phonographic and photographic records'.[40] Spencer and Gillen described the material technology of the Arunta in their first extensive study of the Arunta people, *The native tribes of Central Australia* (1899). This and their later work, *The northern tribes of Central Australia* (1904), contain a number of photographs and drawings of tools, containers, weapons and ornaments. Martin has taken these items from the anthropology text, and placed them in the hands of her Aboriginal characters.

Drawing upon the work of these anthropologists, Martin represents Iliapa's father, Erungara, as a wise old man and an 'Oknirabata', a great teacher of traditional ways.[41] Already somewhat displaced from his position of authority by disputes among the Arunta, he pronounces upon the degradation of Aboriginal tradition as a result of the white invasion:

> Before the white men came we were a great people. The old men were held in honour; they took care of the holy things, and trained the boys to be young men, and taught them the laws of the Arunta. They taught them how to bear pain and hunger, and how to cast the fear from them; they taught them how to kill the birds of the air and of the water, how to snare the great beasts and the small; what things may be eaten, and what should not be touched. They taught them the days of corroboree and the dance, and the days of going without food. They taught them of their relations on the side of the father and the mother, telling them what women they may marry, and what women they must not look at. Now the young are as crows that pick up a bone and a mate as it pleases them.[42]

Erungara represents the past of the Arunta people, and significantly he dies in the course of the story.

Moving from this notion of a great past, Martin also represents the position of contemporary Indigenous people, then living in colonial society around the turn of the nineteenth century. They are portrayed as having to operate in two different worlds, whose demands are different and possibly even contradictory. In white-dominated society they will often be misunderstood. The white people, even those who are well-disposed towards them, do not necessarily understand their situation of having to manoeuvre between two worlds. Martin shows the incommensurability of black and white knowledges and situations in colonial society. Iliapa's husband Nabulka decides to go into hiding when he realises that a corrupt white policeman wants to arrest him for a murder of which he is innocent. He wants to explain his departure to his white boss. But his friend Jim counsels against informing 'the Master', saying: 'Nabulka might tell from now until the sun is high and the white man would not see how it could be.'[43] In other words, the white man could not possibly understand why the Aboriginal man would flee if he were innocent.

Martin emphasises that Indigenous people are at a disadvantage in the white political and cultural arenas. Throughout the text, she differentiates the language of the Aboriginal characters, depending on whether they are speaking to white people or to other Aboriginal people. Thus, when the white 'Mistress of Balkara' station tells Iliapa that her husband is angry that Alibaka has gone off without telling anyone, Iliapa retorts: 'The Master heard one big lie; me want to see him and tell him'.[44] The move to broken English is particularly marked because only a few pages earlier, when she had confronted Yukuta, the Indigenous man who helped steal her son away, Iliapa had used standard English. There she had shown great presence of mind to cleverly force Yukuta to tell her Alibaka's whereabouts.[45]

Similarly, when the woman Polde explains to a white woman her fitness to accompany Iliapa on the trek to recover her son, she says in broken English', Me bin all the way to Labalama two o' 'ree time... My coolie he die there las' year'.[46]

This pattern, which is followed consistently throughout the work, serves to show the articulateness of the Aboriginal characters when talking among themselves and to suggest the power and culture differentials when they are with the much more powerful white characters. When the Aboriginal characters speak in broken English they appear infantile and foolish, whereas in interactions with other Aboriginal people they exhibit a wide range of characteristics and competencies. This different use of language indicates Martin had some understanding of the complexities of the historical situation of Aboriginal peoples.

Martin also shows her readers that Indigenous people have social values and attitudes that make them unwilling to merely fall into line with the powerful values and assumptions of settler society. On a few occasions she even suggests an Indigenous critique of white society and habits; for instance, in Nabulka's wariness of European-style work discipline:

> I can ride, muster cattle, and look after sheep; I can help to dig wells and clean out tanks, and put up fences. But after a time I am tired of the white man and his ways, saying always to-day what must be done tomorrow, or when the next moon comes. When I get tired I want to go Bush — to hunt and fish and snare birds, to lie down when I want to, and get up when I wish.[47]

Aboriginal characters reflect critically upon the ways and characteristics of the white people, who are thus momentarily decentred.

However, the power relations between Indigenous and non-Indigenous peoples in Australia, as represented by Martin, mean that Indigenous people have to submit to those with power, who may also be corrupt. Simon, the white man who takes Alibaka away, drinks with a policeman, who tries to cover up for his friend. In Martin's view, Indigenous people inhabit a lawless and arbitrary world in the white-dominated pastoral zone. When Iliapa and Polde finally find Alibaka, they want to get him away from Simon. They think of confronting Simon directly, but Iliapa reminds Polde of their relatively powerless position:

> Keep still, Polde…we are only two black women. I have often heard my father say that many of the white people have been wicked and cruel to the blacks, and there has been no one to stand up for them and to say: 'You must not do this.' Black women and girls and boys have been stolen away, and when black men have gone to get them back, they have been shot down like wild dogs.[48]

While this is the only occasion in the book when Martin makes such a clear statement of the injustice with which Aboriginal people have to contend, it is nevertheless a powerful description of contemporary reality. *The incredible journey* was published before the Coniston massacre of 1928 made white Australians more aware of the ongoing violence of Australian race relations.[49]

Like a number of Australian feminist critics of governmental policies towards Aboriginal peoples in the 1920s and 1930s, Martin depicts Aboriginal women as victims of both white men, who could steal their children away, and of 'traditional' men and 'traditional' practices such as child betrothal.[50] One reason that Iliapa lost her son was because the 'traditional' man, Yukuta, wished to punish her family. As she and Polde travel across the desert to recover Alibaka, they have to evade Aboriginal men who might pose some danger to them. Hearing men's voices near their camp one night, they slip away under cover of darkness. Polde's fear relates to traditional rivalries between men: 'If it is the men of the Ring-necked parrot, they will knock me on the head, because Loatjira killed one of their boys; if they are men of the Plum-tree, they will take me away, because my cousin stole one of their girls.'[51]

This representation of Indigenous women as victims within their own society is congruent with the views of contemporary white women who were active around Aboriginal issues. Women are seen as needing to be rescued from 'traditional' men.[52] Similarly, when the women enter a cave that Martin identifies as an 'Ernatulunga', or the sacred storehouse of some Arunta men, Iliapa implores Polde:

> Let us get away as fast as we can; something awful might happen to us… Do you know that with the Aruntas, no women or boys are ever allowed to look on the things that belong to the spirit people? If the Rock-Pigeon Men found us here, or knew that one of us touched the Churinga, they would kill us on the spot, or else put out our eyes with a fire-stick.[53]

In fact the Rock-Pigeon Men are so enraged that the women have 'dared to enter our storehouse, where they treated the holy things of our forefathers like bits of old bark lying under a tree' that they pursue them.[54]

The history of Aboriginal people that Martin writes assumes a progress in which Indigenous people become more like non-Indigenous people, with Indigenous people adopting the regular work patterns of white society. Iliapa is the Indigenous woman of the future. The Mistress finds her 'so steady and useful', and wants her to work with her in the household, where she will be much more useful than Polde: 'Iliapa does not learn so quickly, but then she does not get tired, and want to go away. She is happy to go on doing things day after day, and does not forget.'[55] Nabulka is also a reliable worker. While employers may need to allow these young Aboriginal people to 'go Bush' at certain times, they are seen as potentially steady workers for their white bosses.

Furthermore, Martin's 'history' assumes that Indigenous people should and will develop an individual sense of responsibility, and that an individual conscience will replace what she terms the old collective ways. The old man Erungara adheres to 'the tribal feeling of right and wrong' and has 'no sense of wrong in planning a death according to the old custom'.[56] On the other hand, the younger Nabulka is seen as developing a Western-style individual conscience. Nabulka plans to murder another Indigenous man, Ingunta, for killing his brother, but when he discovers Ingunta has been killed by someone else, he is moved by 'an emotion akin to individual conscience': 'I waited and longed with all my heart to touch my enemy for death, yet when I found him dead, it is as if I could weep for wishing him harm.'[57] For Martin, the future for Indigenous people is to become like Nabulka and Iliapa: faithful and reliable workers on the stations, which are run by white bosses.

The incredible journey, while honouring in part the power and complexity of Indigenous culture, affirms the influential contemporary discourse of progress which predicted their passing away from history. The reprieve, she suggests, is for Aboriginal people to become modern and enter the white economy and society, albeit on its lowest rung. Thus *The incredible journey* is a work of recuperation for the white project of colonisation.

But it also contests and refutes powerful and destructive contemporary ideas about Aboriginal motherhood, thereby striking at a central plank of government policy of colonising Aboriginal peoples in the 19th and early 20th centuries. Simply put, she equates Aboriginal motherhood with white motherhood. Her relationship with her mother and perhaps different relationships with some of her brothers and nephews appear to have impelled her to write and publish this work, which was so out of keeping with current thinking. Now, as the Australian white public begins to acknowledge the cruelty of the decades-long policy of child removal, the message in *The incredible journey* may finally be heard.

Notes

1. This chapter contains material used in some of my earlier publications, including 'The brothers up north'.
2. Records of the Highland and Island Emigration Society, ref. A3077, 163, Mitchell Library, Sydney.
3. Allen 1988.
4. Fison & Howitt, p. 30. See also Foster, pp. 140–60.
5. For recent discussions of Christina Smith see Nettelbeck 2001 and Haggis 2001.
6. The 'Arunta' to whom Martin refers are a people she has represented, drawing upon her own experience and also her reading of Spencer and

Gillen's work on Aboriginal peoples of Central Australia. In a note on terminology at the beginning of his book, Patrick Wolfe explains: 'Since the terms "Arunta" and "Aranda" recur throughout the book, it should be noted that the descendants of Spencer and Gillen's original informants are the Arrente people of central Australia.' Wolfe 1999.

7. Martin 1923, p. 85.
8. Martin 1923, pp. 11–12.
9. Paisley 2000, p. 134 and Haebich 2000, pp. 233, 333.
10. Haebich 2000, p. 321.
11. Sheridan 1995, p. 129.
12. Martin 1923, p. 81.
13. Martin 1997.
14. Martin 1923, p. 150.
15. Martin 1923, p. 262.
16. Haebich 2000, p. 312–41. The Ngarrindjeri people were active on this issue. In December 1923, Mr EN Kropinyeri, a Ngarrindjeri man, wrote a memorial to the state parliament against a recent act, the *Aborigines (Training of Children) Act 1923* (SA), which increased the power the Protector of Aborigines had over children. Here he invoked 'the army of motherhood', arguing that 'The only piece of artillery which that army possesses is the weapon called love.' *South Australian Register*, 21 December 1923. Part of the memorial is reproduced in Allen et al. 1989, pp. 222–23.
17. Martin 1923, pp. 24, 25.
18. Martin 1923, p. 25.
19. Report from travelling inspector, 14 June 1893, WA Aboriginal Protection Board No 995 Accession 495, State Record Office of Western Australia (SROWA), Perth.
20. A series of photographs taken by CH Powell at Mundabullangana in 1898 also shows housemaids, women and children transporting river water in barrels drawn by donkeys, and drawing water from a well. JS Battye Library of West Australian History, BA1373/67 3000P-3019P, State Library of WA, Perth.
21. Report from travelling inspector, 14 June 1893, WA Aboriginal Protection Board No 995 Accession 495, Correspondence and Reports, SROWA, Perth.
22. Allen 2001, pp. 17 & 21.
23. Department of Aborigines Accession 652, 961/11, 962/11, 1407/11, SROWA, Perth.
24. Forrest, pp. 196, 316; Allen 2001.
25. West Australian Legislative Council 1896, *Debates*, 15 October, p. 1047.
26. Allen 2001.
27. Macmillan archives: publishing records, archives of the Macmillan Press on microfilm, Part 1, readers' reports (Cambridge, Chadwyck-Healey, 1982) A43, v. 1188 (1906–07), pp. 44.

28. Archives of Grant Richards: 1897–1948 (Cambridge, Chadwyck-Healey, 1981), microfilm A 855.
29. Grant Richards' correspondence with Catherine Martin between 29 June and 2 November 1922 can be seen in Grant Richards' publishing archives at A 532, 840, 855, 867, 879, 880, 922, 950, 967 and 988.
30. This new title must have decided upon at a very late date. An author's proof copy of the Cape book bearing the title 'Back of Beyond' is held among the remnants of the author's library in Adelaide. Indeed, my own copy of the book, stamped 'Colonial Edition' has the former title, 'Back of Beyond', atop all the pages in the text. The title *The incredible journey* appears only on the title page and cover.
31. Letter from Michael Bott, keeper of archives and manuscripts, University of Reading Library, 4 June 1993, in possession of the author.
32. *TLS*, 18 October 1923, p. 688.
33. *Argus*, 17 December 1923, p. 3.
34. Private communication with the late Miss Jean Bethune Loudon Cook, c. 1986, copy in possession of the author.
35. Martin 1923, pp. 6–7.
36. Martin 1923, p. 7.
37. Martin 1923, p. 8.
38. Martin 1923, p. 15.
39. Martin 1923, p. 28.
40. *Adelaide Observer*, 26 July 1902, p. 33 and 2 August 1902, p. 35.
41. 'Oknirabata means a great instructor or teacher, who is at the present day applied to the wise old men who are learned in tribal customs and teach them to the others, It is a name only given to men who are both old and wise.' Martin 1923, p. 98. See Spencer & Gillen 1968, p. 187, n. 1; also, pp. 420 & 653.
42. Martin 1923, p. 53.
43. Martin 1923, p. 92; Moreton-Robinson 2000.
44. Martin 1923, p. 111.
45. Martin 1923, p. 108.
46. Martin 1923, p. 115.
47. Martin 1923, pp. 62–63.
48. Martin 1923, p. 260.
49. Markus 1990, pp. 1–5.
50. Paisley 2000, p. 155.
51. Martin 1923, p. 145.
52. Holland 2001, p. 33.
53. Martin 1923, p. 159. Re Churinga, see Spencer & Gillen 1968, pp. 145ff & p. 648.
54. Martin 1923, pp. 212–13.
55. Martin 1923, p. 82.
56. Martin 1923, p. 56.
57. Martin 1923, pp. 55 & 56.

References

Aboriginal historians for the bicentennial history 1788–1988, working party (Wayne Atkinson, Marcia Langton, Doreen Wanganeen & Michael Williams), 1981, 'Aboriginal history and the bicentennial volumes', *Australia 1939–1988: A Bicentennial History Bulletin*, no. 3, ed. AW Martin, Australian National University, Canberra, pp. 21–25.

Akerman, K & J Stanton 1994, *Riji and Jakoli: Kimberley pearl shell in Aboriginal Australia*, monograph series 4, Northern Territory Museum of Arts and Sciences, Darwin.

Allen, Margaret 1998, 'Catherine Martin: an Australian girl?', in Debra Adelaide (ed.), *A bright and fiery troop: Australian women writers of the nineteenth century*, Penguin, Ringwood, pp. 152–64.

——2001, 'The brothers up north and the sisters down south: the Mackay family and the frontier', *Hecate*, vol. 27, no. 2, pp. 7–31.

Allen, Margaret, Mary Hutchison & Alison Mackinon (eds) 1989, *Fresh evidence, new witnesses: finding women's history*, Stateprint, Adelaide.

Amin, Shahid 1995, *Event, metaphor, memory: Chauri Chaura, 1922–92*, Berkeley University Press, Berkeley.

Anderson, Warwick 1996, 'Disease, race and empire', *Bulletin of the History of Medicine*, vol. 70, no. 1, pp. 62–7.

——2002, *The cultivation of whiteness: science, health and racial destiny in Australia*, Melbourne University Press, Melbourne.

Annas, Marrianna 1997, 'Art originality and authenticity', *Periphery*, no. 32, p. 4.

Attwood, Bain & Andrew Markus 1999, *The struggle for Aboriginal rights*, Allen & Unwin, Sydney.

Attwood, Bain & Andrew Markus in collaboration with Dale Edwards & Kath Schilling 1997, *The 1967 Referendum, or when Aborigines didn't get the vote*, AIATSIS, Canberra.

Austin, Tony 1990, 'Cecil Cook, scientific thought and "half-castes" in the Northern Territory, 1927–39', *Aboriginal History*, vol. 14, no. 1, pp. 104–22.

——1993, *I can picture the old home so clearly: the Commonwealth and 'half-caste' youth in the Northern Territory 1911–39*, Aboriginal Studies Press, Canberra.

——1997, *Never trust a government man: Northern Territory Aboriginal policy 1911–39*, Northern Territory University Press, Darwin.

Baldwin, James 1984, 'On being "white"…and other lies', reprinted in *Black on white: black writers on what it means to be white*, ed. DR Roediger, Schocken Books, New York.

Ball, Megan 1992, 'The lesser of two evils: a comparison of government and mission policy at Raukkan and Point Pearce, 1890–1940', *Cabbages and Kings*, no. 20, pp. 36–45.

Bandler, Faith 1983, 'Birth of the Fellowship', in *The time was ripe: a history of the Aboriginal–Australian Fellowship (1956–1969)*, eds Faith Bandler & Len Fox, Alternative Publishing, Sydney, pp. 1–16.

——1989, *Turning the tide: a personal history of the Federal Council for the Advancement of Aborigines and Torres Strait Islanders*, Aboriginal Studies Press, Canberra.

Bandler, Faith & Len Fox (eds) 1983, *The time was ripe: a history of the Aboriginal–Australian Fellowship (1956–1969)*, Alternative Publishing, Sydney.

Bartlett, Francesca 1999, 'Clean, white girls: assimilation and women's work, *Hecate*, vol. 25, no. 1, pp. 10–37.

Barwick, Diane 1978, 'And the lubras are ladies now', in *Women's role in Aboriginal society*, ed. Fay Gale, Australian Institute of Aboriginal Studies, Canberra.

Bashford, Alison 2000, 'Is White Australia possible? Race, colonialism and tropical medicine' *Ethnic and Racial Studies*, vol. 23, no. 2, pp. 248–71.

Bates, Daisy 1972 (1938), *The passing of the Aborigines: a lifetime spent among the natives of Australia*, John Murray, London.

——1972, *Tales told to Kabbarli: Aboriginal legends collected by Daisy Bates, retold by Barbara Ker Wilson*, Angus & Robertson, Sydney.

——1985, *The native tribes of Western Australia*, ed. Isobel White, National Library of Australia, Canberra.

——1992, *Aboriginal Perth and Bibbulman biographies and legends*, ed. PJ Bridge, Hesperion Press, Carlisle.

Bell, Diane 1983, *Daughters of the Dreaming*, Spinifex Press, Melbourne.

——1987, 'Aboriginal women and the religious experience', in *Traditional Aboriginal society: a reader*, ed. WH Edwards, Macmillan, Melbourne.

——1988, '"Choose your mission wisely": Christian colonials and Aboriginal marital arrangements on the northern frontier', in *Aboriginal Australians and Christian missions*, eds Tony Swain & Deborah Bird Rose, Australian Association for the Study of Religions, Adelaide, pp. 338–52.

——1998, *Ngarrindjeri Wurruwarrin*, Spinifex Press, Melbourne.

Bennett, Mary 1927a, *Christison of Lammermoor*, Alston Rivers, London.

——1927b, 'Notes on the Dalleburra Tribe of northern Queensland', *Journal of the Royal Anthropological Institute of Great Britain and Ireland*, vol. 57, pp. 399–415.

——1930, *The Australian Aboriginal as a human being*, Alston Rivers, London.

——1935, *Teaching the Aborigines: data from the Mt Margaret Mission*, City & Suburban Print, Perth.

Berndt, Ronald 1951, *Kunapipi: a study of an Australian Aboriginal religious cult*, FW Cheshire, Melbourne.

Berndt, Catherine & Ronald 1951, 'An Oenpelli monologue: culture contact', *Oceania*, vol. 22, no. 1, September, pp. 24–52.

——1988, *The world of the first Australians: Aboriginal traditional life, past and present*, Aboriginal Studies Press for AIATSIS, Canberra.

——1993, *A world that was: the Yaraldi of the Murray River and the Lakes*, Melbourne University Press at the Miegunyah Press, Melbourne.

Black, Roman 1964, *Old and new Australian Aboriginal art*, Angus & Robertson, Sydney.

Blackburn, Kevin 1999, 'White agitation for an Aboriginal state in Australia (1925–29)', *Australian Journal of Politics and History*, vol. 45, no. 2, June, pp. 157–80.

Brock, Peggy 1993, *Outback ghettos: a history of Aboriginal institutionalisation and survival*, Cambridge University Press, Melbourne.

Brock, Peggy 1995, 'Aboriginal families and the law in the era of segregation and assimilation, 1890s–1950s', in *Sex, power and justice: historical perspectives on law in Australia*, ed. D Kirby, Oxford University Press, Melbourne, pp. 133–49.

Brown Gribble, John 1884, *Black but comely*, London.

Brubaker, Rogers & Frederick Cooper 2000, 'Beyond "identity"', *Theory and Society*, no. 29, pp. 1–47.

Burton, Antoinette 1994, *Burdens of history: British feminists, Indian women, and imperial culture, 1865–1915*, University of North Carolina Press, London.

——2003, *Dwelling in the archive: women writing house, home and history in late colonial India*, Oxford University Press, London.

Bush, Connie 1990, 'Boo-roon-joo (a story of the Ruined City and a country nearby called Wunmurrie or War-Lun-Dooer-Pa)', *Australian Short Stories*, no. 32, Pascoe Publishing, Apollo Bay, Vic.

——1995, 'Ted Heathcock' in the *Drum*, Northern Territory Police Journal.

Capell, A 1960, 'The Wandarang and other tribal myths of the Yabuduruwa Ritual' in *Oceania*, no. 30, p. 3.

Caruana, Wally 1993, *Aboriginal art*, Thames & Hudson, London.

Cato, Nancy 1993, *Mr Maloga*, University of Queensland Press, Brisbane.

Chaudhuri, Nupur & Margaret Strobel (eds) 1992, *Western women and imperialism: complicity and resistance*, Indiana University Press, Bloomington.

Cheater, Christine 1993 'From Sydney schoolgirl to African queen mother: tracing the career of Phyllis Mary Kaberry', in *First in their field*, ed. Julie Marcus, Melbourne University Press, Melbourne, pp. 137–51.

——2000, 'JB Cleland and the search for the essential Aborigine', in Martin Crotty et al. (eds), '"A race for a place": eugenics, Darwinism and social thought and practice in Australia', *Proceedings of the History and Sociology of Eugenics Conference*, University of Newcastle, 27–28 April 2000, pp. 85–90.

Choo, Christine 2001, *Mission girls: Aboriginal women on Catholic missions in the Kimberley, Western Australia, 1900–1950*, University of Western Australia Press, Perth.

Christiansen, J 1991, *They came...and stayed: a history of Hervey Bay*, R&J McTaggart & Co., Hervey Bay, Qld.

Clark-Lewis, Elizabeth 1994, *Living in, living out: African-American domestics in Washington DC, 1910–40s*, Smithsonian Institute Press, Washington DC.

Cole, Anna 2001, 'The glorified flower: race, gender and assimilation in Australia, 1937–1967', PhD thesis, University of Technology, Sydney.

Cook, CE 1927, *The epidemiology of leprosy in Australia*, Commonwealth Service Publication, no. 38.

Cooke, CMT 1927, 'Australian Aboriginal women', *Report of the British Commonwealth League Conference*, the Women's Library, London, p. 30.

——1930, 'The status of Aboriginal women in Australia', *Proceedings of the Second Pan-Pacific Women's Conference*, Melbourne, pp. 127–37.

Cooper, Frederick & Ann L Stoler 1989, 'Introduction: tensions of empire: colonial control and visions of rule', *American Ethnologist*, vol. 16, no. 4, pp. 1–13.

Cubillo, Franchesca Alberts 1998, 'Grass castles: the making of an Aboriginal artist. Elizabeth Durack and Eddie Burrup', *Periphery*, no. 34, autumn, pp. 6–8.

Cullwick, Hannah 1984, *The diaries of Hannah Cullwick, Victorian maidservant*, ed. Liz Stanley, Virago, London.

Curthoys, Ann 1993, 'Identity crisis: colonialism, nation and gender in Australian history', *Gender & History*, vol. 5, no. 2.

Daley, Caroline & Melanie Nolan (eds) 1994, *Suffrage and beyond: international feminist perspectives*, Auckland University Press & Pluto Press, Auckland.

Davidoff, Lenore & Catherine Hall 1997, *Family fortunes: men and women of the English middle class*, Routledge, London.

Davidson, WS 1978, *Havens of refuge*, University of Western Australia Press, Perth.

Dodson, Patrick 2000, 'Beyond the mourning gate: dealing with unfinished business', Wentworth Lecture, 12 May, AIATSIS, Canberra, viewed 3 February 2005, <www.aiatsis.gov.au/lbry/dig_prgm/wentworth/a317361_a.pdf>

Douglas, Mary 1984 (1966), *Purity and danger: an analysis of concepts of pollution and taboo*, Routledge, Oxford.

Dubinsky, Karen 1999,'The spectacle of race at Niagara Falls' in *Gender, sexuality and colonial modernities*, ed. Antoinette Burton, Routledge, New York.

Duguid, Charles 1972, *Doctor and the Aborigines*, Rigby, Adelaide.

Durack, Mary 1983, *Sons in the saddle*, Constable, London.

Dyhouse, Carolyn 1981, *Girls growing up in late Victorian and Edwardian England*, Routledge & Kegan Paul, London.

Elkin, AP, Papers, Box 69, Folder 1/12/153, Fisher Archives, University of Sydney.

Elkin, AP 1971, *Yabuduruwa at Roper River Mission*, 1965 (in AIATIS collection).

Ellinghaus, Katherine 1997, 'Racism in the Never-Never: disparate readings of Jeannie Gunn', *Hecate*, vol. 23, no. 2, pp. 76–95.

Ely, Bonita 1980, *Murray/Murrindi*, Experimental Art Foundation, Adelaide.

Evans, Julia, Patricia Grimshaw & Ann Standish 2003, 'Yuwalaraay women and attachments to land on an Australian colonial frontier (caring for Country)', *Journal of Women's History*, vol. 14, no. 4, pp. 15–41.

Evans, Raymond 1992, 'A gun in the oven: masculinism and gendered violence', in *Gender relations in Australia: domination and negotiation*, eds Kay Saunders & Raymond Evans, Harcourt Brace Jovanovich, Sydney, pp. 197–218.

Fison, FL & AW Howitt 1880, *Kamilaroi and Kurnai*, George Robertson, Melbourne.

Forrest, K 1996, *The challenge and the chance: the colonisation and settlement of north-west Australia 1861–1914*, Hesperian Press, Perth.

Foster, Robert 1984, 'The Bunganditj: European invasion and the economic basis of social collapse', MA thesis, Adelaide University.

Fox, Len 1983, 'Pearl Gibbs: a tribute', in *The time was ripe: a history of the Aboriginal–Australian Fellowship (1956–1969)*, eds Faith Bandler & Len Fox, Alternative Publishing, Sydney, pp. 41–46.

Gapps, Stephen 1993, 'Mr Ardill's scrapbook: alternative sources for biography', *Public History Review*, no. 2, pp. 99–107.

Gardner, PD 1993, *Gippsland massacres: the destruction of the Kurnai Tribes 1800–60*, Ngarak Press, Victoria.

Gibson, Eva 1992, 'Kancubina-Kiang-oo-panny', *Northern Territory dictionary of biography*, vol. 2, Northern Territory University Press, Darwin, p. 104.

Gilbert, Kevin 1983, 'Pearl Gibbs: Aboriginal patriot', *Aboriginal History*, vol. 7, no. 1, pp. 5–9.

Gill, Merri 1996, *Weilmoringle: a unique bi-cultural community*, Development & Advisory Publications of Australia, Dubbo.

Goodall, Heather 1983, 'Pearl Gibbs: some memories', *Aboriginal History*, vol. 7, no. 1, pp. 20–22.

——1988a, 'Pearl Gibbs', in *200 Australian women: a Redress anthology*, ed. Heather Radi, Women's Redress Press Inc., Sydney, pp. 211–13.

——1988b, 'When Anthony Fernando went to confront his colonisers', *Land Rights News*, September, pp. 32–33.

——1990, '"Saving the children": gender and the colonization of Aboriginal children in NSW, 1788 to 1990', *Aboriginal Law Bulletin*, vol. 2, no. 44, pp. 6–9.

——1995, 'Assimilation begins in the home: the state and Aboriginal women's work as mothers in NSW, 1900-60', in special ed. *Labour History*, no. 69, pp. 75-191.

——1996, *Invasion to embassy: land in Aboriginal politics in New South Wales, 1770-1972*, Allen & Unwin, Sydney.

Gooding, Janda 1995, 'Elizabeth Durack', in *Heritage: the national women's art book — 500 works by 500 Australian women artists from colonial times to 1955*, ed. Joan Kerr, Craftsman House, Roseville East, pp. 334-45.

Grant, Arch 1992, 'Ruth Sabina Heathcock', *Northern Territory dictionary of biography*, vol. 2, Northern Territory University Press, Darwin, pp. 92-93

Grey, George 1841, *Journals of two expeditions of discovery in the north-west and Western Australia, during the years 1837-38 and 39*, Boone, London.

Grimshaw, Patricia et al. 1994, *Creating a nation*, McPhee Gribble, Melbourne.

Haebich, Anna 1988, *For their own good: Aborigines and government in the southwest of Western Australia*, University of Western Australia Press, Perth.

——2000, *Broken circles: fragmenting Indigenous families 1800-2000*, Fremantle Arts Centre Press, Fremantle, WA.

Hage, Ghassan 1988, *White nation: fantasies of white supremacy in a multicultural society*, Pluto Press, Sydney.

Haggis, Jane 1990, 'Gendering colonialism or colonising gender? Recent women's studies approaches to white women and the history of British colonialism', *Women's Studies International Forum*, vol. 13, no. 1/2, pp. 105-15.

——2001, 'The social memory of a colonial frontier', in *Gender in the contact zone*, ed. Margaret Allen, special issue of *Australian Feminist Studies*, vol. 16, no. 34, March, pp. 91-99.

Hall, Catherine 1992, *White, male and middle class: explorations in feminism and history*, Polity Press, Cambridge, pp. 1-40.

——2002, 'Introduction', in *Civilising subjects: metropole and colony in the English imagination 1830-1867*, University of Chicago Press & Polity Press, Cambridge, pp. 1-22.

Hall, Richard 1998, *Black armband days*, Vintage, Sydney.

Hall, Stuart 1996, 'Ethnicity: identity and difference', in *Becoming national: a reader*, eds George Ely & Ronald Gigor Suny, Oxford University Press, New York, pp. 345-46.

Hall, Victor C 1968, *Sister Ruth*, Neville Spearman, London.

Hammerton, AJ 1999, 'Pooterism or partnership, marriage and masculine identity in the lower middle class, 1870-1920', *Journal of British Studies*, no. 38, pp. 291-321.

Hankins, Carla E 1982, 'The missing links: cultural genocide through the abduction of female Aboriginal children from their families and their training for domestic service, 1883-1969', unpublished BA (Hons) thesis, University of New South Wales, Sydney.

Hargrave, John 1980, *Leprosy in the Northern Territory of Australia with particular reference to the Aborigines of Arnhem Land and arid regions of the Northern Territory*, Northern Territory Department of Health, Darwin.

——1984, *Leprosy in tropical Australia*, Northern Territory Department of Health, Darwin.

Harris, John 1927, 'Some servitudes of women', *Report of the conference of the British Commonwealth League*, June, p. 21.

Harris, John 1990, *One blood*, Albatross Books, Sydney.

——1993, 'Losing and gaining a language: the story of Kriol in the Northern Territory', in *Language and Culture in Aboriginal Australia*, eds M Walsh & C Yallop, Aboriginal Studies Press, pp. 145–54.

——1998, *We wish we'd done more: ninety years of CMS and Aboriginal issues in north Australia*, Openbook, Adelaide.

Haskins, Victoria 1998a, '"Lovable natives" and "tribal sisters": feminism, maternalism, and the campaign for Aboriginal citizenship in New South Wales in the late 1930s', *Hecate*, vol. 14, no. 2, pp. 8–21.

——1998b, '"My one bright spot": a personal insight into relationships between white women under the NSW Aborigines Protection Board apprenticeship policy, 1920–1942', PhD thesis, University of Sydney.

——1998c, 'Servants in suburban Sydney: the NSW Aborigines Protection Board and the policy of sending Aboriginal girls to Sydney, 1883–1940', in *Urban life, urban culture: Aboriginal/Indigenous experiences*, ed. George Morgan, Gcolangullia Centre, Sydney, pp. 166–79.

——2001, 'On the doorstep: Aboriginal domestic service as a "contact zone"', *Australian Feminist Studies*, vol. 16, no. 34, pp. 13–25.

——2003, '"Could you see to the return of my daughter": Aboriginal fathers and daughters under the NSW Aborigines Protection Board apprenticeship policy in inter-war NSW', *Australian Historical Studies*, vol. 34, no. 121, April, pp. 106–21.

Heilbrun, Carolyn G 1998, *Writing a woman's life*, Ballantine Books, New York.

Hill, Ernestine 1945, 'Wings to Borroloola', *Walkabout*, 1 October.

——1973, *Kabbarli: a personal memoir of Daisy Bates*, Angus & Robertson, Sydney.

Holland, Alison 1995, 'Feminism, colonialism and Aboriginal workers: an anti-slavery crusade', in *Aboriginal Workers*, eds A McGrath et al., special ed. *Labour History*, vol. 69, November, pp. 52–64.

——1999, '"Saving the Aborigines": the white woman's crusade. A study of gender, race and the Australian frontier, 1920s–1960s', PhD, University of New South Wales, Sydney.

——2001a, 'The campaign for women protectors: gender, race and frontier between the wars', *Australian Feminist Studies*, vol. 16, no. 34, March, pp. 27–42.

——2001b, 'Wives and mothers like ourselves? Exploring white women's intervention in the politics of race, 1920s–40s', *Australian Historical Studies*, vol. 31, no. 117, October, pp. 292–310.

Horner, Jack 1938, 'The life and times of Bill Ferguson, 1965–1970', *Sun*, Wednesday, 4 August, MS4112, Australian Institute of Aboriginal and Torres Strait Islander Studies, Canberra.

——1974, manuscript for *Bill Ferguson: fighter for Aboriginal freedom*, 'The life and times of Bill Ferguson, 1965–1970', MS4112, Australian Institute of Aboriginal and Torres Strait Islander Studies, Canberra.

——1983, 'Pearl Gibbs: a biographical tribute', *Aboriginal History*, vol. 7, no. 1, pp. 10–19.

——1994 (1974), *Bill Ferguson: fighter for Aboriginal freedom: a biography by Jack Horner*, Aboriginal Studies Press, Canberra.

Horner, Jack & Marcia Langton 1987, 'The Day of Mourning', in *Australians, 1938*, eds Bill Gammage & Peter Spearitt, Fairfax, Syme, Weldon Associates, NSW.

Horner, Jean 1983, 'We saw a poster' in *The time was ripe: a history of the Aboriginal–Australian Fellowship* (1956–69), eds Faith Bandler & Len Fox, Alternative Publishing, Sydney, pp. 37–40.

Huggins, Jackie 1988, '"Firing on in the mind": Aboriginal women domestic servants in the inter-war years', *Hecate*, vol. 13, no. 2, pp. 5–23.

——1990, 'Response', in *Through white eyes*, eds Susan Janson & Stuart Macintyre, Allen & Unwin, Sydney, pp. 168–71.

——1993, 'Pretty deadly tidda business', in *Feminism and the politics of difference*, eds Sneja Gunew & Anna Yeatman, Allen & Unwin, Sydney, pp. 61–72.

——1995, 'Writing Aboriginal history', paper presented at the State Library of NSW, 25 January.

——1996, 'Experience and identity', *Limina*, reprinted in Jackie Huggins 1998, *Sister Girl*, University of Queensland Press, Brisbane, pp. 120–30.

Hughes, Karen 1986, *Pitjiri: the snake that will not sink*, Ronin Films, Canberra.

——1995, 'Pioneer for humanity', the *Advertiser*, 3 June, pp. 6–7.

——2001, 'The past is in the present and the present is in the past', in *Crossings*, vol. 6.3, Australian Studies Centre, University of Queensland, viewed 1 February 2005, <http://asc.uq.edu.au/crossings>.

Human Rights and Equal Opportunity Commission 1997, *Bringing them home: report of the National Inquiry into the Separation of Aboriginal and Torres Strait Islander Children from their Families*, HREOC, Sydney.

Human Rights and Equal Opportunity Commission with AIATSIS 1997, *Bringing them home: a guide to the findings and recommendations of the National Inquiry into the Separation of Aboriginal and Torres Strait Islander Children from their Families*, AIATSIS, Canberra.

Jacobs, Jane 1996, *Edge of empire: postcolonialism and the city*, Routledge, London.

Jacobs, Margaret D 1999, *Engendered encounters: feminism and Pueblo cultures, 1879–1934*, University of Nebraska Press, Lincoln.

Jacobs, Patricia 1986, 'Science and veiled assumptions: miscegenation in WA 1930–37', *Australian Aboriginal Studies*, no. 2, pp. 15–23.

Jayawardena, Kumari 1995, *The white woman's other burden: Western women and South Asia during British rule*, Routledge, London & New York.

Jenkin, Graham 1979, *Conquest of the Ngarrindjeri*, Adelaide, Rigby.

John, Young children in brief separation series 1969, motion picture, James & Joyce Robertson, Tavistock Institute of Human Relations, London. Distributed by Concord Video & Film Council, Ipswich, UK.

Jones, Jennifer 2000, 'The black communist: the contested memory of Margaret Tucker', *Hecate*, vol. 26, no. 2, pp. 135–45.

Jose, Nicholas 2002, *Black sheep*, Hardie Grant Books, Melbourne.

Kaberry, Phyllis 1939, *Aboriginal woman: sacred and profane*, Routledge & Kegan Paul, London.

Kate, Young children in brief separation series 1967, motion picture, James & Joyce Robertson, Tavistock Institute of Human Relations, London. Distributed by Concord Video & Film Council, Ipswich, UK.

Kettle, Ellen 1991, *Health services in the Northern Territory: a history, 1824–1970*, vol. 1, North Australian Research Unit, Australian National University, Darwin.

King, Marion 1985, 'Daisy Bates: a guide to the literature', evaluative bibliography compiled for the degree of Bachelor of Social Sciences (Librarianship), Royal Melbourne Institute of Technology.

Kingsley-Strack, Joan 1892–1983, Papers, National Library of Australia, Canberra.

Kleinert, Sylvia & Margo Neale 2000, *Oxford companion to Aboriginal art and culture*, Oxford University Press, Melbourne.

Koven, Seth & Sonya Michel (eds) 1993, *Mothers of a New World: maternalist politics and the origins of welfare states*, Routledge, New York & London.

Lake, Marilyn 1993, 'Colonised and colonising: the white Australian feminist subject', *Women's History Review*, vol. 2, no. 3, pp. 377–86.

——1994, 'Personality, individuality, nationality: feminist conceptions of citizenship 1902–1940', *Australian Feminist Studies*, no. 19, autumn, pp. 25–38.

——1996, 'Frontier feminism and the marauding white man', *Journal of Australian Studies*, no. 49, pp. 12–20.

——1998, 'Feminism and the gendered politics of antiracism, Australia 1927–1957: from maternal protectionism to leftist assimilationism', *Australian Historical Studies*, no. 110, pp. 91–108.

——1999, *Getting equal: the history of Australian feminism*, Allen & Unwin, Sydney.

——2000, 'The ambiguities for feminists of national belonging: race and gender in the imagined Australian community', in *Gendered nations: nationalisms and gender order in the long nineteenth century*, eds Ida Blom et al., Berg Publishers, Oxford, pp. 159–76.

——2001a, 'Eldershaw Memorial Lecture: founding fathers, dutiful wives and rebellious daughters', *Tasmanian Historical Research Association papers and proceedings*, vol. 48, no. 4, pp. 268–79.

——2001b, 'Radical daughters', *Age*, 8 March, p. 1–2.

——2002, *Faith Bandler: gentle activist*, Allen & Unwin, Sydney.

Lind, MA 1988, *The compassionate memsahibs: welfare activities of British women in India, 1900–1947*, Greenwood Press, Westport, Connecticut.

Link-Up (NSW) & Tikka Jan Wilson 1997, *In the best interest of the child? Stolen Children: Aboriginal pain/white shame*, Aboriginal History Incorporated, Canberra.

Lockwood, Douglas 1973, *I, the Aboriginal*, Rigby, Adelaide.

Long, Jeremy 1970, *Aboriginal settlements*, Australian National University Press, Canberra.

Lovejoy, Arthur O 1965, *The great chain of being: a study of the history of an idea*, Harper & Row, New York, pp. 183–86.

Macilwain, Margaret, 'Cooke, Constance Mary Ternent (1882–1967)', *Australian dictionary of biography*, supplementary volume, forthcoming.

Markus, Andrew 1990, *Governing savages*, Allen & Unwin, Sydney.

Marshall a-Kithibula, Bessie 1992, 'The death of Horace Foster at Manangoorah', in John Bradley with Jean Kirton & the Yanyuwa community, *Yanyuwa Wuka: language from Yanyuwa country, a Yanyuwa dictionary and cultural resource*, ePrints@UQ, University of Queensland Cybrary, viewed 3 February 2005, <eprint.uq.edu.au/archive/ 00000072/ 01/yanyuwatotal.pdf>, pp. 609–14.

Martin, CEM 1890, *An Australian girl*, 3 volumes, Bentley, London.

Martin, CEM 1892, *The silent sea*, 3 volumes, Bentley, London.

Martin, CEM 1923, *The incredible journey*, Cape, London.

Martin, CEM 1997, '*Breaking the law': small tales of early Australia*, no. 5, with an introduction by Margaret Allen, Mulini Press, Canberra, originally published in *The Observer Miscellany* (Adelaide), 1879, pp. 849–63.

Mattingley, Christobel (ed.) 1988, *Survival in our own land: Aboriginal experiences in 'South Australia' since 1836, told by Nungas and others*, Wakefield Press, Adelaide.

Maynard, John 2003, 'Fred Maynard and the awakening of Aboriginal political consciousness and activism in 20th-century Australia', PhD thesis, University of Newcastle.

McClintock, Ann 1997, *Imperial leather: race, gender and sexuality in the colonial contest*, Routledge, New York.

McGregor, Russell 1993a, 'The concept of primitivity in the early anthropological writings of AP Elkin', *Aboriginal History*, vol. 17, no. 2, pp. 95–104.

——1993b, 'The doomed race: a scientific axiom of the late nineteenth century', *Australian Journal of Politics and History*, vol. 39, no. 1, pp. 14–22.

——1997, *Imagined destinies: Aboriginal Australians and the doomed race theory, 1880–1939*, Melbourne University Press, Melbourne.

McLeod, Hugh 1977, 'White-collar values and the role of religion', in *The lower middle class in Britain 1870–1914*, ed. G Crossick, Croom Helm, London.

Midgley, Clare 1992, *Women against slavery: the British campaigns, 1780–1870*, Routledge, London.

Midgley, Clare (ed.) 1998, *Gender and imperialism*, Manchester University Press, 1998.

Miller, James 1985, *Koori: a will to win. The heroic resistance, survival & triumph of Black Australia*, Angus & Robertson, London.

Minault, G (ed.) 1982, *The extended family: women and political participation in India and Pakistan*, Chanakya Publications, Delhi.

Moreton-Robinson, Aileen 2000, *Talkin' up to the white woman: Indigenous women and feminism*, University of Queensland Press, Brisbane.

Morgan, M 1986, *A drop in a bucket: the Mount Margaret story*, United Aborigines Mission, Victoria.

Morphy, Howard 1998, *Aboriginal art*, Phaidon, London.

Morphy, Howard & Francis 1984, 'Myths of Ngalakan history: ideology and images of the past in Northern Australia', *Man*, vol. 19, no. 3, pp. 459–79.

Morris, Barry 1989, *Domesticating resistance: the Dhan-Gadi Aborigines and the Australian state*, Berg Publishers, Oxford, pp. 130–32.

Morris, HF & JS Read 1972, *Indirect rule and the search for justice: essays in East African legal history*, Clarendon Press, Oxford, pp. 227–28.

Mudrooroo 1995, *Us mob: history, culture, struggle: an introduction to Indigenous Australia*, Angus & Robertson, Sydney.

Muecke, Stephen & Adam Shoemaker (eds) 2001, *David Unaipon, legendary tales of the Australian Aborigines*, The Miegunyah Press, Melbourne.

Nettelbeck, Amanda 2001, '"Seeking to spread the truth": Christina Smith and the South Australian frontier', *Australian Feminist Studies*, vol. 16, no. 34, March, pp. 83–90.

Newman, Louise Michele 1999, *White women's rights: the racial origins of feminism in the United States*, Oxford University Press, New York.

Paisley, Fiona 1993, '"Don't tell England!": women of empire campaign to change Aboriginal policy in Australia between the wars', *Lilith*, no. 8, summer, pp. 139–52.

——1995, 'Feminist challenges to White Australia, 1900–1930s', in *Sex, power and justice: historical perspectives on law in Australia*, ed. D Kirkby, Oxford University Press, Melbourne, pp. 252–69.

——1997a, 'No back streets in the bush: 1920s and 1930s pro-Aboriginal white women's activism and the trans-Australia railway', *Australian Feminist Studies*, vol. 12, no. 25, pp. 119–37.

——1997b, 'White women in the field: feminism, cultural relativism and Aboriginal rights, 1920–1937', *Journal of Australian Studies*, no. 52, pp. 113–25.

——1999, '"Unnecessary crimes and tragedies": race, gender and sexuality in Australian policies of child removal', in *Gender, sexuality and colonial modernity*, ed. Antoinette Burton, Routledge, New York, pp. 134–47.

——2000, *Loving protection? Australian feminism and Aboriginal women's rights 1919-1939*, Melbourne University Press.

——2002, 'Cultivating modernity: culture and internationalism in Australian feminism's Pacific age', *Journal of Women's History*, vol. 14, no. 3, autumn, pp. 105–32.

Parry, Suzanne 1992, 'Disease, medicine & settlement: the role of health and medical services in the settlement of the Northern Territory, 1911–1939', PhD thesis, Department of History, University of Queensland, Brisbane.

Pascoe, Peggy 1990, *Relations of rescue: the search for female moral authority in the American West, 1874-1939*, Oxford University Press, New York.

Pateman, Carole 1989, *The disorder of women: democracy, feminism and political theory*, Polity Press, Cambridge.

Patten, JT & W Ferguson 1938, *Aborigines claim citizen rights! A statement of the case for the Aborigines Progressive Association*, the Publicist, Sydney.

Pepper, Phillip 1980, *You are what you make yourself to be: the story of a Victorian Aboriginal family, 1842-1980*, Hyland House, Melbourne.

Perry, Adele 2001, *On the edge of empire: gender, race, and the making of British Columbia, 1849-1871*, University of Toronto Press.

Pierson, Arthur T 1907, *George Muller of Bristol*, James Nisbet & Co. Ltd, London.

Pines, Dinora 1993, 'Pregnancy and motherhood: interaction between fantasy and reality', in *A woman's unconscious use of her body*, Virago Press, London, pp. 59–77.

Procida, Mary 2002, *Married to empire: gender, politics and imperialism in India, 1883-1947*, Manchester University Press, New York.

Radi, Heather (ed.) 1988, *200 Australian women: a Redress anthology*, Women's Redress Press Inc., Sydney.

Read, Peter 1999, *A rape of the soul so profound: the return of the stolen generations*, Allen & Unwin, Sydney.

——2003, 'One hundred years of Aboriginality', *Psychoanalysis Downunder*, online journal of the Australian Psychoanalytical Society, issue no. 3, viewed 3 February 2005, <www.psychoanalysisdownunder.com/PADPapers/pap3/onehundred_pr.htm>.

Reynolds, Henry 1998, *This whispering in our hearts*, Allen & Unwin, Sydney.

Rich, Adrienne 1979, *On lies, secrets and silence: selected prose, 1966–78*, Virago, London.

Richardson, Paula 1992, 'Point Pearce: history of the Point Pearce Mission Station, South Australia', *Cabbages and Kings*, no. 20, pp. 25–35.

Riddett, Lyn 1991, 'Guarding civilisation's rim: the Australian Inland Mission sisters in the Victoria River district 1922-1939', *Journal of Australian Studies*, no. 30, pp. 29–44.

——1993, '"Watch the white women fade": Aboriginal and white women in the Northern Territory, 1870–1940', *Hecate*, vol. 19, no. 1, pp. 73–93.

Roberts, Tony 2005, *Frontier justice*, University of Queensland Press, Brisbane.

Rollins, Judith 1985, *Between women: domestics and their employers*, Temple University Press, Philadelphia.

Ross, Ellen 1993, *Love and toil: motherhood in outcast London, 1870–1918*, Oxford University Press, London.

Rowley, CD 1980 (1974), *The destruction of the Aborigines*, Penguin Books, London.

Ruddick, Daisy, Kathy Mills & Tony Austin 1989, "Talking about cruel things": girls' life in the Kahlin Compound', *Hecate*, vol. 15, no. 1, pp. 8–22.

Ryan, Judith with Kim Akerman 1993, *Images of power: Aboriginal art of the Kimberley*, National Gallery of Victoria, Melbourne.

Sabbioni, Jennifer 1993, 'Aboriginal history', *Tasmanian Historical Studies*, vol. 4, no. 1, p. 8.

Salter, Elizabeth 1971, *Daisy Bates: great white queen of the Never Never*, Angus & Robertson, Sydney.

Sansom, Basil 2001, 'Irruptions of the Dreamings in post-colonial Australia', *Oceania*, vol. 72, no. 1, September.

Saunders, Suzanne 1989, *A suitable island site: leprosy in the Northern Territory and the Channel Island Leprosarium*, Northern Territory Historical Society, Darwin.

——1990, 'Leprosy propholaxis in Australia', *Aboriginal History*, vol. 14, no. 2, pp. 169–81.

——1991, 'A duly qualified medical practitioner: health services in the Northern Territory, 1911–1939' in *Peripheral visions: essays on Australian regional and local history*, ed. BJ Dalton, James Cook University, Townsville, pp. 251–69.

Sayers, Andrew 1994, *Aboriginal artists of the nineteenth century*, Oxford University Press, New York.

Scanlon, Tony 1986, '"Pure and clean and true to Christ": black women and white missionaries in the north', *Hecate*, vol. 7, nos 1–2, pp. 83–105.

Scott, J 1985 *Weapons of the weak: everyday forms of peasant resistance*, Yale University Press, London.

Scott, Joan Wallach 1988, *Gender and the politics of history*, Columbia University Press, New York.

Sekuless, Peter 1978, *Jessie Street: a rewarding but unrewarded life*, University of Queensland Press, Brisbane.

Sheridan, Sue 1995, *Along the faultlines: sex, race and nation in Australian women's writing 1880s–1930s*, Allen & Unwin, Sydney.

Sinha, Mrinalini 1998, 'Refashioning Mother India: gender, caste and national identity in India in the 1920s and 1930s', Conference of the International Federation for Research in Women's History, June/July.

Spencer, Baldwin & FJ Gillen 1904, *The northern tribes of Central Australia*, Macmillan, London.

——1968 (1899), *The native tribes of Central Australia*, Dover Publications, New York.

Spivak, Gayatri & Sneja Gunew 1986, 'Questions of multiculturalism', *Hecate*, vol. 12, no. 1–2, pp. 136–42.

Standish, Anne 1999, 'Devoted service to a dying race?', in *Citizenship, women and social justice*, eds J Damousi & K Ellinghaus, Melbourne University Press, pp. 52–59.

Stanner, WEH 1991 (1968), *After the Dreaming*, ABC Books, Sydney.

Stern, Daniel N 1985, *The interpersonal world of the infant: a view from psychoanalysis and developmental psychology*, Basic Books, New York.

Stoler, Ann Laura 1989, 'Making empire respectable: the politics of race and sexual morality in 20th-century colonial cultures', *American Ethnologist*, vol. 16, no. 4, pp. 634–60.

——1997, *Race and the education of desire: Foucault's history of sexuality and the colonial order of things*, Duke University Press, Durham & London.

Stretton, Pat & Christine Finnimore 1991, *How South Australian Aborigines lost the vote: some side effects of Federation*, Old Parliament House, Adelaide.

Summers, Carol 1991, 'Intimate colonialism: the imperial production of reproduction in Uganda, 1907–1925', *Signs*, vol. 16, no. 4, pp. 787–807.

Sweet, Georgina 1930, 'Women and international relationships', Proceedings of the *Second Pan Pacific Women's Conference*, Honolulu, pp. 335–42.

Taffe, Sue 2001, 'Witnesses from the conference floor: oral history and the Federal Council for the Advancement of Aborigines and Torres Strait Islanders', *Journal of Australian Studies*, no. 67, API Network & University of Queensland Press, Brisbane.

Taplin, George 1859–1879, Journal: five volumes as typed from the original by (Taplin's granddaughter) Mrs Beaumont, Mortlock Library, Adelaide.

Taylor, Dr and Mrs Howard 1911, *Hudson Taylor in early years: the growth of a soul*, China Inland Mission, London.

Thomas, David 2002, 'What Professor Cleland did on his holidays: collecting expeditions to Central Australia as Indigenous health research, 1925–39', *Health and History*, vol. 4, no. 2, pp. 57–79.

Thompson, Donald 1983, *Donald Thompson in Arnhem Land*, compiled and introduced by Nicolas Peterson, Currey O'Neil, South Yarra.

Thonemann, HE 1949, *Tell the white man: the life story of an Aboriginal lubra*, Collins, London & Sydney.

Tucker, Margaret 1983, *If everyone cared: autobiography of Margaret Tucker, MBE*, 2nd edn, Grosvenor, London.

Walden, Inara 1991, 'Aboriginal women in domestic service in New South Wales, 1850 to 1969', BA Hons thesis, University of New South Wales, Sydney.

Walden, Inara 1995, '"That was slavery days": Aboriginal domestic servants in New South Wales in the twentieth century', *Aboriginal Workers: Labour History*, no. 69, eds Ann McGrath & Kay Saunders, University of Sydney, pp. 196–207.

Ware, Vron 1992a, *Beyond the pale: white women, racism and history*, Verso, London.

——1992b, 'Moments of danger: race, gender, and memories of empire', *Journal of History and Theory*, vol. 4, no. 3, pp. 116–37.

Wetherell, David 1996, *Charles Abel and the Kwato Mission of Papua New Guinea, 1891–1925*, Melbourne University Press.

White, Isobel 1985, *The native tribes of Western Australia/Daisy Bates*, National Library of Australia, Canberra.

—— 1993, 'Daisy Bates: legend and reality', in *First in their field*, ed. J Marcus, Melbourne University Press, Melbourne, pp. 47–66.

Williams, Ross 1998, 'Why should I feel guilty?' Reflections on the workings of guilt in white–Aboriginal relations', *Australian Psychologist*, vol. 35, no. 2, pp. 136–42.

Wilson, Andrew 2003, 'Indigenous culture: exploring the past to inform the present: Aboriginal family history and state records', paper presented to the History Trust of South Australia, Renmark conference, 24–25 May.

Winnicott, DW 1980 (1971), *Playing and reality*, Penguin Books, London.

Wolfe, Patrick 1999, *Settler colonialism and the transformation of anthropology: the politics and poetics of an ethnographic event*, Cassell, London.

Woodruff, PS 1951, 'Obituary, Frank Sandland Hone', *Medical Journal of Australia*, vol. 1, pp. 919–22.

Woollacott, Angela 1998 'Inventing Commonwealth and pan-Pacific feminisms: Australian women's internationalist activism in the 1920s–30s', *Gender and History*, vol. 10, no. 3, November, pp. 425–48.

——2001, *To try her fortune in London: Australian women, colonialism and modernity*, Oxford University Press, Melbourne.

Index

www.ingramcontent.com/pod-product-compliance
Lightning Source LLC
Chambersburg PA
CBHW020314290526
45785CB00007B/2783